A HEART
TO KNOW THEE

A Practical Summa of the Spiritual Life

"And I will give them a heart to know me, that I am the Lord: and they shall be my people, and I will be their God: because they shall return to me with their whole heart."
(Jeremias 24:7)   *Douay Version*

A HEART
TO KNOW THEE

A Practical Summa of the Spiritual Life

by E. J. Cuskelly, M.S.C., S.T.D.

NP

The Newman Press • Westminster, Maryland

1963

Imprimi potest: L. McDougall, M.S.C.
Superior Provincialis

Nihil obstat: Bernard O'Connor
Censor Deputatus

Imprimatur: D. Mannix, D.D.
Archiepiscopus Melburnensis
November 11, 1961

In humble gratitude,
I dedicate this book
to the Virgin Mother
of God

Preface

"I have come so that they may have life and have it more abundantly" (Jn. 10:10). We who have begun to live in Christ dream our recurring dreams of a more abundant life. We feel the need of deepening our knowledge of God, of making our minds more alert to the calls of His love and our hearts more ready to respond. At times, at least, we feel that we "should be doing more for God." In our search for fuller living, we turn to the books that have been written to help us in our need. We all find help for a time; some of us may even have all our questions answered. But there are many (and for them this book is written) who, in their reading, find their high hopes waver, or who hope on, not knowing clearly how their hopes will be fulfilled.

We read theologically exact accounts of the supernatural life: we must live a life of grace; we must practice all the various virtues, theological and moral; the gifts of the Holy Spirit must function more fully. Yet, although we know this is true, it seems far removed from what we live and feel and do. We go on, hoping that the "supernatural apparatus" is functioning, although we have little assurance that it is. Authors tell us that to advance in perfection we must follow faithfully the inspirations of the Holy Spirit; we must be attentive to His voice. We listen, and all we hear is—silence! There are books that exhort us to the higher ways of sanctity, which speak of the ascent of Mount Carmel and the lofty flights of the soul.

Few of these stock phrases seems to fit our lives, which seem so very ordinary. We resign ourselves to the lower ways, not seeing how we can be classed among the "chosen souls." There is a more modern class of book on the spiritual life that helps us even less, for it goes in for all the technical jargon of psychology. It makes us wonder how much of what we thought was spiritual life is really reducible to subconscious urges, instincts, and complexes. Then, some day, we come upon a book that is alive and warm and which seems to make good sense. It may give us fresh heart; but if we do not see how it fits in with the certain theology of the spiritual life, a lingering doubt about its value will prevent us from accepting it fully.

Whence this book. It is an attempt to comply with a request once made for a book on the spiritual life "theologically sound, yet not theologically heavy." The request is not easy to satisfy, for to some extent soundness and solidity go together.[1] The desire, however, is understandable; it is also fairly widespread. Pious books are many, but their theological value is not always in evidence.

There are many good theological works on the spiritual life. In these—as in all works of science—technical and abstract terms are frequently common. It would seem that there is room for a work which tries to express the certain doctrine of the spiritual life in terms which will have more meaning for less speculative minds.

In the study of spiritual theology above all, St. Thomas's principle holds true: "Our intelligence cannot and must not be content with a rational analysis wherein reality is subjected to a process of successive abstraction."[2] Spiritual theology is a practical science. If it remains in the realms of technicalities and abstract terms, it will not help as much as it should to true Christian living. This statement may be illustrated by an example from philosophy. Philosophers teach that in any thought process the active intellect abstracts an impressed species from the phantasm, and then imprints an expressed species on the possible intellect; a mental word is thus formed as a result of this process of intellection. This may be the exact philosophy of a thought process, but no nonphilosopher can understand it. Nor will such knowledge help anyone think—not even a philosopher! Further, in our thinking, we do not consciously make these steps. We just think! Similarly, a description of the faculties and powers of our "supernatural organism," theological though it be, does not help many live for God. Spiritual theology must show us how these truths can become part of our conscious living. This is frequently not done; the failure to do so is a defect in some writing.

Dom Chapman once wrote that all spiritual authors disagreed with one another and that he disagreed with all of them. Of course, he knew this to be an exaggeration. But his exasperation has been shared by others in search of a spiritual doctrine which was clear, certain, and practical.

Some of the causes of such dissatisfaction are:

(a) Many works are too technical and abstract.

(b) Others make frequent use of stock phrases and pious jargon ("chosen souls," "higher ways of sanctity," etc.) without showing what they mean in the twentieth century.

(c) There is often a failure to show how the "supernatural" or "spiritual life" blends with the rest of human activity. Often the impression is given that, unless we manage to give a spiritual color to "nonspiritual" tasks by consciously doing them from a right intention, they do not contribute to sanctification or merit.

(d) Certain works on the "psychological" aspects of the

spiritual life also use a jargon which many do not understand. Some also give the impression that psychology is a substitute for spirituality.

(e) Many do not realize that making our conscious aim "pursuit of perfection," "striving for sanctity," "striving to be a saint" is very likely to lead to discouragement or disillusion. Being told to aim at growing in charity is too general a directive that is not much more helpful. "Love God and do what you will" is sufficient as a practical directive for a saint, but not for anyone else.

It would, of course, be absurd to say that all, or even the greater part, of spiritual writing suffered from one or more of these defects. But the defects appear often enough to leave many people uncertain in spiritual matters. It would be presumptuous to think that one could solve all the problems of the spiritual life. There have, however, been recent trends of theological thought which throw new light on spiritual theology and contribute considerably to its intelligible unification, and to the clarification of some difficulties. Frequent requests for the notes used in lectures on spiritual theology (as well as the suggestions that they be published) have led to the writing of this work. I hope that it will be as helpful as others have assured me it will.

As the subtitle of this book indicates, it does not even attempt to cover the whole field of spiritual theology; some important questions are not treated.[3] It is hoped, however, that it will be a unity in itself, that it will complement the knowledge of those already familiar with the more standard studies of the spiritual life, and serve as an introduction for beginners.

In giving notes and references (and in omitting any fur-

ther bibliography than that contained in such notes), I
have kept in mind the general aim of this work:

(a) that it be theologically sound—hence a certain number
of notes and references;

(b) that it should not seem to be too specialized for the
nontheologian—hence, notes limited in number.

Croydon   E. J. CUSKELLY, M.S.C.
December 8, 1961

NOTES

 1 The reader is urged not to skip the first chapters as being too
solid, for they are a necessary key to the understanding of many questions of the spiritual life.

2 This is M. Chenu's summary of St. Thomas' principle, *"In Boe-
thium"* (q. 6. art. 1), in *Is Theology a Science?* Twentieth Century Encyclopedia of Catholicism (New York; Hawthorn, 1959).

3 A notable omission is that of the liturgy; but there are so many
good books in English, written recently by experts, that I have judged
it unnecessary and unwise to attempt a summary treatment.

Contents

[xiii]

[xvii]

A HEART
TO KNOW THEE

A Practical Summa of the Spiritual Life

Chapter 1

THE SPIRITUAL LIFE
IN ITS PSYCHOLOGICAL CONDITIONS

"Grace perfects nature." A simple sentence and easily said, but its perfect understanding is high wisdom indeed. Its misunderstanding has been the cause of many failures along the way to perfection and the attempted justification of many errors in the field of spiritual theology.

Spiritual theology may be described as the study of grace bringing nature to perfection. Better still, it could be said to be the study of grace perfecting the human person. For life is dynamic, and while "nature" frequently suggests a more static concept, "person" indicates human nature in its dynamic functioning.

A recent definition of spiritual theology as "the theological study of the evolution of the spiritual life in its psychological conditions,"[1] is in itself, by contrast with older descriptions ("the Science of the Saints," "the study of Christian perfection"), indicative of a different stress in the study of spiritual theology. It is a recognition of the fact that spiritual theology must take into account the conclusions of sound psychology. Grace is a sharing in the divine life—divine life, but human sharing; hence there are two factors which must be studied in themselves and

[1]

harmonized or blended in the perfection of human living for God.

Much has been written in recent years on psychological theories and discoveries in relation to religion. So much has been written, in fact, that many fear that there is a tendency to reduce the spiritual life to psychological phenomena. Hence, in some quarters, there is a distrust of the psychological approach to the study of the spiritual life. The distrust is to some extent justified. Father A. Gemelli, O.F.M., as a priest with degrees in psychology, medicine, and surgery, and thus eminently qualified to speak on the subject, judged it necessary to write a word of warning for "those clergy, who, impelled by a zeal for the good of souls, have rashly accepted the conclusions of psychoanalysis, or worse, have themselves applied psychoanalytical treatment to neurotics who have had recourse to them, or even, in some cases have had themselves psychoanalyzed."[2]

Certainly it is an error to accept rashly all the "findings" of the various schools of modern psychology. It is an error, also, to think that the spiritual life can be explained in psychological terms.

On the other hand, it is a mistake to think that what the human mind can know of human nature, through sound psychological research, is of no use in matters of religious life. "The more urgent problems of spiritual direction occur precisely in the realm of psychology. Those who refuse to consider the psychological aspect completely suppress the examination of these problems, and thus inevitably leave them unsolved."[3]

There has been, in recent years, a certain amount of exasperation among doctors and psychologists and the representatives of religion. Medical experts thought that appeals were made to religion and faith, when application of sound psychological principles would have been more to the point, whereas spiritual leaders regarded psychology as an attempted substitute for religion.

Fortunately, reasons exist for better mutual understanding. Knowledge of human nature, at which psychology aims, can be a help to those who work for the education of humanity to deeper Christian living. Furthermore, through the course of centuries in trying to save and sanctify human nature, the Church has learned a lot about humanity. She has incorporated into her laws and directives many sound psychological principles. Most of the masters of the spiritual life have been rather shrewed psychologists with a wonderful understanding of human nature. One has only to think of St. John of the Cross, St. Teresa of Avila, St. Francis de Sales, for example, to realize this.

On reflection, this is just what one would expect. As another doctor writes:

The best text-book for the study of psychology is the human heart. . . . Three-quarters of psychology is recognizing in other people what is present in yourself; in seeing your sinfulness and weakness in their sinfulness and weakness; in remembering your heartache in the story of their heartache. Human nature is a mystery forever unknowable; not two examples of it are alike; each preserves its separate mystery and dignity. Yet human nature is also built upon the same general plan. If otherwise, any science of psychology would be impossible. The majority of joys and sorrows that afflict mankind are common. . . . In the recesses of their hearts, men and women are more alike than they are perhaps willing to admit.[4]

The saints knew themselves well; the Church under the guidance of the Spirit has the mission of leading men to the fullness of perfection. Hence, we must not think that a knowledge of human nature in its motives and self-deceits and the reasons for failures of development have been *discovered* by modern psychology. This is well illustrated by one psychologist's research to discover the deepest drives of human nature. He pursued his study among certain opposed classes: Negroes and whites in the United States, workers and capitalists, etc. He found that, generally, members of one class considered the opposite class as anxious for money and for power and as indulging in illicit sexual gratification. He reasoned that when you feared (and sometimes envied) your "enemy," you would accuse him of having what you felt you would like to have, but from which you were deprived by laws, circumstances, or convention. Thus he concluded that three of man's deepest unreasoned urges were for money, power, and sex.[5] Now the results of this modern research were summed up long ago by St. John in the New Testament, when he said that what was in the "world" was "the concupiscence of the flesh, concupiscence of the eyes, and the pride of life" (I John 2:16), i.e., the same three urges. For centuries the Church has regarded the most perfect practice of self-control as the opposite of these three: the practice of poverty, chastity, and obedience.

It would, however, be foolish to think that modern psychology can teach us nothing. It may be a "refining of the methods of common sense to understand the motivations of the acts of others,"[6] but it teaches us quickly what common sense would take a lifetime to learn. And much of what it teaches, many of us can be very slow to learn because of one other fact—well-known to common sense—our strange blindness to see ourselves as others see us, as well as our tendency to "judge others by ourselves." This latter tendency may succeed in teaching the more discerning among us "three-quarters of psychology," but not the other quarter.

From all this, I wish to draw only one conclusion: To understand our spiritual life, to see what grace should help us to be, we can utilize most profitably what we learn from psychology. Not only can we do so, but we must, if our thoughts about certain aspects of the spiritual life are not to remain abstract theorizing.[7]

The aim of this book is to express the main teachings of spiritual theology in a way in which its harmonious unity is apparent, and which outlines a living, simple, yet virile spirituality. Since spiritual theology is "the theological study of the spiritual life in its psychological setting," we shall treat of: (a) the principles of the life of grace; (b) certain of the sound conclusions of psychology. (We shall try to develop both of these divisions in less technical terms.) Finally, (c) we will show how these elements fuse into a vital unity.

The spiritual life is the life of the whole human person, living for God in and through the nature that God gave him, with his individual temperament and characteristics. It could be said that spiritual theology is the study of the development of the Christian personality. This is the study of the human person as he comes to full maturity under the perfecting influence of the grace of Christ through personal contact with the Three Divine Persons. The life we are given at baptism is one of personal intimacy with God our Father, and Jesus Christ His Son, and the Spirit of personal love. The purpose of this book is to show how the spiritual life in all its details is best seen as a living unity if studied in this personal context. It is in this context, too, that we understand more fully how our natural knowledge of the human person harmonizes perfectly, in theory and in practice, with our revealed knowledge of the personal character of grace.

NOTES

[1] Gabriel of Mary Magdalene O.C.D., *The Spiritual Director* (Westminster, Md: Newman, 1952), p. 61.

[2] *Psychoanalysis Today* (New York: Kenedy, 1955), p. 53. A recent instruction of the Holy See sounds a similar note of caution.

[3] Gabriel of Mary Magdalene, *op. cit.*

[4] R. E. Harvard, M.D., "Religious Sisters," *Blackfriars* (London, 1950).

[5] Dr. Gregory Zilboorg, "Christian Asceticism and Modern Man," *Blackfriars* (London, 1955).

[6] Dr. Alexander, quoted in "Direction Spirituelle et Psychologie," *Etudes Carmélitaines* (Paris: Desclée de Brouwer, 1951).

[7] It is most instructive to note that psychological balance is one of the factors carefully weighed in the study of causes of canonization. *See* Gabriel of Mary Magdalene: "Present Norms of Holiness," in *Conflict and Light* (New York: Sheed and Ward, 1953).

Chapter 2

GRACE AND PERSON

The key to a vital grasp of the truths taught by spiritual theology is an understanding of the fact that "the theology of grace can be wholly explained in personal categories."[1] The standard textbook treatment and the older catechism teaching follow these lines: "Sanctifying grace is a quality inhering in the substance of the soul; the infused virtues are proximate principles of operation; the gifts of the Holy Spirit are receptive potencies; actual graces are transitory helps of illumination and inspiration. These various elements go to make up our supernatural life, considered as a principle of operation within a being. They are all graces, because they are gifts of God, God's favor bestowed on us." We accept these truths, but we understand very little of what they mean in terms of ordinary conscious living. This speculative study of the static aspects of the supernatural life is very necessary. But for our spiritual life, we must translate these speculative truths into a more living language, studying the dynamic aspects of grace. Or perhaps it would be better to say that we must set forth clearly and strongly the vital truths of Scripture and tradition that speculative theology sets out to safeguard by exact, technical expression.

1. The Supernatural

Throughout the history of the Church, one of the prime concerns of theologians has been to safeguard the supernatural, to insist that supernatural life is God's gift, first and last. But the *supernatural*, as a term, has very little positive meaning, even for the theologian. It means only (with all its precisions) what is "above created nature," "not natural to man," "not in any way due to creatures." These are largely negative concepts. When we come to living a spiritual life, insistence that it is above nature tends to leave us with the impression that the supernatural is completely beyond our understanding and quite outside the realm of experience.

Positively, we can express the reality of the supernatural life by saying that it is God's taking us into a relationship of personal friendship, knowledge, and love with the Three Divine Persons.[2] This life will reach its perfection in heaven in the beatific vision. However, the beatific vision, the goal of our life, is not just "seeing God" in the sense that a TV-conditioned modern might understand that phrase. It is rather our being taken into the heart-filling happiness of intimate personal union with the three perfect Persons.[3] Everything that we know of personal union in love should give us some knowledge—shadowy, distant, imperfect, yet nevertheless true—of what this eternal, all-absorbing, ecstatic union with the Three Divine Persons will be. In order to give some idea of it, Scripture appeals to every possible human relationship of personal knowledge and love: friendship, marriage, and family life in all its aspects. Instead of thinking of the supernatural as lifting us above our natural capabilities, we can say with equal truth and more intelligibly that it consists of being drawn into personal intimacy with a personal God.

[8]

From this point of view, it is easy enough to see what theologians stress by the more technical term *supernatural:* something to which a creature has no rights, for which he has no natural capacity. Man has no capacity for sharing God's knowledge and love unless God gives it. Friends must meet on terms of some sort of equality, and in this case man must be lifted up to God. Man has no rights nor claim to personal friendship. We know this even from human affairs. All invitations to personal friendship are freely given. I cannot walk up to someone, especially of a higher station in life, and announce that I am to be his special friend. We wait for the gift of friendship to be bestowed. In more romantic days, the example of a prince bestowing his love on a beggar maid was used to illustrate the complete gratuity of the bestowal of a personal love. When there is question of the God of infinite majesty calling His sinful creatures to share His love and friendship, the sheer "grace" of it is more clearly evidenced. As St. Augustine said, "Grace because it is given *gratis.*"

A most important point, much stressed in recent theology, is the "immanence" of the supernatural. This refers to the truth that the supernatural is in perfect harmony with all our deepest human aspirations. "Grace perfects nature"—along a line or direction in which it already naturally tends. There are well-known examples that are used to illustrate what is meant by the "supernatural life." Taking life as "a principle of operation within a being," authors explain that for a higher operation, you need a higher principle, a higher life—one that is above your nature and, therefore, *super*-natural. As examples they say that a cabbage would need a higher nature to be able to walk; a cat would need extra powers if it were to enjoy an opera. We, if we are to know and love God as He knows and loves Himself, must be given a super-nature.

[9]

Such examples are useful, as far as they go. But they do not go far enough. A cat does not want to enjoy an opera; should it become capable of doing so, it would cease to be a cat. But man does want to know and love God, and when he is enabled to do so on an interpersonal level, he becomes more perfectly a man. The supernatural is not adequately grasped unless it is seen as responding to a man's natural aspirations and in perfect harmony with them. The "personal" character of grace helps us see this. Much more will be said on this point later. For the time being it is sufficient to note that, although it is evident that personal friendship with God is something to which man has neither right nor claim, it is nevertheless something to which (when its possibility is made known) his whole nature responds, and which brings his nature to perfection.[4]

Furthermore, it is important to note that, to understand what is meant by the supernatural, it is not necessary to have a clear knowledge of what is called the state of pure nature, nor to know what man's happiness would have been had he not been called to the beatific vision. We must hold that God could have created us without making our destiny a face-to-face vision of God.[5] Theologians suggest different possibilities. It is an interesting problem, but we have no practical need to solve it.[6] We know that God created us for the beatific vision—for eternal personal union with Himself. We never had any other destiny. We must not think of God creating our human "nature" and then, as a kind of afterthought, deciding to lift us up and destine us for the beatific vision. Man was created for the supernatural! Because of this it is almost impossible to draw a clear line between the natural and the supernatural. Man as he is, body and soul, is made for the vision of God, and there-fore his whole being is in some way orientated toward that goal. This is of the utmost importance for the spiritual life. The failure to realize it has sent authors to all sorts of inanimate examples to try to explain the supernatural life. They give descriptions of boats with oars and sails, cars without petrol, etc., all purporting to illustrate the life of grace. But the God who made us for personal union with Himself has given us—in the human nature that He gave us, with our natural need for love and friendship and personal union with another—the best way of knowing what sharing in His personal life does mean.

Man was created for the supernatural. This is most important for the spiritual life. There are many who tend to think of "the supernatural life" as lived only in prayer and in what we do with conscious reference to God. I wonder how much of our thought is influenced by this tendency to separate the natural and the supernatural. We tend to think that God made human nature and then, as it were, changed His plans, deciding that He would not, after all, let man live according to merely natural norms to gain a natural happiness. He *elevated* him to a supernatural state. We almost think of God as making the best of a bad job, as if it would have been so much better had He not made us the way we are. This means that in practice we tend to think that a part of us only is directed toward God—the supernatural. We must, as it were, take care lest the rest stop us from tending toward God. The supernatural must drag an unwilling nature along a road that is too high for it. This of course is wrong. Not much of it would be explicitly formulated. But it influences the attitude of many people more than they realize. We shall see later how necessary a right outlook is on this fundamental point. Let us repeat: God willed to create man for personal union with Himself, an imperfect union on earth but brought to perfection in heaven. With that end in view, an all-wise Creator, who does nothing uselessly or aimlessly, created the human race. Body and soul He created them, male and female, to His own image and likeness, that their whole living might be for Him and lead them to Him at last.

2. Sanctifying Grace

Sanctifying grace, faith, and charity are "the beginnings of eternal life in us," because thereby we enter into a relationship of personal friendship with God. The reception of grace and charity is called justification. Textbooks treat of the realities of justification in the following order:
(i) Justification is an internal renovation of man.
(ii) In justification, a created gift is infused into man's soul: a physical quality, an entitative habit inhering in the substance of the soul.
(iii) As a result, man is made a sharer of the divine nature, an adopted child of God; and God comes to dwell within him.
(iv) Further (and this by way of corollary), man becomes a friend of God.

This may be good theology; but it is more alive, more in accord with the order of revelation—and better theology— to put things the other way: God wants us to enter into a personal relationship with Himself, fully in heaven, but in reality, even now. He wants to make us His children, to unite Himself to us in friendship and personal presence, sharing His life of knowledge and love. To bring this about God must give us new powers: the created reality of grace and the virtues whereby man is internally renewed.

For St. Paul (to cite only one of the New Testament writers), "grace is not a thing, but God loving and giving Himself, or, if you wish, his relation of charity and gener-

osity towards men. Whence you can call grace the super-
abundant gift of salvation. . . ."[7] It was to make us sons
that God sent out His Son on a mission to us (Gal. 4:4 ff.),
to lead us into intimate friendship with Himself.

We are taught to invoke God with the name which Christ
used in speaking of his Father: *Abba*. It is also the word which
Jesus used in regard to St. Joseph. In their prayers the Israel-
ites said, "Abi, Father," while the term *Abba* is intimate and
familiar, corresponding with the French *Papa*. (The English
equivalent would be "Daddy." While reverent usage would
not permit most of us to use this title in our dealings with
God, it should at least be given serious thought, coming as it
does from the pen of Paul, writing under divine inspiration.
No more striking way could have been chosen to express the
degree of intimacy to which we are called by grace.) It follows that, in daring to pronounce such a name, the Christian
does not appeal to the loving and helping providence of God
the Creator, but precisely to this relation of paternity, by
which God gives him a share in His own nature and calls him
into the family circle of the Trinity: "You are no longer
strangers or exiles then, or aliens; the saints are your fellow-
citizens, you belong to God's household" (Eph. 2:19).[8]

One writer[9] gives an illustration that is excellent in
this context. As the parents of an idiot child look on this
child whom they have begotten, their deepest desire is that
it should share their life—their human life of knowledge,
love, laughter, and family happiness. With its malformed
brain cells, however, it is capable of no more than a sub-
human, animal-like attachment. It lives in its own self-
centered world, apart. An inner transformation, giving it
a higher human power of knowing and loving, is needed
if it is to break through the barrier of its own closed existence to share the love and friendship of its parents, living
fully as their child and their image. The application of this

analogy to God and His grace is evident. The tremendous truth is that God longs for men (who fail to recognize the lower level on which they live) to share the life of knowledge, love, and delight which is the life of Father, Son, and Spirit. But unless a man is lifted out of his own closed world, he cannot share this personal life of God. To make this sharing possible, the God who created us to His image gives us new powers to know and love Him on a "divinely personal level": grace and the virtues, an inner transformation. This also makes it clear why theologians at the Council of Trent so strongly fought Luther's teaching that grace brought no internal change to man. If none were given, we should be like the poor unfortunate child, condemned forever to have no personal knowledge or love for God, our Father. But where the love of a human father is helpless, the love of God is charged with power, able to pour new life into the soul He has created, so that it can live fully as His child in His image. God's grace is life giving and uplifting.

We could well return to an ancient definition of grace by the greatest of theologians. St. Thomas Aquinas writes of grace as the *potestas fruendi divina Persona*, i.e., "the power of enjoying and delighting in the Divine Persons."[10] It would be difficult to find a phrase that better expressed the reality of created grace.

3. Faith

The theological virtues take on their fullest meaning when considered in this personal context. Charity and hope will be treated later on. In concluding this chapter, however, it would be well to stress the personal character of faith—briefly only, since it has been widely treated in recent years.[11] As a reaction against errors that tried to empty faith of any intellectual content or which opposed faith to reason, the Catholic Church has had to insist that by faith we accept as true whatever God says. She has had to insist also on the infallible teaching authority of the Church. For quite a few Catholics, then, faith has come to mean, almost exclusively, a tenacious adherence to the truth of propositions put forward by the Church, to be believed on the authority of God revealing. God makes known certain truths; this is revelation. We accept them as true; this is faith. Faith tends to be more a matter of the intellect than of the whole human person.

In its living reality, the call to faith and justification is God's invitation to man to enter into a relationship of personal friendship. God does not come to us bearing two tablets of stone, the one with a set of commandments to be kept, the other with a set of propositions to be believed. Divine revelation is not first and foremost making known a truth to which we assent. It is God making Himself personally present to man in the Word that He utters. That this might not remain mere phraseology, let me explain it by an example. Think of a counterpart of Robinson Crusoe, alone on an island, not knowing where he is, not knowing where to go, and unable to go anywhere. One day the silence of his solitude is broken by the sound of a human voice. His first reaction is not that something is being said to which he should listen and assent. First of all, he thrills to the presence of a person, for the voice reveals a personal presence before it reveals anything else. It reveals also the possibility of salvation from his sorry plight, and hope will arise in his heart. Mixed with it will be a loving gratitude if (as we shall postulate for the sake of our illustration) the voice is the voice of one who has come of set purpose to seek out and save him.

God's revelation is similar to that. For this reason in

man's living response, faith, hope, and love are mingled; the living reality cannot be reduced merely to an assent of the intellect. If it were merely that, it would not be real justifying faith at all. God does not reveal a message that has no effect on our lives. Were the content of His message merely, "Two and two are four," "matter is the principle of individuation"—propositions to which we had to assent—it would leave us sitting on the sand. But to men lost in the hopelessness of their own sin and weakness, God comes, making Himself personally present in His plan to free us from darkness and the shadow of death. He reveals His own nature in the beauty of an infinite, saving love, making known His will to raise us to a share in the personal life and intimacy that belongs to the Divine Persons. Faith is acceptance of God, acceptance of His plan of salvation. Christian faith is the acceptance of Christ, the Word incarnate, the "Revealer of the Father" with all the demands of His love.

St. John has a most enlightening phrase when he describes how he and his fellow-Christians were justified: *Et nos credidimus caritati* (I John 4:16). Not just belief, but "we have believed in his love," in God's love for us. For St. Paul, too, "the object of the Christian faith will be to believe in the love of God who pardons sin, and makes all things help to secure the good of those who love him."[12] God's revelation does contain propositions to be assented to as true. But these are a very special set of propositions, expressing God's personal self-revelation. In human life, a young man's proposal of marriage is a statement of a truth; it is also a very special self-revelation, the revealing of his mind and heart, of his most intimate personal life. God's self-revelation bears a similar stamp: It is God making Himself known to us in the desire that we should meet Him in the personal encounter of conversion, giving Him our love, willing to share in His life. Faith means that "we have learned to recognize the love God has in our regard, and to make it our belief" (I John 4:16). It is, of course, in Christ that we see and accept this love. "What has revealed the love of God, where we are concerned, is that he has sent His only-begotten Son into the world, so that we might have life through him" (I John 4:9). St. John's whole Gospel is written to show how the Word, who in the beginning lived in close intimacy with His Father, came to reveal to men something of that intimate knowledge and love which was His, and which He willed to share with men.[13]

It is, strictly speaking, charity that justifies us. But as St. Thomas says, there could be no charity or love of friendship toward God unless men were called to share in God's personal life. There could be no charity in man unless he believed in the love of God for him, in God's will that man should share in His life and love, at least in the general sense that God is the Rewarder of those who seek Him. From the fact that he knows that he is called to share in the personal life of God and wills to accept that call, a love of charity must arise in man. Charity necessarily flows from a real belief in God's love.[14]

Faith is "an act of the intellect assenting," as every textbook says. It is more. For in its living context it is the freely willed assent of the whole human person to the call of a personal God. In the unity of that personal assent, faith, hope, and charity are blended:

Biblical faith is the acceptance of the alliance which God offers to man. Faith which God asks of man is analogous to that which husband and wife give to one another and which unites them forever. This profound analogy is more than mere metaphor: for by this full faith which is confidence and fidelity, man comes to a true knowledge of God, to that concrete knowledge which only perfect intimacy gives, that which unites husband and wife. This is what God himself said to his people by the mouth of Osee: "And I will espouse thee to me in faith: and thou shalt know that I am the Lord."

Since the coming of Christ, the call of God is new; new because God speaks to us through His Son; new because God invites us to share in the love which unites him to his Son, and to become his children. . . . Faith, our reply to this new call, acceptance of Christ . . . opens our souls to the charity of Christ . . . (and there follows) a renewed hope, the hope of a child of God, his confidence in his Father whose love he shares, because he has given himself to this love, and already shares in it."[15]

NOTES

[1] I. Alfaro, S.J., "Persona y Gracia," *Gregorianum*, XLI (1960), 5 ff. I have developed this point in some articles in the *Australasian Catholic Record*, XXXVIII (1961), most of which are reproduced (with some modifications) in this work.

[2] E. Mersch, S.J., *The Theology of the Mystical Body* (St. Louis: Herder, 1955), pp. 455 ff.

[3] R. Troisfontaines, "Le Ciel," *Nouvelle Revue Théologique*, 82 (1960), 225 ff.

[4] L. Malevez, S.J., "La Gratuité du surnaturel," *N.R.T.*, 75 (1953), 561 ff.; 673 ff. I Alfaro, S.J., "Transcendencia y immanencia de lo sobrenaturel," *Gregorianum*, XXXVIII (1957), 5 ff.

[5] The Encyclical *Humani generis* says only that God could have created man without destining him to the beatific vision.

[6] G. de Broglie, S.J., *De Fine Ultimo Humanae Vitae* (Paris: Beauchesne, 1958), pp. 183 ff.

[7] C. Spicq., O.P., *Vie Morale et Trinité Sainte selon St. Paul* (Paris: Ed. du Cerf, 1957), p. 27.

[8] *Ibid.*, pp. 53 ff.

[9] L. Trese, *Many Are One* (Chicago: Fides, 1952), p. 3.

[10] *Summa Theologica*, Pars I, q. 43, a. 3—Holy Spirit; a. 4, ad 1—the Father; a. 5 ad 2—the Son. Cf. q. 38, art. 1.

[11] J. Mouroux, *I Believe* (New York: Sheed and Ward, 1957). E. Joly, *What is Faith?*, Twentieth Century Encyclopedia of Catholicism (New York: Hawthorn, 1958). T. Barosse, "The relationship of love to faith in St. John," *Theolo-*

gical Studies, 18 (1957), 538 ff. "Christianity, Mystery of Love," *C.B.Q.,* 20 (1958), 137 ff.

[12] Spicq, *op. cit.,* p. 28.

[13] John 1:2 *(pros ton Theon,* indicating intimacy). 1:13—*in sinu Patris,* a term indicating special intimacy, e.g., conjugal, as in Num. 11:12; Deut. 13:6.

[14] *S.T.,* II–II, q. 23, a. 1.

[15] Lacan, "Les Trois qui demeurent," *Recherches de Sciences Religieuses,* XLII (1958), 321 ff.

Chapter 3

GRACE AND THE DIVINE PERSONS

---

1. Indwelling: Personal Presence

For fuller Christian living, it is most important to regard grace not chiefly as an effect produced in us, but as a power to live in personal contact, by knowledge and love, with the Three Divine Persons. Our Lord's teaching on the indwelling of the Trinity underlines the closeness of this union, and this mystery of God's nearness to men has been the focal point of the prayer of many of the saints.

All theological explanations of this mystery must remain inadequate, but we must always try to understand something of it in order that we might live it more fully. To my mind, the most satisfying explanation of the meaning of the mystery is again the personal explanation. This has a double element. The first is that grace is directed toward our being present to God by our personal meeting with Him.

God is present in the soul not only as efficient cause, producing faith and love, but also objectively after the manner of a friend with whom it converses and whom it keeps with it. . . . The movement of the creature, says St. Thomas, "does not stop at the gifts received from God, but tends onwards, to Him who gave the gifts" (*I. Sent.* d. 14, q. 2, art. 1). All the supernatural spontaneity which it receives from the Trinity acting in it as a unique efficient Cause, the holy soul uses, even on earth, to raise itself up to the meeting with this supreme object, ineffable, possessed in mysterious intimacy, which is the Three Divine Persons. For the presence of efficiency results from the divine essence common to the Three Divine Persons, but the presence of meeting is with the Three Persons as distinct. The whole Trinity is thus present in a new objective manner to the soul who lives in charity.[1]

In this passage, Father Journet expresses the fact that all the realities of grace and the virtues are given to us that we might know and love the Divine Persons. But most of us are accustomed to think of God as already present to us, even before we consciously know and love Him. We do speak of persons being present to us when, even though they are physically absent, they fill our minds and hearts. God abides in us, and we abide in God. Our abiding in God, from the point of view of our active living is evidently, as St. Thomas insisted, by our knowledge and love of Him. This is the way persons are "present" to one another. Such presence is not merely a matter of physical nearness, but a union in knowledge and love.[2] We have an expression, "He's not with us," which we apply to someone physically present when in thought or will he is separated from us. Two strangers in the same train compartment who do not know each other nor speak to each other are not personally present to each other. Personal presence is through union of mind and will. God is pure spirit, and any special presence to Him of intellectual creatures must be by way of knowledge and love.

But when we think of the Divine Indwelling, it seems evident that our knowledge and love of God are not the whole of it. The active exercise of our knowing and loving would seem to be toward God who is already present.

Many theologians say that God, who is always present in us by the presence of immensity (since God is present everywhere), is not really present to us personally until we know Him by faith and love Him by charity.[3] To my mind this is not sufficient. Christ, speaking of this special presence, says: "We will come to him, and make our continual abode with him" (John 14:23); in this, clearly, He implies a special coming, and in a later passage, a special sending of the Holy Spirit. The obvious meaning of Our Lord's words seems to go further than a mere presence of efficient causality or presence by immensity.

Explained in terms of personal reality, the Indwelling takes on a meaning for our spiritual life which it does not have if God is thought of as being present merely as efficient cause, even of supernatural gifts. We do not, in this sense, have devotion to a cause! We can, therefore, profitably modify Journet's view, given above. As he stresses, and as St. Thomas insisted, the created reality is caused in us precisely in order that we may freely tend to a meeting with the Three Divine Persons in a mysterious intimacy of loving friendship. However, it must be remembered that friendship is a *mutual* meeting in knowledge and love, a *mutual* giving and receiving. Toward friendship with God, we cannot take the first step: "He has first loved us" (I John 4:10). If we keep this in mind, we can see how created grace is more than our ability to know and love God present in us as in all creatures by a presence of immensity or even present as a cause of special supernatural gifts in us.

Created grace is the effect of God's personal approach to men. This personal approach is the special coming of which Our Lord spoke. God can give us grace only if He looks on us with a new special knowledge and love: only if He makes a new personal approach to us, becoming present to us in a new, personal way. Strictly speaking, of course, the newness can involve no change in God. But it is true to say that God comes to us in a new and special knowledge and love if there are new effects produced in us. As St. Thomas says: "The knowledge of God is the cause of things"; "The love of God creates and infuses goodness into things."[4]

This is the essential difference between created love and divine love. We see that people are good, and our love is a response to their goodness. God loves, and the result of His love is goodness produced in creatures. Thus it is true that God's infusing of supernatural realities into the human soul is the result or term of God's special knowledge and love. These realities are given for one purpose: that we might use them to live in personal friendship with God. Hence, God's gift of them is clearly His coming to us, making Himself present to us in a personal approach. Here we can see how vital was the necessity of insisting against the Reformers that justification must necessarily involve a renewal of man's soul. For to say that God looks on us with a special knowledge and love must mean, if it is to have any meaning, that there is a new created effect of His knowledge of us and love for us.[5] But for our spiritual living, it is more necessary to insist that the giving of grace makes it really true that in justification God becomes present to us, by coming to us in a personal approach, with a special knowledge and love.

For the full concept of meeting with God in friendship, or of indwelling as the mutual personal presence of God and man, a twofold step is involved (as is the case in any personal friendship): (a) God must first make Himself present as a friend in a personal approach to us; (b) then man recognizes and responds to this personal approach, actively knowing and loving God in friendship, living in His presence.

In heaven this living in God's presence will be continuous and uninterrupted. On earth it is not so; but there is still a true dwelling together, since friendship is an atmosphere in which we live. And if we are not always consciously living with God, He is always with us, as father and friend.

Scripture speaks of God being present in us as in a temple. This obviously conveys two ideas which fit in well with what we have just said:

(a) God personally, permanently present—waiting to be the object of man's worship and attentive love. This permanent personal presence is by means of God's gift of grace which, of its very nature, is an invitation to turn in loving adoration to the God who has come to dwell within us.

(b) The homage of man. In this life such homage cannot be uninterrupted. It will be given in proportion to one's fervor and as necessary human occupations allow.

The "personal presence" of God in us will be more perfect as we grow in knowledge and love of Him, exercising that knowledge and love more continually.[6] Still, since "God has first loved us," the Three Divine Persons are continually present to all who are in the state of grace.

2. Children of the Father

In recent theological articles, much discussion has centered around the question of whether, because of grace and the Divine Indwelling, we have special ontological relations to the Three Divine Persons as distinct, or one relation only to God as one in essence. If God is regarded as being present as efficient cause, there is an obvious difficulty against special relations, arising from the truth that created effects come from the Trinity acting as one principle.[7] One writer even suggests a relation that is "absolutely one and virtually threefold," ultimately founded on quasi-formal causality. One argument advanced in favor of this is: "the practical consequence . . . a devotional life more genuine and sincere. . . ." Certainly, devotion is dogmatic truth in action. But I do not think that many will find their devotional life helped or hindered by the virtualities of their ontological relationships.

There are other certain theological truths that can help us here. As we have seen, St. Thomas wrote that grace is the power of delighting in the Three Divine Persons. Three Persons are really present in the just soul in their personal reality. Ontological relations do not necessarily dictate the quality of "personal" relationships. For example, according to St. Thomas, my relation of sonship to my parents is ontologically one, since it is as one principle that they beget me. But my father and mother are two distinct persons. If my mother is a delightful person and my father a self-centered, inconsiderate scoundrel, my relationship of personal knowledge and love will be lived according to their personal qualities. It will not be dictated solely by my ontological relation.

While the theological discussions continue, we may continue to use the grace which is ours: our power of enjoying and delighting in the three distinct Persons who come to us and make their abode within us. The Father, as Christ taught us, we shall approach as our Father, too: "I am going up to him who is *my* Father and *your* Father" (John 20:17). Our divine sonship we shall look upon as a sharing in the Sonship of Christ, "destined from the first to

[25]

be moulded into the image of his Son, who is thus to become the eldest-born among many brethren" (Rom. 8:29). The Spirit we shall regard as the personal love of God who is given to us, making it possible for us to be united to the Father and Son in personal love: "The love of God has been poured out in our hearts by the Holy Spirit, whom we have received" (Rom. 5:5). "If uncreated grace is but the personal self-giving of God to us . . . if in God there is no other personal Being than Father, Son, and Holy Spirit, there is no other possible personal self-giving of God than the giving of the Divine Persons."[8]

At least since the days of Pope Leo XIII, most of us (unless we are Scotists) like to think that St. Thomas is not against us in matters of theology. In this particular question, St. Thomas is often quoted as saying that we are sons of the Trinity. In his writings, however, St. Thomas has two lines of thought which some say he did not synthesize perfectly. Mersch[9] sums up the two series of texts as follows: (a) The juridical conception of divine adoption, regarded from the viewpoint of the act producing it. Since this is in the realm of efficient causality, it is common to all Three Persons, and any special role attributed to the different Persons is merely a matter of appropriation. The act of making us God's children is common to all three Persons. (b) The theological or mystical conception of adoption which, regarding the Persons to whom we are personally united by grace, considers them as distinct.

Rondet[10] sees these two currents as St. Thomas's inheritance from two distinct traditions: (a) that of St. Augustine and the Latin Fathers; (b) that of the Greek Fathers.

St. Thomas may have neglected to synthesize these two lines of thought. Perhaps he thought they did not need synthesizing. Be that as it may, our life of grace will be knowing and loving the divine Persons as they are in themselves. In the beatific vision, we shall be united to them as they are in themselves, in their personal distinctness.[11] Our life of grace is the beginning of that same life of personal union with the divine Persons. Our personal knowledge and love of each Person will have this in common: It will be tinged with gratitude for the life that each has given us. But it is as Father that the Father, source of all divine life, gives us a share in that life; the Son gives us life as He possesses it—His personal life of sonship; the Spirit, as the gift of personal love.

3. Sharing Christ's Sonship

Christ as man was full of grace and truth, and of His fullness we have all received. Our grace is a sharing in His fullness of grace. Grace has the personal quality of making us sons of the Father, for this was the personal quality it had in Christ. Our grace is *gratia Christi*, the grace of Christ, not only because He merited it for us, but because it shapes us to His likeness. In His human soul, grace has a personal characteristic—that of sonship—which it should produce, in lesser measure, in our souls.

If we regard grace as the power of living a personal relationship with the divine Persons, it is not difficult to see the function of grace in the human soul of Christ. In Him there is one Person—the divine Person of the Son. In His human nature He could not have any personal relationships with the Father and Spirit other than those He possessed from all eternity. His whole personality was to be the only-begotten Son of the Father. He is a Person only insofar as He is the Son of God. Created grace was infused into His soul so that, in and through his human nature, He

might live the only personal life He could have—that of
the Son of God. The explanation of the function of grace
in the soul of Christ is as simple and sublime as that. This
created grace was given Him to make it possible to live,
as man, a personal relationship with the other divine Persons. As the eternal Word, He possesses eternal immutable
relationships with the Father and Holy Spirit. Created
grace is a lifting of the human faculties so that the Son of
God can live through them His personal life of sonship.
It would not be possible for this one divine Person to have
personal relationships with Father and Spirit other than
those He had from all eternity. If grace is given His
humanity it must be a grace of sonship. St. Thomas said
that such grace was a necessary consequence of the Incarnation.[12] For, through merely human acts, Christ could not,
in His human nature, know and love Him as His Father;
could not live in His human nature the personal life of
sonship which was His. And so He was given grace; and
the whole spiritual life of the man Jesus, as the Gospel of
St. John shows, was this living from the Father and for the
Father. Of His fullness we have received. Our grace is a
sharing in His grace of sonship. He lives in us His life of
sonship, which we must try to make more deeply and
personally our own.

4. The Spirit of Love

Scripture tells us something of the role of the Spirit in
our lives. Speculative theology has been able to do little
to give us any further understanding. The Spirit of God is
somehow identified with the personal love of God that
is poured forth in our hearts (Rom. 5:5) to help us live as
children of God. We know that the Holy Spirit is, as it
were, the mutual personal love of Father and Son—They

love one another in the Spirit. Their personal love is poured out on us—we receive the Holy Spirit. And, from the point of view of our exercise of love, the Spirit of God is given to us to lead us in our active movement of love toward Father and Son. We cannot understand much more than that. Perhaps here theology must be content to repeat, without clarification, the teaching of St. Paul.[13] If the whole of the Christian life can be summed up in charity, it can also be summed up in the work of the Spirit of love, leading, enlightening, and strengthening us in the way of love.

5. Divine Personality

Speculative theology tells us that a divine Person is a "subsisting relation." We have a philosophical definition of person which is satisfactory in its way and in its place. For the purposes of our study of the spiritual life, we shall try to express it in less abstract terms.

In ordinary conversation, if you are asked to describe someone, to say what sort of a person he is, you will give a description of his personality by indicating his way of acting toward other people, his attitude toward them, his relations with them. You will say that he is kind or domineering, a recluse, etc. Furthermore, a person has as one of his fundamental and essential characteristics the ability to enter into friendly relations with other persons. This property is limited to beings who are persons. "Impersonal" is a word we use of someone who has no friendliness in his dealings with others. It is a word we use of an interview or letter in which there was no note of friendly regard.

Human personality is fashioned after the divine. A divine personality is essentially and totally a relation to another Person or Persons. We can never understand this of course. But we can grasp something of its meaning by thinking about all the fine qualities that go to make up a human personality. To grasp something of what is meant by a divine Person and the richness of divine personality, we should not start from the rather tenuous philosophical notion of "relation," and then pass to the "subsisting relations," which, as speculative theology says, are the divine Persons. This, though theologically correct, is too abstract for the spiritual life.

All the richness of a personality, generous, kind, devoted, self-forgetful, thoughtful of others; all the finest qualities of persons we know are gathered together and multiplied to the infinite in the divine Persons, whose very personal life and reality is that "being for another," or "being in relation to another" which is given by theologians as the description of a divine Person. This truth may be somewhat abstruse, but its implications for the spiritual life and for spiritual theology are immense. It should be given much thought.

6. The Personality of Christ

Hundreds of books have been written in an endeavor to penetrate the mysterious depths of the personality of Christ. The purpose of this small section is to make one point only: that the essence of the perfection of Christ's personality was His living entirely for Another. This is the necessary consequence of the Incarnation: The one Person in Christ was the Son of God. As we have just said, divine personality is to be for Another—and, in the case of the Son, from Another.

In the human life of Christ it is this same thing that is most characteristic of Him: looking to His Father from

whom He had received all that He was, to whom He gave
all His love, seeking only to know and do His will: "I do
always the things that are pleasing to him" (John 8:29);
"My food is to do the will of him who sent me" (John
4:34). St. Paul sums it all up in one simple phrase, *Non sibi
placuit* (Rom. 15:3): He did nothing just because it was
His own good pleasure, but all things were the result of
looking to the Father and doing His will.

Toward men, the love of God, the divine agape, translated into human terms, can be summed up as a wonderful
regardfulness for others as persons.[14]

This divine regardfulness for the rights and possibilities of
every human being is essentially His character. . . . Christ is
God indeed; Christ has all knowledge and all power; He has
all things given into His hands. But all these gifts He uses in
order to give eternal life to the humblest and poorest, in order
that He may be loved by the simplest, in order that He may
strengthen the weak reed, in order that He may re-kindle the
poor smoking flax.[15]

NOTES

[1] C. Journet, *L'Eglise du Verbe Incarné* (Fribourg, 1951), II, 511 f.

[2] B. Lonergan, S.J., *Personarum Divinarum* (Rome, 1957), pp. 229 ff.

[3] V.g. Garrigou-Lagrange, Gardeil, etc.

[4] *Summa Theologica*, I, q. 14, art 8; I, q. 20, art. 2.

[5] *S.T.* I, q. 43, a. 3, ad 2.

[6] For an excellent exposition of a spirituality centered around the
divine indwelling, *see* M. Philipon, O.P., *The Spiritual Doctrine of
Sister Elizabeth of the Trinity* (Westminster, Md.: Newman, 1947).

[7] Pius XII, *Mystici corporis*, A.A.S. 35 (1943), 321.

[8] J. Alfaro, S.J., "Persona y Gracia," *Gregorianum*, XLI (1960), 5 ff.

[9] *Theology of the Mystical Body* (St. Louis: Herder, 1955), pp. 353
ff.

[10] *Gratia Christi* (Paris: Beauchesne, 1948), pp. 333 ff.

[11] Constitution *Benedictus Deus*, D.B. 530.

[12] *S.T.* III, 9. 6, art. 6. This whole question has been more fully

treated by Catherinet, O.P., "La Sainte Trinité et notre filiation adoptive," *Vie Spirituelle*, 39 (1934), 113 ff. Dom Marmion centered his whole spiritual teaching around this doctrine.

[13] C. Spicq. O.P., *Vie Morale et Trinité Sainte selon St. Paul* (Paris: Ed. du Cerf, 1956), c. 4.

[14] C. Spicq. O.P., *Agapé dans le Nouveau Testament*, 3 Vols. (Paris: Gabalda, 1958).

[15] Dom A. Vonier, O.S.B., *The Personality of Christ* (London: Longmans, 1922), pp. 218–219.

Chapter 4

HUMAN PERSONALITY

As we pointed out in Chapter I, it is necessary, for a true knowledge of spiritual theology, to study the spiritual life in its psychological setting. Grace is a sharing in the divine life, but it is shared and lived by the human person. God-given and God-directed, it must nevertheless be lived according to the laws of human nature. It will, if it develops truly, bring the human personality to a fuller human richness and maturity. The call of God to more perfect living cannot be a denial of all the meaning He gave to human nature by creating it such as it is. Hence we must consider some of the sound conclusions of the psychology of human personality.

A human person is an *individual existing in a free human nature*. *Personality* is a term in common use. It is easier to describe than to define. By personality we mean the human person considered in the exercise and control of his dynamic qualities, in his way of existing, acting, and reacting in all the circumstances of life; his reasoned and willed control of emotional drives, his acceptance of responsibility, etc. One definition of personality is: "The organized emergent totality of a human organism's individual characteristics, dispositions, values, and attitudes that regulate his adjustments to self and environment."[1]

1. Development of Personality

We shall not attempt to list all the factors which influence the development of a human personality; we shall, rather, consider some of the main lines of its growth and perfection. This chapter, then, will be a summary and a simplification. It can be that without distortion, for as Alexander wrote: "Psychoanalysis (and psychology) is a refining of the methods of common sense to understand the motivations of others." The refinements of common sense can be translated back into concepts and general lines which can be understood by anyone endowed with common sense, even if he have no knowledge of the more detailed and technically expressed findings of psychoanalysis and psychology. In less technical terms, we shall outline some of the more important aspects of the development of human personality. Different aspects of the one living unity, they are not mutually exclusive. It is useful, however, and even necessary, to consider the question from different approaches.

(a) EMOTIONAL MATURITY

A good deal of insistence is placed on the necessity of coming to emotional maturity if a human person is to develop as he should. The general line of such maturing is simple enough. As a man reaches his full human perfection, he must be characterized by the rule of his highest faculties over the other drives of his nature. Reason and will, man's noblest faculties, must rule his course of action and regulate his reactions to persons, objects, and events. Yet it is evident that a human being begins his development well before the awakening of reason. Instincts, animal urges, emotions play a great part in dictating his earliest ways of acting. Desire, fear, anger, etc., are the "motive" forces, that move him in his actions and reactions.

Then, as he comes to the age of reason and lives according to the dictates of right reason, he has to learn to moderate and control his instincts, the urges of animal nature, and his emotional drives and reactions. He must learn to integrate these forces of his nature with the higher, controlling forces of reason and will. As he does so, he is said to develop emotional maturity. This is a vast field, especially in the study of its details, and much has been written on various points. For our purposes, it is sufficient in this chapter to indicate the general principle, which is simple enough for anyone with some knowledge of human nature.

(b) ACCEPTING RESPONSIBILITY

This is obviously one of the important factors in human development. It is regarded by some as the chief indication of adulthood. The adult knows that he is responsible for his actions. He acts after reflection and, having done so, accepts responsibility for his actions. "I did not do it on purpose," "It was not my fault" are typical excuses of the child.

An adult assumes his responsibilities, whatever they may be and, in assuming them, becomes more perfectly a mature human person. It is a common view that university students and those in other similar categories are "irresponsible." The very word has a note of immaturity in its meaning. It is only by facing up to one's responsibilities in life, realizing what they are, accepting and carrying them out, that the human person can attain to maturity.

[35]

(c) FACING REALITY

This also is frequently given as a characteristic note of the adult. Its meaning, too, is simple enough. The child lives in a world of fantasy, dreams his dreams of the beautiful, the good, and the true, dreams of "living happily ever after." His horizons are unlimited, and the world seems full of possibilities for unalloyed pleasure and happiness.

The realities he must learn to face are the realities of the limitations of all created things: the imperfection of his own nature and possibilities, of other people, of society; the realities of life's difficulties which must be surmounted. Men must learn to live what Freud called "the suffering common to mankind." It is a natural thing that the young should experience an instinctive recoil from the hard realities of life. The real will always be less perfect than the ideal, and disillusionment is, in some measure at least, a fact of life.

Those who cannot resign themselves to accepting this difference between the ideal and the real are the dreamers, or those who in one of many possible ways take refuge from hard realities. The possibilities of this "escape from reality" are manifold. But again, it is sufficient to note the general principle and to leave more detailed examination until later.

(d) DEVELOPMENT OF AUTONOMY

The development of a reasonable independence, liberty, or autonomy is regarded as a necessity for the maturing of the human person. The child is, of necessity, dependent. The adult is one who has freed himself from the dependence characteristic of the child. There are various aspects of this attaining to liberty. A useful observation is that the word *liberty* comes from the Latin word for *free will*. In the true sense, then, a man attains full human liberty only by freeing himself from the tyranny of his lower impulses, instincts, and emotions, subjecting them to the rule of his will enlightened by reason. A man is not free until he is master of himself. In this sense, then, personal autonomy or liberty depends upon emotional control.

Then there is social autonomy. A man is of course dependent on others, on his milieu, for much of what he is. He must belong to a group, and he must be dependent on authority. The anarchist is still following childish impulses. It is not mature to rebel against all the ideals and customs of the group to which one belongs, on the plea of being independent. Nor is there real maturity in imagining that all decisions of authority are perfect, that all the ways of thinking of our society are the best possible. Man accepts the reality of society and the various groups of society. He also accepts the reality of their limitations. He can live with the limitations, accept the limited wisdom of their decrees, knowing that nothing created is perfect. One of the marks of the adult is his ability to admit authority exercised by people who have obvious limitations. A characteristic of the young is that the faults of those in authority make them reject authority. They have not yet freed themselves from the childish tendency to suppose that mother and father are perfect, and that authority is exercised by right of perfection.

The main steps in man's growth to full liberty, particularly in the choice of the good, must necessarily be considered in spiritual theology, for they have important consequences in many fields of the spiritual life, as we shall see later.

The will has a natural attraction to the good in general. Yet in regard to particular goods, there are all sorts of possibilities. Choice of one means rejection of another. The possibilities are infinite—before we make a practical choice. Each choice rules out something of what was possible in the abstract. Furthermore, with the awakening of reason, each individual person, in accordance with his individual character and as his early training fits him more or less to assume the burden of liberty, will have the more or less difficult task of mastering his feelings and emotions, instinctive desires, fear, attraction, anger, repulsion, sadness, etc. All these urge him to act in certain ways, while his reason is not yet able to judge clearly enough the sets of "values," which should be the norms of "good" action.

The first step, then, in acquiring liberty to do good in the various circumstances of life is by imitation. We imitate others; we accept their norms of action: their "do's and don'ts." Our way of acting is imposed from without. It must be; this is a necessary step in education. And so, by accepting as a reasonable norm for good action what others tell us is best, we transcend the original state of indeterminateness with regard to good and evil. Thus, although in a yet imperfect fashion, we develop a certain liberty: a rule of the will according to the norms of reason. (It should be well-noted that this is the first stage for all "beginners"—beginners on the way to perfection, beginners in religious life, beginners in the way of prayer. The following stages are also verified in these same fields.)

Man first frees himself from the tyranny of emotions and instincts by submitting them to reason and will according to certain norms which come in the first place from his parents and teachers. He learns by imitation, by the imposition of a set of values from without. As he develops, he comes to a new step in the development of liberty, autonomy, or independence. He realizes that in many things he must make his own judgments, his own decisions, and his own choices. He will be faced with the choice between different possibilities. Choosing one will mean rejecting the others. He will then be responsible for the consequences of his choice. There will be a certain risk involved in some of his choices—risk of error and its consequences, the risk of failure. Hence there is always a certain anxiety connected with freedom and the full acceptance of liberty.

Typical of such instances is the crisis of adolescence when a young man realizes his growing autonomy and his ability to choose for himself. If he shirks the responsibility of choice, remaining overdependent on his parents, he renounces his personal development to maturity. This overdependence is more likely to occur in girls than in boys. Another failure is the opposite: complete rejection of all that has been gained, of all the norms and values learned from others.

A reasoned facing of the demands of freedom, conserving what is of value in what we have received, adapting ourselves to new circumstances, decisive thinking in weighing all the factors involved, accepting responsibilities, accepting the risk, challenge, and renunciation which every choice involves, making the choice as adults, leaving the shelter of a dependent childhood—these are the characteristic acts of the adult.

We come, however, to realize that the good can be achieved in various ways. We have our own talents, potentialities, and personal qualities which must be developed. When we realize this, we see that it is impossible for us to be true to ourselves if we are content to remain forever in forms of moral goodness or perfection which we have borrowed from others. At least we should realize this. Each of us has his own personal destiny that he must face with full responsibility. And here man goes through a process parallel to natural maturing. Liberty takes responsibility with it—responsibility for the choice made, and the necessary rejection which every choice implies. There is risk in choice. Man will be tempted to avoid the risk. If he chooses to stay in the shelter of cut-and-dried ways of acting, which have become comforting, he chooses to remain in an immature moral or spiritual state.

This facing up to fuller liberty and to responsibility with its inherent risk and anxiety is, in many parts of the spiritual life, the turning point between advance and failure to progress. What makes it a more difficult point to pass is the human tendency to rationalize; man's great capacity to mistake illusions for realities, to find reasons for doing what costs less effort or entails less risk. Man does not like to admit that he lacks moral courage. He can find all sorts of reasons for not taking risks and he can *justify* these reasons. Unless he realizes these truths, a man in such circumstances can be governed by automatic character reactions. The developed personality will know what way his natural inclinations will take him; he will force himself to consider the situation objectively, in the light of reason and grace, and will act accordingly. And in acting he will develop his personality and his spiritual life. The man who has not a strong personality, who is dominated more by his character and temperament, will choose the less mature course of action, less reasoned, less perfect.

(e) FULFILLMENT OF BASIC PSYCHOLOGICAL NEEDS

This is another point much stressed by psychologists in their study of the development of the human personality. We must be content to note it here. It will be considered in much greater detail in later chapters.

(f) INTERPERSONAL RELATIONSHIPS

Many regard this as the best approach in studying the development of the human personality, since it includes many of the other aspects we have listed. For the purposes of this work, it is worth treating at greater length. It is quite certain that, to a large extent, the human personality attains its perfection when a man recognizes and responds to the demands, rights, and needs of other persons. If he does this according to right reason, he must exercise and develop control of reason and will over instincts and emotions. He must develop a sense of responsibility, etc. From this aspect, the main stages in the development of the human personality are the following:

1. THE INFANT. Self is the center of his existence. Other persons are regarded only as ministers to his needs, satisfying his wants.

2. THE CHILD. His consciousness awakens to others as individual "centers in themselves," as persons with their own personal demands and rights, and his consequent duties toward them. Acceptance of these personal demands of others is the first real step in the development of his human personality. There are demands of duty which he is constrained to accept—at first more from various emotions, such as fear, than from reason and will. There are demands of love, which he is urged to accept out of generosity and in an answering love. A good education shows these two to be one: The demands of duty are to be embraced out of unselfishness, love, or respect for other persons.

3. THE ADOLESCENT. He becomes conscious of his relative freedom and independence, his liberty to enter into personal relationships with others, according to his free choice. Hitherto, in his friendships outside the family he either chose his parents' friends as his own or needed parental approval. He also becomes aware of his liberty to accept the rights of other persons and the moral person of society. He may reject them, by his power to assert his ego, disregarding the claims of other persons.

4. The *young man* usually marries, and thus enters into exclusive personal relationships with another, transcending self by giving himself to another; making the center which regulates life a common one: common to husband, wife, and children, whose needs and welfare are placed first in his conscious living. It is a well-known fact that selfishness and self-centeredness are certain to ruin a marriage or, at best, to reduce its happiness and warp the human personality. (The equivalent "transcending self" is often found in devotion to one's parents, the needy, or "others" in some way.) Thus altruism is the measure of one's developing a mature and full personality.

5. Even in the *family*, there must be, according to psychologists, no closed and selfish family circle, but an interested "attachment to the human enterprise."

6. As these interpersonal relationships open a man's mind and heart to the demands of love or duty toward others, he achieves his fullness as a human personality in proportion to his self-forgetfulness. He really finds his own good by striving for the good of others, respecting the worth of other persons considered as such. It is interesting to see that psychologists require for maturity "a giving rather than a receiving attitude," "leaving egotism and competitiveness behind . . . realizing that hostile aggressiveness, anger, hate, cruelty, belligerency are weakness (as are trouble-making and childish criticism), and that gentleness, kindness, and good will are strength."

Note how each of these successive steps in the development of human personality is one further step in "self-forgetfulness"; each involves something further in the way of "self-renunciation." The more momentous steps of adulthood and marriage demand that the human person face and accept his responsibilities with all attendant risks, conquering his anxiety, and accepting the consequences of his actions. Marriage demands the surrender of oneself to the love of another and the unselfish acceptance of all the sacrifices which that love will ask.

In the same line of interpersonal relationships—beyond the realms of mere psychology, although psychologists do take it into account—is man's meeting with a personal God. God has His personal demands—again of duty and of love, with the two viewed correctly only if considered as coinciding. This last step is from the "natural" to the "supernatural"; for its attainment it demands the help of grace. More will be seen later of the need and role of grace. For the time being, we wish to stress that this last step in interpersonal relationships is in perfect harmony with all man's development as a human person. Therefore, all his "natural development" is in view of this last step, which was the first in the order of God's intention in creating and fashioning the human person. This meeting need not, of course, come after all the others in point of time. Those who as adults face the personal step of conversion (either initial conversion to the faith, or a second conversion to closer personal intimacy with God) will see the depth of the separating gap insofar as they have become attached to self in one form or another, or formed hindering personal attachments. For all of them, the transition will follow a course parallel to that of any passing beyond the limits of one's comfortable, self-contained world: attraction, yet aversion; wanting to have, yet fearing to lose. This transition can take place in two ways:

i. Perceiving the demands of a person who has rights and who will punish if those rights are not respected; acceptance of these demands from a sense of duty, or from fear of punishment: "unless you shall do penance, you shall all likewise perish" (Luke 13:3).

[43]

ii. Perceiving and responding to the appeal of a person who loves.

Both are free responses; the first is far from the maturity of faith, for it is parallel to the early responses of the child in the natural order. It is the fear which is cast out by perfect love. But, in both cases, we are aware of and respond to the demands of a Person above us; and in both cases there is a consent to the demands of God as our personal good.

Various consequences of this truth will be discussed in the course of the following chapters. In concluding this section, I think it necessary to stress that the importance of these points for ascetical theology and the spiritual life can hardly be exaggerated.

2. Obstacles to Personal Development

(a) PSYCHOLOGICAL

Emotional immaturity, refusal to accept responsibility, inability to face reality, exaggerated dependence—all these are indications of a lack of personal development. All these things, again, have an infinite variety of possible details, but we do not wish to study them here. Our main point here is a general one: that as personal development is, from one aspect, coincidental with self-forgetfulness, so is failure to develop equivalent to self-centeredness and egotism.

Here it should be useful to make a few observations with regard to neuroses and "preneurotic tendencies." A neurosis is really a breakdown of the personality, for it means that the reason and will have ceased to exercise their control of one or other of the emotional fields. As the great French psychiatrist Ernest Dupré said, the study of mental diseases is instructive for anyone who has to deal with people, because these abnormalities are only the exaggerations of inclinations to be found in all of us. I do not wish to dwell on the abnormal, but merely note that we all have preneurotic tendencies. These, unless controlled, can be obstacles to the development of our personality, even if they do not actually lead to a neurosis. They will also, as we shall see later, be obstacles to fuller living of the spiritual life.

"It must be noted that for all neuroses there is a universal basis: the tendency to autoanalysis, self-seeking, introversion." Preneurotic tendencies, then, are also tendencies toward self-centeredness and away from self-forgetfulness. Further, all flight from responsibility, all avoiding of decisions, all emotional immaturity is a failure in that renunciation of self which is necessary for personal development. These failures result from an effort to keep secure the concept of self which we have evolved: fear that *we* might fail, *self*-defense, imposition of *self*.

Further, it is now generally recognized that many psychoneurotic disorders originate in poor interpersonal relationships[2]: the failure to recognize, accept, and adjust oneself to the rights of other persons—either as individuals or a group.

(b) SIN

If grace perfects the human person, then sin, the effects of sin, and inclinations to sin would seem, logically, to be obstacles to the development of the human personality. And so they are; although, of course, in spiritual theology, they are seldom studied under that precise aspect, for they are considered more as obstacles to spiritual growth.

It is, however, most interesting and instructive to confront what the psychologists say about obstacles to personality development with the biblical concept of sin. There is far more to sin than transgression of a law. Its first aspect is that it is disobedience—rejection of the rights of a personal God, a refusal to respect His demands. It is, therefore, a nonacceptance of the basic interpersonal relationship between man and God. It is also called a sin of pride; it is self-assertion. It is man's wanting to be, *of himself,* what he can be only in dependence on God. It is man's claiming an unlimited autonomy. It is man's closing himself in his own universe, making himself, his own wants and desires, the supreme law of his universe. He thus sets up an unreal concept of self; sin is self-justification.[3] These are the ideas which are contained in the description of the sin of our first parents, which was the exemplar and cause of all subsequent personal sin.

For St. Paul,[4] sin is a force within man urging him to seek his own satisfaction, to reject the demands of a personal God, preferring himself as supreme norm, closing him in upon himself so that he is no longer open to the demands of God's grace, refusing to surrender to His love.

It is small wonder, then, that spiritual writers have always seen pride (self-exaltation) and selfishness as the only obstacles to perfection. St. Thomas said that the only obstacle to the love of God was love of self.[5] It is instructive to see that various forms of pride listed by spiritual authors practically coincide with the summaries of preneurotic tendencies of the psychologists. Doctors speak of "mental constitutions"—the particular constitutions of certain classes of character or temperament which predispose them toward personal lack of balance and eventual neurosis or psychosis along a particular line. These again practically coincide with what spiritual authors give as "predominant tendencies" expressed in categories of pride or concentration on self. The following division, given by Felix Duffey,[6] is as good a summary, from both the "spiritual" and "psychological" points of view, as I have seen. It could be quite profitably compared with the "Mental Constitutions" classified in *Medical Guide to Vocations* by Drs. Biot and Galimard.

1. PRIDE OF SENSUALITY: an inner cleverly concealed urge to pleasure. When this tendency colors thought and action, the affections are inclined to run away with reason; pleasure of the senses attracts so strongly that the observance even of simple duties is neglected. There is a strong romantic tone in the working of the imagination. There may even be a pronounced tendency to affectionate gestures and facial expression, sometimes carrying over into soft and flattering speech; it reaches a danger point when it develops into sensual friendship.

2. PRIDE OF TIMIDITY: sometimes walks in the garb of humility. As G. K. Chesterton said, "We are too proud to be prominent." Its worst effect is the vice of human respect. Essentially self-centered, it broods in silence and lacks the power to confide in anyone. It has too great a regard for the opinion of others, and a fearfulness of what others will think of possible failure. It sometimes makes people omit the good they should do, or not avoid the evil they should avoid, only because of what others may think of them. At times it makes one critical of others, branding them as "show-offs," or making one say, "I could do much better," "I would never make that stupid blunder." It lacks the courage of a frontal attack.

3. PRIDE OF SENSITIVITY: the world's injured ones. This pride causes them to detect insult and injury where they are never intended. This tendency shows itself in what is properly called touchiness. The person possessing it is generally kindly disposed toward all, but his temperature drops when his emotional nature is rebuffed. Somewhat

sentimental, the sensitive person cannot understand harder heads; he may give room to jealousy when attention is paid to others rather than himself. Easily wounded at the lack of response to his attentions, he has the tantrums of a child who seeks attention and does not find it. Unstable, he is given to fits and starts in his enthusiasms.

4. PRIDE OF COMPLACENCY: an exaggerated notion of one's own excellence. Ignoring the fact that God is the Author of all good in them, these people excuse their own failings; others are the cause of their shortcomings! Day-dreamers, they conjure up triumphs in the world of their own imaginings, neglecting the job on hand. Often they are boastful, and this is a way of concealing their own ignorance. They show off by witty sayings and loquacity, playing the clown only to have the eyes of all focused upon them; they preen themselves on their prowess in sport, singing . . . anything.

5. PRIDE OF AUTHORITY: a tendency to bossiness, the ambitious desire always to beat down the opposition in order to acquiesce in one's own will and way. Two of its chief manifestations are anger and stubbornness. It has the character of bludgeoning others into the ways it has traced and will brook no delay in having its commands obeyed. Those who possess this trait in marked degree are generally contemptuous of the opinions of others and do not hesitate to wound their sensibilities. Their audacity is not bravery but rashness to attain their ends, come what may. Leadership, in itself a good thing, for them means domination. Their zeal is generally zeal without knowledge and is imprudent.

3. Overcoming the Obstacles

All the principles of sound education, in the full sense, are directed to overcoming the obstacles to human development of personality. Psychotherapy applies the principles of psychology for the treatment of neuroses and maladjustment.

Again I wish to note only a general principle. If for neuroses and preneurotic tendencies there is a universal basis of autoanalysis, self-seeking, and introversion, then overcoming the obstacles will consist in general in insisting on the opposite. "Obviously, then, the direction to be given to these people is to distract them from their self-contemplation, to suppress their preoccupation with self so that they can develop a salutary exterior activity."[7]

This general principle again coincides with a general principle of spiritual theology. Negatively, a person overcomes the effects of sin by ceasing disobedience, by leaving his self-seeking and self-preferment to accept the demands of a personal God and to consent to *be* only what God wills him to be. Positively, he surrenders himself completely to the call of God's love, seeking to do His will, striving for His glorification, his eyes lifted to the Lord, his trust in His providence. Then, too, since the Second Commandment is like to the First, and he must love his neighbor as himself as the test of his love for God, it will be a law of love to regard others as the persons they are and to strive for their real personal good.

4. The Christian Personality

The steps in the development of the human personality are steps in the development of the Christian personality. For the person to whom grace comes in early life, grace which undoes the effects of sin will help this natural development, provided it is given full play. The person who, although he may not even think of God, develops toward full maturity of personality with its essential characteristic of unselfishness, will be preparing himself to be able to respond to the call of grace, and thus reach fuller perfection.

Grace perfects the human person, leading him to a further perfection along the line that nature brings him. The last step is a continuation in the same direction, and all that goes before is ultimately a seeking of the personal God who, as St. Augustine said, "is loved knowingly or unknowingly by all things capable of loving." But the last step is beyond the human person, unless he is further drawn by the divine Persons themselves, lifting him above the closed circle of "nature," strengthening him for the risk involved in this self-surrendering step into the unknown. This last step in the line of our self-perfecting is:

(i) harmonious with and perfective of all our natural tendencies, which is all the more so since the Incarnation brings it about that all our human response toward the man Christ becomes supernatural as soon as we recognize and accept His Person.

(ii) Like all responses to other persons, it is self-forgetting and self-denying.

(iii) It is an assimilation to, and a sharing in, the "personal life" of God, a complete "for Another-ness."

(iv) It reaches its fullest possible perfection in the ecstasy (*exstasis*—going out of oneself) of our union with God, which, in an active sense, is the complete giving of self to the Divine Persons, and in a passive sense, allowing ourselves to be possessed completely by another's love.

NOTES

[1] A. Schneiders, *Personal Adjustment and Mental Health* (New York: Holt, Rinehart and Winston, 1958), p. 566. Pope Pius XII, in his discourse to the Thirteenth Congress of Applied Psychology, said: "We define personality as the psychosomatic unity of man insofar as it is determined and governed by the soul."

2 J. Magner, *Personality and Successful Living* (Milwaukee: Bruce, 1954), c. VI.

3 S. Lyonnet, S.J., "Quid de natura peccati doceat narratio Gen. 3," *Verbum Domini*, 35 (1957), 34 ff.

4 S. Lyonnet, "De natura peccati quid doceat N.T," *Verbum Domini*, 35 (1957), 332 ff. *See also, Le Péché,* Series Présence Chrétienne (Paris: Désclee de Brouwer, 1951).

5 *S.T.,* II–II, q. 34, art. 5.

6 *Testing the Spirit* (St. Louis: Herder, 1957).

7 "Direction Spirituelle et Psychologie," *Etudes Carmélitaines* (Paris: Desclée de Brouwer, 1951), pp. 274, 321–322.

Chapter 5

ACTUAL GRACE—PERSONAL ATTRACTION

"Man is born many and dies one." His development is one of unification: controlling the various forces of instinct and emotion within himself by submitting them to the control of reason and will. All this is in view of something higher: that his reason and will may be guided by the Spirit of God. For only those who follow the lead of God's Spirit live as children of God (Rom. 8:14). The teaching of spiritual theology is not directed first and foremost toward perfecting the human personality. It is to help men to give themselves completely to God's Spirit of love.

There is a "unanimous teaching of spiritual authors that fidelity in following the inspirations of the Holy Spirit is the first and essential condition for any progress in perfection, and that real perfection and sanctity cannot exist without habitual docility to the Holy Spirit, who directs the soul by these inspirations."[1]

The necessity and importance of actual grace, for beginning and advance in the spiritual life, are truths that we hold most strongly. Since actual grace is of such importance, it is also supremely useful to understand the nature and function of grace in our lives. Theology teaches that actual graces, which are illuminations of the mind and inspirations of the will, are necessary for an adult to do anything in preparation for justification; necessary, too, for those in the state of grace to persevere; necessary for any real advance in the spiritual life. We hold firmly to these truths, even though many of us may not understand much about them. In this chapter we seek further understanding.

Pelagius must really bear the blame for the fact that the main text for actual grace became "Without me you can do nothing" (John 15:5). The absolute necessity of grace had to be strongly defended against the Pelagians, of course, but it was not altogether fortunate that actual grace (all grace in fact) was thenceforth spoken of, almost exclusively, as the power to do things. The key text for an understanding of the nature and function of actual grace is another sentence of Christ, "Nobody can come to me without being attracted towards me by the Father" (John 6:44). We have seen that revelation is God's making Himself known in His own personal life, and inviting man to enter into relations of personal friendship with Him. Faith is man's learning "to recognize the love God has in our regard and to make it our belief" (I John 4:16). If we remember this, we shall see that some theological problems can be examined from a slightly different angle—to our fuller understanding of the grace that is given us. These are the problems of the relation of faith and reason, the necessity of grace for faith and justification, and, in general, the exact role of actual grace at all the stages of a man's journey from infidelity to the vision of God.

In the last chapter we have considered the various steps in a man's interpersonal relationships, in which the final, crowning step was the acceptance of the demands of a personal God. Thinking of actual grace in this context will mean much more to most of us than the concept of grace as the power to do things. Seeing the function of grace at these various stages will help us understand the present function of grace in our spiritual lives. For the grace that runs through man's life from the first stirrings toward justification to the highest mystic states is the same vital reality of God's drawing the human person, through different stages, toward closer personal union with Himself.

1. Grace Preparing for Faith

The fact that grace is necessary for anyone to make an act of divine faith has been defined by the Church more than once. The explanation of this truth is not always easy to grasp. Catholics, to whom the faith is so obviously true, often ask of those without the faith: "But why can't they see that it is true?" Ultimately we have to reply that faith is a gift of God, and leave it at that. In the theology of faith, a much-discussed problem is that of the precise role of grace and reason in the act of faith. The problem is more obvious than the solution. It is, briefly this: The Church teaches that reason can prove that God exists; that, as supreme Truth, He can neither make a mistake nor deceive us.[2] Reason can also prove the fact that God has revealed certain truths. Why then cannot the human mind, which can work out all these things, assent to the truth of what God reveals? This would seem to be a perfectly logical conclusion: Since God has certainly revealed these things, they must be true. Yet the Church also teaches that for an act of faith, by which we assent to the truths which God has revealed, grace is absolutely necessary. One attempted explanation is that faith is supernatural, therefore beyond our natural powers, and hence needs grace or an extra power to do things. This is true, but it gives us no enlightenment as to what grace does. Various deep and intricate solutions of the problem have been proposed. None has been universally accepted.[3]

Let us remember that faith is more than a matter of seeing the force of arguments; it is not merely a question of assenting to truth. Faith does not remain in the realm of abstract truth; it passes into the personal order. "I accept this truth with all the personal implications it has for me." "I surrender to the call of a personal God, whose claims are supreme and universal." "What characterizes most clearly this 'new man' (of whom St. Paul wrote) . . . is the loss of his autonomy."[4]

A human parallel, which sheds some light on this question, is a decision to marry. Normally speaking, all the intellectual reasoning in the world will not get a man to relinquish his autonomy to the extent that he must in marriage. The effective and necessary help for him to do that in his experience of a personal attraction toward someone else. It must be an attraction strong enough to make him want to forsake the attachments which he must renounce, particularly the attachment to his own independence—to himself. If, for example, a girl is attached to the career which she has chosen—a career with an opera company— and also attached to the leading tenor of that company, you would be wasting your time trying to prove to her that it would be better for her to marry someone else toward whom she experiences no attraction whatsoever. A necessity, if she is to accept your "arguments," is that she should experience a personal attraction toward a third person, strong enough to make her give up her other personal attachments, and ready to "go out of herself" to give her love and life to another.

The application to faith should be simple enough. Actual graces, in the accepted phrase, are "illuminations of the mind and inspirations of the will." But these are not mainly to show us that arguments prove something, nor that we ought to do something (although they are this). They are first of all and necessarily, as St. Thomas says, "the instinct of the divine operation moving a man's *heart* to believe,"[5] a personal attraction, a being drawn to Christ. Faith is a vocation, being called as persons and making a personal response. Now, in any vocation—to priesthood or religious life—it is not enough to see that priesthood or religious life are good things. Any good Catholic sees that. Nor is it enough to see that I ought to be a priest or religious. There is, over and above the reasoning process, a mysterious attraction that touches my heart. This is the grace of vocation. Speculatively, of course, it could be analyzed into illumination and inspiration. It is lived as a personal attraction in the field of personal experience.

The grace of vocation to the faith is of the same sort. Unless that attraction of the heart is given by God, since it is "natural" to cling to one's own personal autonomy, man will not let himself see the force of the arguments which exist. "You do not come to me because you do not will to believe" will always hold true. The "not willing" can be caused by any form of natural attachment: to one's own egoism or selfishness, or to anything we fear we may have to renounce if we respond to the drawing of Christ to unconditional surrender. Here, there is another psychological case of man's facing up to the unknown, with the risk involved, to forsaking "self" and the ways in which he has grown comfortable. Man can think of all the reasons why he does not want to take this step; he can rationalize his lack of courage, can blind himself with all sorts of specious reasoning. The light of God's grace has to cut through his blindness; his will must be inspired and drawn toward Christ.

Actual grace is as simple as that: It is the personal attraction of the Divine Persons drawing the heart of a man. It is supernatural; it comes from God as His free gift; man has no right to it, but it is in perfect harmony with the deepest personal longings of his being. Man cannot take the first step toward personal friendship with God unless he be first drawn toward personal intimacy with God. Theology speaks of "elevating grace," of God elevating man to a higher plane of operation. It is in this personal context that this has most meaning. It is lifting man above the lower plane of his own self-centered existence to center his love on a personal God. For, of himself, he is like a mentally defective child; his life is on a lower level than the divine. He must be lifted up to share in the personal life of God. The Council of Trent taught that man must prepare himself for justification and faith. This necessary preparation is a man's progressive detachment from his own autonomy and egoism so as to allow his mind and will to be shaped by God's grace toward the likeness which must exist if there is to be any true friendship between himself and God.

Theology speaks of *gratia sanans* (healing grace) and *gratia elevans* (elevating grace). The first regards grace as given to heal man's weakness and proneness to sin; the second stresses the function of lifting man up to God, or toward union with Him. It is the general opinion of theologians that these are really two functions or aspects of one and the same grace. Actual grace, as this personal attraction, appears as obviously elevating, because it lifts man above his own closed circle of selfish interests. Any movement toward real personal friendship does that. And when it is a response to the personal love of God, it lifts him into the sphere of the divine. We have seen that sin, according to the biblical notion, is man's setting himself up as the final end of his existence, centering his activity around himself; pride of disobedience is a refusal to listen to the personal demands of God. He can only be "healed" from sin and its effects by the opening of his soul to God's demands, i.e., only by being drawn to center his love and will on another—the personal God for whom he is made. Sin is an assertion of self, making "what I want," "my own will and preferences," the deciding norm of activity, even should it conflict with the will of God. It is closing one's heart to the demands of God's love, shutting ourselves up in the closed little circle of our own egoism. Therefore, no grace can heal our nature from sin and the effects of sin unless it opens our souls to the personal demands of God; unless it elevates us to a personal relationship with God, drawing us to forsake our egoistic self-centeredness by drawing us to surrender to the personal demands of God.

2. Freedom under Grace

How can a man be free if he *needs* grace before he can make any move toward faith and justification? He cannot move unless God first give him the movement of grace; yet if God moved him, does he freely move himself? There is little need to say how much this problem agitated the minds of theologians. Yet, in the concrete sphere of human action, is it such a problem? Let us take a human parallel again. Does a man fall in love with a tree or a statue? Of course not. To fall in love, it is absolutely necessary for a man to be attracted by another person, perceived and recognized as a person. A man cannot fall in love unless he is moved by this personal attraction—or better, by the person who attracts him. Yet the splendor of human love is that it is free: a freely-willed and total self-giving to another person. You may, if you wish, speculate how this necessary movement still leaves man free. But, in the order of life, men will go their way and freely fall in love, which they could not do unless they were first drawn to another person.

If grace is a personal drawing of man's heart to God, it is also a necessity which, nevertheless, leaves him free. This is so obvious that one wonders why it presented such a problem, or rather one sees that speculation about living realities must not be too far removed from life. Grace may remain a mystery, but it is the mystery of human love. In this case, the love is for divine Persons from whom the attraction comes as a necessary "supernatural" grace.

This is, of course, not to decry speculative theology, but to insist on the necessity of thinking of actual grace in terms that can have real meaning for our spiritual life. Nor do we wish to say that this is a sufficiently deep theological explanation of grace, or grace and freedom. But it is a theological explanation that gives us some real light on the nature of grace and its function in our lives.

3. Actual Grace after Justification

This part of the theology of actual grace has the greatest meaning for spiritual theology, but what we have discussed is necessary for understanding the role of grace in the spiritual life. There is a paralled between God's calling people to faith and charity and His calling them to a special degree of charity. There is no *essential* difference between grace in the soul of a recently converted sinner and grace in the soul of a saint. God calls the sinner to conversion; He calls the converted to a more fervent life; He helps the recent convert hold fast to the grace he has received; He helps the fervent in their ascent to higher sanctity. Actual graces are given all along the line.

A question which generally puzzles the student of theology as he goes through his textbook is this: If the role of grace before justification is to elevate man's faculties, what is the need and purpose of actual grace after his faculties are permanently elevated by sanctifying grace and the virtues? Some authors give an example of a boat with sails (the virtues) which needs the wind (movement of actual grace) to set it sailing. This example is not very enlightening. Furthermore, it and other similar examples give the impression that actual grace after justification is not the same sort of grace as actual grace before justification. From the personal aspect that we have been considering, there is no such difficulty. Actual grace, we know, is needed in order to persevere in the state of grace, and special graces are needed if we are to grow in Christian perfection. These graces will be of exactly the same sort as those given to a man who is not yet in the state of grace. We still have need of healing grace to bind our wills closer to God, strengthening them against sinful attractions by a contrary drawing closer to union with God. The force of egoism, the inclination toward selfishness, remains with us, for it is part of our heritage of original sin. Pride and self-seeking are constantly recurring movements of the natural man.

From another point of view, the need of actual grace after justification is the ordinary human need of continually renewed personal contact with the person we love, if our love of friendship is to endure and be constantly lived in all things. When the person we love "dwells in light inaccessible" to mere human knowledge, there will obviously be a need of supernatural light and inspiration. The grace which, in the first place, draws toward a love of friendship with Another, by that very fact draws toward harmony of wills, with man transcending self. Between

God and men that harmony of wills must eventually be absolute, in all things. In this life the harmony will never be completely absolute with complete surrender of the whole man in all his being without the least trace of reluctance. Growth in perfection means approximating to that conformity. This is effected by God's drawing of our wills to more intimate personal union.

Scattered through the lives of all Christians who sincerely try to live for God are the high times of God's special calls, akin to the call to faith. Because of this kinship, they have, if accepted, received the parallel name of "conversions." They can be "vocations," in the more restricted sense of vocation to the priesthood or religious life. Within or without the framework of these more restricted forms of life, they will be always, for layman, priest, or religious, calls to closer intimacy with God. There will be the "personal attraction" to closer intimacy, with its appeal to man's freedom. The man who is called will again be confronted with an invitation to a further transcending of self, a further self-renunciation, a further step into the unknown, the land into which God calls him. There will be again the risk involved in the full acceptance of liberty, in giving up all ways, even in things spiritual, to which he has become accustomed. Here again, if he is not of the stuff of which saints are made, man will have all the old repugnances to this further self-surrender. He will, again, unless he has learned to be utterly honest and sincere with himself before God, find all sorts of reasons for not going further in his reply to God's call. He will again to able to "rationalize" his refusal, and again will need the light of God's grace to cut through his own darkness. He will need to have his heart and will drawn to closer intimacy with God—by a further "personal attraction" of actual grace.

[61]

4. Internal and External Graces

Paul planted and Apollo watered, but it was God who gave the increase. Unless God moves the heart of a man by His grace, no external grace of preaching or teaching can bring him to faith or virtue. Yet God wills that the faithful should work for the spread of the faith, and it is through their efforts that He brings others to the faith. External grace and internal grace work together. Just how they do is one of the mysteries of the workings of grace. However, there is one aspect which it is important for us to consider. It is often said that sanctity converts more people than learning. People are brought into the Church more through kindness received than through arguments as to the truth of the Church. It is impossible to see why this should be, if faith is thought of merely as an assent to truth and grace as an enlightenment of the mind to see the truth, or the power to perform higher acts. The personal character of grace brings some understanding of these truths, with important practical consequences for our own lives and apostolic work.

Internal grace and external graces (preaching, etc.) will work in harmony. If internal grace is a personal attraction toward God and Christ, those external things will be most in harmony with it that bear most clearly the mark of personal attachment to God. The pagan, the sinner, or any prospective convert will see in the lives of those who influence them the reality of a personal dedication to God. They will see it more clearly the more strongly it exists in the persons they know, the greater the personal sanctity of those with whom they come in contact. It does not require much learning to be able to convey to others the inescapable evidence of personal attachment—the Curé of Ars is historic proof of that. No amount of eloquent reasoning will give the same impression of personal conviction and attachment. This is true of any human relations. In ordinary life, a well-phrased proof of the fact that I *should* like some person will move me far less than will the statement of someone whom I know and respect who says simply, yet with utter conviction: "He is the kindest and most wonderful person I know." The parallel with the faith is evident.

With St. Paul, and with the Book of Wisdom, I shall take it for granted that all men, if they allow themselves to think without prejudice, can know that God exists.[6] If they, then, in the lives of those they know and respect, see the unmistakable fact of a personal attachment to God— a God who, by His grace, draws them to Himself—they will be drawn externally, also, to their own personal meeting with God. They will be drawn, too, through the kindness and fraternal charity of those they meet. When this real charity appears to them as the result of a conviction that they have a great personal worth in the eyes of God, their hearts are prepared to respond to His personal call.

As the Vatican Council taught[7] the Church herself is a sign of her divine origin. I doubt if her value as a sign is brought out sufficiently by constructing a statistical, syllogistic argument to provoke an intellectual assent. This is often done and doubtless has its value. But the Church is principally a sign in that, in her and her living members, those outside can experience the living reality of personal contact with God. Protestants will be brought to her only if they see her as the point of their fuller personal contact with Christ.

It is thus clear, too, why a child who comes from a home in which God was a personal reality, whom he early learned to meet, will have a deeper and stronger faith than one who learned more of the "truths" of his faith but has not met with persons who live the personal reality of real friendship with Christ. From this it would obviously follow that the chief value of Catholic educational systems is that, in our schools, the children see this personal contact with Christ and dedication to Him as a treasured reality in the lives of those who teach them. The value of these realities, for those who come from careless homes, can be beyond calculation. All this must make us who, in schools or any branch of the apostolate, are to be witnesses to Christ, reflect on the effectiveness of our personal witness. It is perhaps pertinent to recall a text from St. John (8:29) who relates how, when Christ spoke of His personal attachment to the Father, many believed. There were no signs or miracles. Christ said: "He who sent me is with me; he has not left me all alone, since what I do is always what pleases him. While he spoke thus, many of the Jews learned to believe in him." Commentators on the passage see this as one of those cases of utter conviction and personal dedication that are the most persuasive of all arguments. For a spirituality of the apostolate, the consequences of this truth are most important. They will be treated later.[8]

5. Salvation of the Infidel

There is one final problem of theology that may be capable of solution along the same lines: the salvation of those who never hear the Gospel. This may seem somewhat far removed from practical spiritual theology. Nevertheless, it also has its practical import, as we shall see later. How can these people assent to a truth which they never hear? Yet faith is an assent to truth. The problem seems a knotty one. For St. Thomas and those of his time, however, it did not seem any great problem: They hear "interiorly or exteriorly."[9] As we have seen, faith is not just an assent to a proposition; it is a personal surrender to God. And so it has been suggested[10] that when, to a man who by the light of his natural reason can know the existence of God, there comes the personal attraction of actual grace (which must come to every man), it draws him to recognize the personal demands of God who rewards those who seek Him. If then, under the drawing of grace, he submits to and accepts the personal demands of God, he thus passes into a personal or supernatural relationship with the God whom he has met as a person, recognizing and embracing His claims.

There is much from the theology of grace and the relationship of faith and reason which has been omitted from this chapter. The omission in no way implies a failure to realize the importance of what has been omitted. But an exposition of other aspects is outside the scope of this work. My purpose was to show how a view of grace, seen in its living, personal reality, throws light on some of the problems of grace, which touch us closely. It does not solve them all, of course, for God's ways differ from ours, and grace will remain forever a mystery. But, seen in this light, it remains a mystery with meaning: the reality of God's personal dealings with us and our personal response. Even the human person must, in his depths, remain inscrutable to all but his Maker—but he is a mystery we can accept, the mystery that we also live.

Before concluding this chapter, we shall give a little thought to the gifts of the Holy Spirit, for actual graces and the gifts are very closely connected.

6. Gifts of the Holy Spirit

It is the teaching of writers on the spiritual life that, as we advance in perfection, the gifts of the Holy Spirit must play a greater part in our spiritual life. Many of us do not have a very clear idea of the gifts and their exact function in the spiritual life. Many theologians do not seem to be agreed on the matter either. Furthermore, there is this practical difficulty: What should we do to foster the operation of the gifts of the Holy Spirit? As all spiritual authors say something about them, giving the usual division and the general nature of each of them, I shall not repeat here what can be found by consulting any one of them.[11] But continuing our personal approach we can get some understanding of the function of the gifts.

The gifts of the Holy Spirit are needed precisely because of the personal nature of the life of grace. If we take our human parallels of interpersonal relationships, we will see that a love of friendship can exist and yet be far from perfect. It may even need to be perfected further if it is to endure. Just think of a child whose desire is to act according to the will of its parents whom it loves. Left to itself, and unenlightened by its parents, it will still judge in a way that is at variance with its parents' wishes, even though it have all the good will in the world. It will judge according to its own self-centered norms, according to its own ideas and preferences. And so it will buy them useless presents and will "help" them in all sorts of hindering ways. Think again of a young married couple who, in spite of their love, can have all sorts of misunderstandings. This will be because they tend to judge "others by themselves." For the sake of harmony, they must develop an understanding, instinctively sensing one another's moods, preferences, etc. Love, as it develops, takes this instinctive understanding with it—a knowing without reasoning what the other thinks and prefers. By a deep personal love, two souls are tuned to perfect harmony and mutual understanding.

The gifts of the Holy Spirit (receptive potencies) give us that instinctive way of sensing the will of God, and of knowing God in that intimate knowledge which follows on love that is deeply lived. As a result, we act more instinctively according to divine norms, which are often not our norms at all. Even with our infused powers of knowing and loving God, and acting according to His will, we often judge His ways from the central point of self. Adopted children of God, taken into the circle of His personal family life, we bring with us our limited norms of judging. Confronted with the choice of the best mode of action, we will tend to choose in a very human fashion unless we are enlightened by our Father, who gives us His Spirit to lead us.

Wisdom is the highest of the gifts. This wisdom in the ways of God comes to us through charity which unites us to God and makes us "one spirit with him" (I Cor. 6:17).[12]

The work of grace is not just to help man submit his instincts and emotions to the rule of reason. This harmony within man is directed to something higher: the rule of the Holy Spirit. Man is united to Him in charity and lives attentive to His personal presence. The gifts shape his soul, his mind and will, to the divine likeness, so that instinctively, because of his oneness in love with the Spirit of Love, he knows and judges according to the mind of God.[13] If a man is to grow in the spiritual life, he must, as authors insist, become more docile to the leading of the Holy Spirit, more faithful in accepting His inspirations; and the gifts must play an ever more permanent role in his life. In practice what does this mean? It means simply this: that we try to live ever more consciously our life of personal intimacy with the Divine Persons, striving to be alert to the calls of God's love, to the least indication of His will. More will be said on these matters later. It was important to see the gifts of the Holy Ghost in relation to actual graces because of the intimate connection between the two.

NOTES

[1] J. de Guibert, S.J., *The Theology of the Spiritual Life* (New York: Sheed and Ward, 1954), p. 110.

[2] Vatican Council; Constitution *De Fide Catholica*, D.B., n. 1794.

[3] R. Aubert, *Le Problème de l'Acte de Foi* (Louvain: Warny, 1958).

[4] C. Spicq, O.P., *Vie Morale et Trinité Sainté selon S. Paul* (Paris: Ed. du Cerf, 1957), p. 40.

[5] *In Joan.*, VI., Lect. 5., n. 3.

[6] Wis. 13: 1–9; Rom. 1:18–32.

[7] Const. *De Fide Catholica*, D.B., n. 1794.

[8] Cf. XIII.

[9] *III Sent.*, d. 23, q. 3, a. 2, ad 2.

[10] J. Mouroux, *I Believe* (New York: Sheed and Ward, 1959), p. 69 f. E. Joly, *What is Faith*, Twentieth Century Encylopedia of Catholicism (New York: Hawthorn, 1958), pp. 108.

[11] A. Tanquerey, *The Spiritual Life* (Tournai: Desclée, 1930), p. 609 ff.

[12] *S.T.*, II-II, q. 45.

[13] This obviously fits in perfectly with the teaching of St. Thomas on the necessity of the Gifts. I-II, q. 68, art 2.

Chapter 6

PERSONAL ENCOUNTER

The spiritual life begins with a personal encounter between God and man—with man "learning to recognize the love of God in our regard, and making it our belief." From these beginnings of faith flow all degrees of the Christian life. If you would know whether a man has lived to the full his life in Christ, you ask first of all if he has grown into the fullness of a personal living faith.[1] The first stage in the Christian life is the acceptance of a personal God and His demands. This takes place for an adult at conversion. For one baptized in childhood, it occurs when he embraces the moral obligations flowing from the faith received at baptism. There is a class of people whose only aim in matters of religion is to do what is necessary to keep God's friendship, respecting His laws in order to be with Him forever in heaven. While they do not strictly limit their conscious aim to this, they have no habitual purpose of developing a more intimate friendship with God. With them, spiritual theology is not a main concern.

Our concern is with others—with those who feel a more imperious need of more intimate personal union with Christ. Many of them may never have formulated this need as a "desire for perfection"; they have never thought of themselves as "striving for sanctity." But under the personal attraction of grace, they feel they should "do more for God." They feel drawn to "live closer to Christ," "to make their lives more worthwhile in God's sight." To all of these the teachings of spiritual theology—and this book—are directed. For they have all heard, in varying degrees of clearness, the call of Christ to be perfect, to grow in charity and in personal friendship with Him.

Man's love for God is not an ethereal, unfelt sort of love—at least not in its perfection. Charity perfects a man in his human power of loving. We will never love God with a fully personal love unless we realize the nature and purpose of the power to love implanted in every human heart.

1. A Heart to Know Thee

St. Augustine, commenting on our being drawn to Christ by the Father (John 6:44), writes: "Give me someone who loves and he will understand. . . . But if I speak to someone cold and without ardour, he will not know what I say."[2] Grace supposes a human power to love. This power was given to man precisely in order that, under the drawing of grace, he might reach a personal love of God. "I will give them a heart to know me," says God through the prophet Jeremias (24:7). It would be an unreal abstraction to see in this merely an infused virtue. It is the whole man who loves, and a heart to know God is a humanly personal power to love, conditioned by the grace of God drawing man's heart to Himself.

One of man's basic psychological needs is the need of loving and being loved. This is a fact on which all psychologists are agreed. It is also a fact that this, as other basic personal needs, can be fully satisfied only in God.

Again St. Augustine's phrase is a byword: "Thou hast made us for thyself, O God, and our hearts are ever restless until they rest in Thee." He saw that man's search for love was, ultimately, a seeking for union with infinite Personal Love—God Himself, "loved knowingly or unknowingly by all things capable of loving." *Sublimation* is a common term for the fulfillment of our needs on a higher level. Often it is regarded as seeking a shadowy substitute for the full-blooded realities we would like to have but which freely, or by compulsion, we renounce. The true notion is, of course, that we are made for God, and our deepest personal needs find fulfillment in Him alone. The higher drama of the soul and its need for God is acted out on a lower level. Our bodily and emotional needs are given us that, in the passing pleasure of their imperfect satisfaction, we might know our need for God and know, although in imperfect fashion, something of the perfect contentment of our whole being which we are to find in eternal union with God.

As we have seen, you cannot oppose nature and grace. To live a life of grace, you must know your own nature. Yet nature—the nature of man—is not pure spirit; it is a combination of spirit, emotion, instinct, and flesh. It is from such a being that human love springs, even though it terminates in the divine. The being who has to live it must know his nature if he is to live it in peace of soul. Errors about human love are multiple. The opposite extremes are: (a) the Freudian concept that all human love is reducible to animal urges; and (b) what is called a "false angelism," the mistaken and impossible notion that a human being can live as if his life of love were purely "spiritual." For those who find their way to God through the natural human fulfillment of their need for love, as well as for those who renounce its natural fulfillment through virginity or celibacy, it is equally important to see the full reality of human love in its relation with the divine.

It may be useful to stress this last point. "There are persons who have an almost instinctive revulsion for everything concerned with the flesh, and flee marriage because of this physical impression. . . . Such a state is not normal."[3] A necessity for a balanced personality, according to spiritual authors and psychologists alike,[4] is "integration of sex." This means that, from the point of view of spiritual theology, there is only one really sane and successful way of living a life of celibacy. This is to see the place of sex in the plan of God, without any false inhibitions about it. This is more than merely accepting the fact that, as older authors said, God has attached pleasure to sex in order that people might take on the responsibilities of family life. Sex must be seen in the context of human personality and personal needs in order that both those who use it and those who renounce its physical use might live a life of deeper personal union with God.

In this matter, for any understanding, you must begin a long way off. If you want to understand what man is, and why he is as he is, you must consider well what he is called to be. When you keep in mind why man was made, then only will you understand why he is made as he is, and what must be his attitude toward the nature God gave him.

We were made for the vision of God—to be lost in an ecstatic, all-absorbing union with the Three Divine Persons of the Trinity, a union that will actuate to the full all our human possibilities of being and acting. Then only will all our seeking be ended, and all our nameless yearnings satisfied, and our restless nature brought to rest at last. For this goal were we created, body and soul, so that all our being and activity is, in some way, orientated toward the possession of God. As we have remarked before,[5] it is most important that we should not tend to think of God creating us body and soul and then, as a kind of afterthought, deciding to give us grace and a destiny to the beatific vision. It is necessary to stress this for, possibly more than most of us realize, we are heirs to attitudes and ways of thought conditioned by an implicit conviction that we could have been much better off had we been differently made. The supernatural thus appears as an atmosphere not native to us, in which we must always move awkwardly, like fish out of water. Knowing that God gives us special powers to live our new life, we are inclined to assume that much of our human nature becomes now a useless appendage which only hinders the higher flights of the soul.

It is of the utmost importance to have the right perspective. The center of the whole picture is an all-wise Creator who wills to share His life of personal intimacy with creatures. This sharing, which is His gift, will also be our conquest, to our own greater dignity and perfection. For this end (and for no other) God created us. An all-wise Creator, He does nothing uselessly; body and soul He made us, male and female, so that in all our living and loving we might grow in the knowledge and love of God.

2. Sacrament of Personal Union

Marriage is a sacrament signifying and giving knowledge of a higher reality. Like all sacraments, it is a sign of things to come, giving in human fashion some knowledge of the fullness of things divine. Here again we must avoid an error. Sacraments are sensible signs of spiritual realities. But we must not think of Christ, as it were, looking around for created things, choosing one, and saying, "We'll use this, and say it is a sign of this particular spiritual reality." It is not by mere chance that marriage, with its measure of human love, can serve as a sign of love without measure. God made it to be a sign. His purpose in creating human beings in such a way that they should marry and be given in marriage was that this "human institution" might serve as a symbol of the divine. It is not merely, nor chiefly, as a contract that marriage is a sacrament. It is a sacrament of personal union, giving some faint idea of what eternal, personal union with God will be. Thus it appears in biblical imagery through the Old Testament and into the New. The mystery of man's union with God, in and through Christ, is "the nuptial mystery" (Eph. 5).[6] Marriage is thus a sign signifying the greater reality of personal union with God. But a symbol is not the reality; the shadow is not the substance. Symbol and shadow bear within themselves the testimony of their own insufficiency. They give a faint foreshadowing of the reality; they are not ends in themselves. The reality they contain points onwards and upwards. Accepted as such it gives contentment and promise. But to see it as a goal which gives "happiness ever after" is to mistake the road for the goal, a mistake which must lead to disillusionment and discontent.

It has never been easy for the human mind to grasp the harmonious blending of spirit and matter in God's creation. Perhaps this is because in human living harmony emerges from conflict. The conflict has made us regard matter and spirit as two principles less connected than they really are. The sacramental system stresses their unity.

It is from their goal in God that all things take their meaning. Christ's revelation of God is that God is triune. Distinction of Persons in unity is the fullness of divine perfection. Father and Son are divine *ex-stases:* Their whole personalities consist of giving themselves to one another in divine delight and, as one principle, breathing forth the ecstatic love of the Spirit of their personal love. Each Divine Person is the image of the other; all are united in personal love and complete "for Another-ness."[7] The goal of all human life is the beatific vision, our divinization. Then we will be taken into the breathless eternity of union with God in personal ecstasy, to be lost in endless wonder in the absorbing love of the Three Divine Persons. Their personal life of intimate knowledge and love will be shared with man, and this sharing will actuate to the full all our powers of being, knowing, and loving, of giving and receiving. In that fullness we find eternal rest.

One of the aspects of all creation is that it is a sharing in the divine. This truth is fraught with mystery, even on the natural level, but it is a fact. All created beings participate in divine perfection or possess imperfectly and incompletely something of the infinite perfection completely possessed by God. Of man alone is it said in the Bible that he is made in the image of God. It is written: "So God made man in his own image, made him in the image of God. Man and woman both, he created them" (Gen. 1: 27). It is not in his isolated individuality, but by his union with other persons that he is most perfectly the image of his Maker, mirroring thus the image of distinction of persons in unity. Different sexes God created them, different and distinct persons, with different personalities. In the merely natural order, man and woman are made for personal union with one another to find themselves fully and to realize the fullness of their own personalities. Marriage is a personal union, spiritual, emotional, physical. It is a mutual, complete self-giving; in its most intimate moments of spiritual, affective, and bodily union it is possessed of an ecstatic and all-absorbing character. The union of husband and wife will be more human and more personal in proportion as each is more conscious and considerate of the individuality and personal dignity of the other. The completeness of their union and self-surrender makes them, as one principle, achieve their human fullness as parents, creating out of love an image of themselves in the personality of their child, united to them in love and embraced in the intimate unity of the family circle.

Marriage is the sacrament of personal union. As a sacrament or sign, it is meant to signify the future eternal personal union of man with a personal God, and the present personal union of grace and the supernatural order. As a sign, it gives knowledge. Through their experimental knowledge of personal union—spiritual, affective, and physical—human persons are meant to derive some knowledge, analogous and imperfect, of what will be the purely spiritual, yet fully actuating, all-absorbing, ecstatic, and perfect union with the three perfect Persons of the Trinity. But it is only a sign and a faint foreshadowing of the eternal reality. It is stamped with the mark of its own insufficiency. Those who seek perfect satisfaction in the created symbol will be frustrated and disillusioned. They will not even see it for what it is. It will not be for them the sacrament that lifts them to higher things.

Here, too, let it be noted, the universal rule holds good. Man finds himself, reaches his perfection as man, by transcending himself. The initial "walking on air," the ending of every romantic novel, is only the beginning. In married life, it is through the sacrifices entailed over the years of the development of their love, through their growth in self-forgetfulness, that man and wife are brought toward their full personal maturity. "Love seems almost like a ruse of nature to gain her ends . . . for, from the external point of view, love is a contrivance for inducing man to perform voluntarily what is most repugnant to him, to know self-sacrifice, nay even, in the end, the sacrifice of love, since it is through absence that all love settles its account."[8]

3. Direct Personal Union with God

Men and women are created with a deeply felt need of personal union with another. This need is known first of all on the natural level. It is a personal, not merely physical, need, including spiritual and affective longings. According to the plan of God, this psychological need of loving and being loved is directed further than any created persons: "Our hearts are ever restless until they rest in thee." For the majority of the human race, the way to a living, personal union with God is indirect—through the created sacrament. And so it is in two stages that they come to a deeper living of their faith and grace which, as St. Thomas says, is "a spiritual marriage of the soul with God."

All actual grace is a personal attraction to God and Christ. The grace of a vocation to virginity or celibacy is, quite simply, a personal attraction to direct personal union with the Three Divine Persons. Without such a grace, it has no meaning; it would be cramping, restricting the development of the human personality, and leading to endless frustration. Under the personal drawing of grace, men and women feel the call to a direct personal union with God, embrace it, will it, and vow it. They feel that they have no need of the created fulfillment to lift them to a life of personal union with God. This does not mean that they do not feel that they make a sacrifice; but it is a sacrifice made for a higher love.

The implications of this are many. First of all, however, it is necessary to point out that, according to the teaching of the Church, virginity is a higher state than marriage and does not cramp human personality.[9] In recent years, writers have done well to extol the worth of marriage—personal and spiritual. It is a sacrament, certainly, rich in signification. But since original sin and its consequences for humanity, the richer a created reality is in personal value and satisfaction on all created levels, especially the physical, the more is man inclined to make it a substitute for the "full contentment" (*satietas plena*) which only God can give. The symbol, instead of lifting him to the divine as it would have done infallibly in the state of innocence, becomes a weight which slows him down in his ascent to a personal union with God in this life. As St. Paul saw clearly, married people are "divided" in heart. The real is never on the same high level as the ideal. However, there is no need for us here to defend the state of virginity nor to prove its superiority over the married state from the point of view of perfection. For one thing, it is not chosen precisely as a "superior state"; and for another, personal sanctity, with which we are concerned, can take no pride in the perfection of its state.

We have said that the reality of marriage is never on the same high level as the ideal. Unfortunately it is often far below it. But it is important to remember that, for those who live a life of celibacy, it is the ideal which is renounced. Normally speaking, one does not renounce marriage because it is less perfect, because of drawbacks to the spiritual life which may be encountered in it. Still less does one renounce it because it is regarded as not worth having. The choice of virginity is a positive thing—an answer to a call. The grace of this vocation is a personal attraction—being drawn directly to personal intimacy with Christ. On Him, Who was "the most perfect among the sons of men," the human affections also can be centered, drawn along in the wake of the spiritual love for the Divine Person in Him. It is not, normally speaking, in cold hearts that such a call can strike a responding chord. "Give me someone who loves and he will understand." And he or she will understand, too, that the answer to the call involves, on the purely human level, the renunciation of all young dreams. Dreams are often idealistic; in renouncing their realization, one may give up more than the real could ever be in fact. But because it is divine love which draws, the greatest of human loves can be foregone.

In a recent best-selling novel, one of the characters says: "We are priests by vocation, and celibates by canonical legislation." The writer was an ex-religious, and in that phrase, perhaps, he reveals a failure to understand his own lost vocation. There may be laws around celibacy, as laws surround human love in marriage. But neither one nor the other is merely, or in essence, a matter of law. Both flow forth from the free gift of love; or else both are almost impossible for human nature to endure, and both are cramping and deadening. Virginity and celibacy are the glad gift of one's heart to God. Without grace, such a gift is impossible. Those who have not experienced the reality of grace will never understand this working of it.

A life of chastity—for the priest or the religious—is not merely a matter of not indulging physical urges and attractions. From the point of view of renunciation, it will be felt most, particularly with the passing of the years, on the affective level. This need of love and companionship will be felt on the natural level, but those who live it will know that it is a need ultimately for God, and one which will not be fully met outside the vision of God. When it is felt—and feel it we must—we must turn to the God who has called us to direct personal union with Himself and ask Him to fill our hearts more fully. When felt as a need for more direct fulfillment, that is what we must expect, for we take our human nature with us. But we live by faith and personal attachment to Christ, and "temptations" can be seen as reminders of our deeper need—our eternal need of personal union with God.

The model of all who live a life of chastity is Christ, the Incarnate Word; next to Him is the Virgin Mother. At the Incarnation, in the power and peace of the Spirit of God, the Spirit of eternal love, the Word, a Divine Person, united to Himself a body and soul of our human nature. In Him, the restless turbulence of human nature was stilled and fixed in the eternal peace of personal (hypostatic) union with the Word. For Christ, as man, marriage was unthinkable. It was not that He despised marriage which He had blessed and made a channel of grace. But as we have seen, marriage is a sacrament: a sign and a steppingstone to personal union with God. The person of Christ had been ecstatically united eternally with the other Persons of the Trinity. In His human nature He possessed the fullness of the vision of God in personal unity and love. He possessed the substance; how could He turn back to the shadows? Mary was the Virgin Mother of God. As such, she was taken directly into unique personal relationship with the Three Divine Persons. Her relationship with the Word who became her Son was at once spiritual, affective, and physical. She, too, was above and beyond the ordinary way of ascent through created signs to personal union with the divine. All those, who through the centuries of Christianity, have followed her example of virginity, have done so because the grace which they received in lesser measure than she, who was full of grace, drew them into personal and direct union with Christ, and through Him with Father and Spirit. In the power and peace of the Spirit, they have been called to live beyond the turbulence of the flesh and all its uneasy seeking. This they will do only if they live in love.

The theology of virginity, especially as expounded by Saints Cyprian, Ambrose, and Augustine, is developed along the lines of the "nuptial mystery." Thus also it appears in the ceremonies and prayers of the liturgy. Its basic inspiration was the theme of Chapter 5 of the Epistle to the Ephesians: the Church is the Bride of Christ; members of the Church are united to Christ in an intimate union of which marriage between man and woman is only a shadow and symbol. This spiritual reality shines forth most clearly in the life of the virgin who, consecrating herself to God, goes to her profession as a bride to her marriage with Christ.

Our liturgy still retains something of this symbolism, particularly in the feast of the Epiphany. In the Vespers antiphon for what used to be the Octave of the Epiphany (now the feast of the Baptism of Christ), three happenings are linked together in what seems something of a coincidence: the Epiphany, with the Wise Men from the East coming to Christ, our Lord's Baptism, and the first miracle wrought by Christ at the marriage feast of Cana. Their linking is not from coincidence, but a spiritual and symbolic unity. In the Eastern Church, January 6th was originally regarded as the Birthday of Christ—the feast of the Nativity. When, later, it was made the feast of the Epiphany, that made no difference, for this was the day when Christ was manifested to all men, and when, in the person of the Magi, all peoples came to Christ. These earthly kings came to offer their gifts at the wedding of God with humanity. Baptism was the Christian's nuptial mystery, and in the East the Epiphany, rather than Easter, was the great day for baptism. Christ, at His baptism, goes down into the waters, to communicate to them the cleansing power of the Spirit of life and holiness. From the cleansing waters of baptism, the Church, the Bride of Christ, is born without spot or blemish, to be united to Christ as His bride. The wedding feast at Cana fits naturally into the whole context.

The Armenian liturgy, to take but one example, expresses the idea of this invitation addressed to those who were to receive baptism: "O you who have been invited to the wedding feast of the heavenly bridegroom, come and receive your baptism at this glorious feast. Robe yourself with the wedding garment woven by the Holy Spirit."

The consecration of virgins and entry into religious life for women has always retained the external expression of this symbolism of the reality of grace and personal consecration to Christ. The heart of the vow of chastity is the vowing of one's heart to God. The other two vows of poverty and obedience are seen correctly as the fuller expression of this gift of self out of love.

The "poor" of the Old Testament and the "poor" whom Christ declared blessed were not those who were just materially destitute. The word had a religious sense, and the "poor" were those who looked to God for everything, wanting only what He gave. Conscious of their need and insufficiency, they turned toward the Source of all being to allay their hunger and thirst for happiness. Those who saw that material possessions could give the illusion that we have filled the void of our own insufficiency renounced such possessions in order that their souls might be open to the influence of God. In religious life, the subject goes for material goods to the superior who, in his or her authority, represents God, so that in this way of acting, one externally professes looking to God for all things, content with what He gives, and wanting most that He give Himself.

[82]

Obedience is one further step in complete personal surrender to God, renouncing one's own will, to be led only by God through the exercise of the authority of His created representatives. It is lived not chiefly as renunciation, but as fullness of personal self-giving.

NOTES

[1] *Code of Canon Law.* Canon 2104.

[2] *In Ioannis Evangelium, Tract.* XXVI, c. 6; P.L. XXXV, c. 1608.

[3] R. Biot and P. Galimard, *Medical Guide to Vocations* (Westminster, Md.: Newman, 1955), pp. 197–198.

[4] *Supplément de la Vie Spirituelle* (1958), n. 46.

[5] Ch. 2.

[6] D. Barsotti, *Vie Mystique et Mystère Liturgique* (Paris: Ed. du Cerf, 1954), pp. 112 ff.

[7] Cf. Chapter 3.

[8] Jean Guitton, *Essay on Human Love* (New York: Philosophical Library, 1951).

[9] The age-old doctrine of the Church was restressed by Pope Pius XII in his encyclical *Sacra virginitas.*

Chapter 7

PERSONAL DEDICATION

---

1. Natural or Supernatural?

Spiritual authors warn us about the danger of being "too natural" in our activities and tell us that we must make constant effort to make our lives more "supernatural." We are told that unless our deeds are "informed by charity" they are worthless for the spiritual life. We know that there are such things as "natural" virtues, as they are possessed by pagans. How are we to know that what we do is not merely the exercise of such "natural" virtues? Do not many of our actions seem to spring from "natural" motives? We get into the way of doing things out of habit, and we derive a certain amount of natural enjoyment out of doing them. Does this mean that what we do is in danger of "degenerating into merely natural activity or activism," as we are sometimes warned?

There can be no doubt that statements and questions such as those we have just listed give rise to doubt and uneasiness. This doubt and uneasiness increase if some of us are engaged in work that does not appear very "spiritual" by nature. We wonder what our lives are really worth (a) in the line of merit, as having value in God's sight, (b) in the way of our own sanctification. We want our lives to be given to God and lived for Him. Our spiritual life begins with that strongly lived personal experience of the gift of self to God. Strong and noble in its beginnings, it seems, then, to cease suddenly—at least as a surge of personal life—and to fall back into the drab, the ordinary, the merely human. Has something gone wrong? Have *we* mistaken the way? Or was our initial mistake an unreal view of the truth? Was that which we thought we saw only the illusion of splendor, with the real thing very ordinary after all?

The answer to such questionings is contained in what we have already seen: the personal character of grace. We must draw out some of its further implications. This can best be done by seeing human parallels. Theologians today are explaining many questions about the nature of the moral life and the necessity of grace in connection with what is called the "fundamental option."[1] We might call this the fundamental, personal choice in life. It is, in a very true sense, that which gives a definite character to the whole of a person's life, automatically influencing further personal choices and the whole direction of one's life and action. If a man chooses to be first and foremost a family man, all his other choices and activities are subordinated to and directed toward his life in and for the family. He need not explicitly formulate his choice by the judgment, "I am first and foremost a family man," but that choice is evidenced in his whole way of acting. He is offered preferment in business—which he refuses almost without thinking because it would take him away too much from the family. He is invited to join a certain club; before deciding, he weighs all the factors. His ultimate decision

rests on the compatibility of club obligations with his devotedness to his wife and children.

By contrast, we may take the case of an actress, first
and foremost a career girl. If her husband stands in the
way of her career, she divorces him on the grounds of
incompatibility. This example is so well known that it
need not be developed.

In the merely human sphere, of course, there can be a
few competing and near-equal choices. But cases of conflicting claims show which one is supreme. Even the
supreme choice will often leave quite a lot of neutral territory. Furthermore, often things will be tolerated which
are at variance (although not seriously) with the fundamental choice.

The supernatural order—from the point of view of the
man who lives it—is the order of personal union with God.
A man enters into it by making his absolutely fundamental
option, or fundamental personal choice for God and His
personal demands. Over and above all others, this will be
the supreme choice to which all others are subject. Nothing will be tolerated in his life that really conflicts with
this. Expressed in this way, the reality of his living for
God is already a great thing in his life, for it rules out all
mortal sin. But for the man who wants to do more for
God, for the person who has experienced a call to a life of
closer intimacy, for the Catholic who wants to live his
faith more fully, there will be more than that. There will
be the decision to have that supreme choice rule his life in
all its details. The most obvious instance of this is a priestly
or religious vocation, for there you have the definite experience of a complete personal dedication to God. With
it goes the wish not to tolerate anything at variance with
this supreme personal dedication. The same applies to anyone who has, in reply to the personal invitation of God's

grace, decided to live a life of closer personal intimacy with Christ. In other words, it applies to all those with whom spiritual theology is concerned.

Now, what norms must they apply in judging the value of their lives? How are they to know whether what they do is "natural" or "supernatural"? They have only to ask: Are their lives, and all things in their lives, a practical way of living out this personal dedication to God? If they are, they are completely supernatural, for they are completely "personal." Again let us consider human parallels. We must do this if we are to have a sensible approach to the whole matter. Some good-willed people have rather distorted notions about this business of "supernatural" motives, as if they have to be thinking about doing things for God in order to make them really "for God." They set off to do something with the best motives in the world, and then they get caught up in their task. When, some hours later, they return to their prayers, they realize that they have hardly thought of God at all, and fear that it has all been time wasted as far as their spiritual life is concerned. On the other hand, they may be given an assignment for which they have no natural liking. They do it, but because of their natural repugnance they feel that they are half-hearted and that the work has no value in the eyes of God. Or, after the deeply experienced beginnings of their personal self-giving to God, they go about ordinary everyday tasks that appear drab and "worldly." They envy the "spiritual life" of others, and fear that the light has gone from their own.

But let us take the human parallel: a husband and wife, whose lives in marriage have been dedicated to one another. Because of his personal dedication the man goes off to the office to earn a living. He will spend most of the day coping with business problems, thinking about his job, exasperated by other people. Except for the early part of his married life, he will not sit down at his desk dreaming about his wife. When he returns from work, his wife—if she be reasonable—will not think he has lacked personal devotedness just because he has not thought of her. If, on the other hand, he does think of her often during the day— and because of so doing, fails in his work, and fails as a provider for the family—she will not want that sort of impractical personal devotion. She in turn will go about the prosaic tasks of cleaning, cooking, and sewing with her mind on her job. All flows from her personal dedi- cation. Were he to return from work to find that the house was untidy, the dinner not prepared, he would won- der why. If she told him that she spent the day just sitting down and thinking of him, he might possibly be pleased the first time. At least by the third day, he would send for the doctor!

We live a life of grace by living our personal dedication to God. But grace does not destroy nor distort our human nature. God does not expect from us an unnatural sort of personal dedication, similar to what we have just described on the human level. Spirituality is not a species of mental acrobatics that enables us to think about God while we are doing some mind-absorbing task which our personal dedication to Him demands. It is living our personal dedi- cation to Christ. This we must do in our human fashion, with full attention given to the task in hand. What if we do not think of God when we get caught up in our work? Why are we doing the work anyway? We would not be doing it were it not for our fundamental personal choice for Christ. What if some of the things we are asked to do fail to stir any natural enthusiasm? Personal dedication cannot make us like all the things which it brings in its train. Nor can it retain forever that initial "honeymoon" quality—not if it's normal. It will settle down to steady, daily devotedness.

If, on the other hand, we develop a natural "liking" for the things we do, there is no need to fear that we thereby lose something of the supernatural character of our motives. St. Thomas taught that we had not developed a perfect virtue until we did things with ease and delight.[2] A man can be naturally temperate, just, and virtuous. These are natural virtues. But these, St. Thomas said, and all theologians agree, are not true virtues unless they are informed by charity. What does this mean? It means simply that unless they are directed toward God by our personal decision to accept His love and live for Him, they are of no value for eternal life; they are not part of any spiritual life. On the other hand, once they become part of our living according to our love for Christ, they are integrated into our "spiritual" lives.[3] There would seem to be no need nor human possibility, ordinarily speaking, of having an actual motive of love in all that we do. That is, there is no need to think explicitly that we are doing this particular thing because we love God. The housewife we mentioned sweeps the kitchen because she loves the members of her family. She does not love them the less if she does not consciously think that she is sweeping the floor out of love for them.

In our supernatural life, which is just our personal life for God, it is the same thing. Once the personal dedication to God comes into a man's life, all his natural virtues are lifted to the supernatural level because they take on a personal character. A man may be just, courteous, or temperate because he thinks it is the gentlemanly thing to do. This is good, but it is all directed toward himself and remains in the natural circle. If he is courteous and temperate out of love for his wife and family, it is better and more noble. If he is all these things because the gift of his life to God demands it, they are all the practices of supernatural virtue, because they are personally directed to God.

Theoretically, it is as simple as that. Positively, it is as straightforward as that. But there are the inescapable negative elements in life. There are all the myriad ways of self-seeking, even when we start to do things from altruism and dedication to God. Hence, in the spiritual life, there must be perpetual vigilance and constant effort to live consciously our personal dedication to Christ. From what we have just seen, this cannot consist in an effort to think of God when dedication to Him demands that we think of the work in hand.

We are so made that although we begin an undertaking gladly and from noble motives, we often feel the work weighs heavily upon us. Caught up by cares and wearied by monotony, we are preoccupied with what the work is doing to us. Or we become proud of the fact that *we* are doing the work. Whichever way it goes, our thoughts tend to center on ourselves: our trials, our work, what we are doing, or what we are doing without because of it. There is something wrong in our spiritual lives when we start to count the cost, when we think of how much we do for God, or how much we give up. At times we may not be able to help thinking of this, but if it becomes a habitual frame of mind, the light has died out of our lives. True love does not count the cost nor make a list of things it puts up with out of love. When you begin to count the cost, you are really beginning to wonder if it is worth the price. In this regard, the only spiritually healthy sentiments are those reflected in the prayer of David: "Wherefore I also in the simplicity of my heart have joyfully offered all these things. . . . O Lord God of Abraham, and of Isaac, and of Israel, our fathers, keep for ever this will of their heart" (I Par. 29:17, 18).

Our constant effort here, as in all things in the spiritual life, must be to transcend self, to look beyond the work to the Person for whom and with whom we work. This is the only way to avoid the danger of routine and depersonalization that lies in wait for every man. All spiritual authors urge us to "raise our minds and hearts to God frequently during the day." The most necessary and most profitable way to do this is to make each thing we do our tribute of personal love to the God to whom we have made our complete personal dedication. "See I am coming to do thy will, O my God."

But what of the things in which we do not feel inclined to count the cost, the things we rather enjoy doing, even naturally speaking? Though, as St. Thomas says, as virtues become more perfect we perform acts of virtue with ease and delight, it is also true that we can enjoy doing things, not because it is virtue to do them, but because we would like to do them for ourselves, even if we were not asked to do them for God. Since human nature is so subject to illusion, are there any means of knowing whether we are doing things for God or for ourselves? It is easier to say that we are doing something for the Lord alone than to be sure that we really are.

There are a few acid tests, given by Our Lord Himself, and stressed by all the masters of the spiritual life.

2. Fraternal Charity

"The mark by which all men will know you for my disciples will be the love you bear one another" (John 13:35). By this will you, and all men know that you seek

Christ's will and not your own, that your life is centered on Christ and not on yourself. St. John, the disciple of love, was even more emphatic: "If a man boasts of loving God, while he hates his own brother, he is a liar" (I John 4:20). *Hates* has to be understood in the biblical sense of refusing to love. It can be a merely negative thing; there is no need for it to develop into the positively conceived attitude which we call hate. If you do not positively love your brother, you do not love God.

For purposes of salvation and keeping the commandments, this can be reduced to a fairly easy minimum. Love of benevolence means wishing someone well—charity means that we wish salvation for all, even our enemies. Even writers on the spiritual life can water things down. One man writes that this does not mean that we *like* our brothers, for love is a matter of the will. Love, the love of charity, is a divinely infused virtue, but it is lived by the human person. If we grow in virtue, it will become a part of ourselves and cannot remain an aloof "wishing well" to another. It will also be more than a fulfilling of a commandment. God commands us to love our brethren. Well, we love God, so we accept His commandments and love others in a detached, impersonal sort of way. Is this the test that we are Christ's disciples? Is this the mark that the "love of God has reached its full growth in our lives" (I John 4:12)? I don't think so. But—more important—neither did St. John, nor did Christ. This minimum may be sufficient to acquire and conserve the state of grace. But it is the bare beginning and nothing like the fullness of charity.

The intimate bond between the love of God and love of others is studied by theologians from the speculative point of view. I wish to point out here that it is a psychological necessity. If we don't love others—our brothers—our neighbors, those with whom life throws us in contact—then we are self-centered. And if we are self-centered, then our life is not centered on God. And if our life is not centered on God, then there is no fullness of charity in our life. It is easy enough to think that we are living for God in all things, not for ourselves. But God is invisible; He does not jostle us or come to us with importunate demands. He waits for us to look to Him, to turn to Him. We do so when we are ready, at our leisure, at our convenience. We tell him that we will do certain things for Him, not for ourselves. We offer Him our day and then go off and live it in the way that we have decided best pleases Him. All for His good pleasure? We hope so. But, "He has seen his brother, and has no love for him; what love can he have for the God he has never seen?" (I John 4:20).

He has seen his brother, and lived with him, been importuned by his demands, thrown out of his routine by him, asked to do what he wants. He has been asked to consider his brother's needs, not his own preferences. "If he steels his heart against his brother, how can we say that the love of God dwells in him?" (I John 3:17). How can he say that his life is not centered on himself?

Self-love is centering our lives around ourselves. Charity is the opposite. St. Thérèse of Lisieux, with the perception of the saints, taught that it was always easier to offer to do things for others than to accede to their requests for help. When we offer to do works of charity, we can retain something of ourselves in what we do. It is what we have thought of doing, what we have decided to do. In a way, it still flows forth from the center of self. But when others ask us to do something, we make their needs, their wants, the center, the norm of our action; and that is complete self-renunciation. Charity does not mean inflicting on others what we decide will be good for them, giving them the things we think they would like. Charity regards others as persons, individuals, "centers-in-themselves." It seeks to approach the practical problem from the point of view of the other person—his needs, his likes. (There should be no need to say that all this is subject to God's will, commandments, right reason, and common sense. If the demands of others are puerile, unreasonable, or not for their good, they merit no consideration. But let us not brand as puerile, etc., what *we* don't like!)

Charity, love for our brethren, is a sharing in the love of God. The love of God does not wait to see the good in others to which it then responds. Charity is a love that goes out to others to do good to them, to benefit them, and by so doing to make them good and lovable. It is a sharing in the "divine regardfulness" which characterized Christ's attitude toward all men. We have said nothing about charity when we have said that we get on well with others. We start to say something about it when we speak of our regard for them as persons, when we think of them as individuals with their own individual worth and claims on our charity. Charity begins when we begin to forget our own needs and likings; when our first thought is for the needs of others, how they can be helped to be themselves, to reach the full development of personality that God wills for them. This is far different from our wanting to make them what we think they ought to be.

It is truly said that we fail in charity if we are indifferent to anyone, even the least of our fellow men. A good practical question to ask is whether we try to see persons from their point of view, their aspirations, longings, hopes, needs, difficulties. Or do we see them only as centers of force that conflict with the concentric circles that surround our own existence? It is not charity if we get on well with those we like and will no harm to those we can't stand.

Charity is far from full as long as there is anyone we "can't stand," except it be for real evil or nastiness of disposition. Why are there others whom we can't stand, anyway? "They get on our nerves"—is a confession that we approach them from our central point of view. "They have nothing in common with us"—except the human personality, individual worth, and personal destiny! Does not this statement really mean: "They do not like the things I like; are not interested in the things I am interested in; don't talk about the things I like talking about"? Does not this mean that we are not interested in them as persons? Then this is a lack of the perfection of charity and a proof of a lingering self-centeredness.

How do we characterize others? Do we think of them as "not interested in the higher things of life," "no appreciation of literature, music, sport"? As long as there is any sort of snobbishness in our attitude toward others, we have not accepted them as persons, with their personal worth, their personal individuality, their personal differences. We think they are imperfect because they do not have what we have, because they don't choose to be interested in the same things as we are.

Even when it is a question of real defects, the same holds good. True love is never blind, but it sees beyond all externals and all defects to the personal worth and the real good. It knows that, in spite of weakness and blindness and all the limitations of human nature, there is a human heart in need of God. Often, that human heart is seeking, in the best way it knows, to give itself to God. But because its way is different from ours, we look upon it with pity and condescension. Charity sees beyond ill manners and uncouthness, and uncleanliness and inconsiderateness. Charity is patient, and charity is kind, not in an attitude of tolerant condescension, but in an appreciation of the real worth there is in every man. In the heart of every saint there was a real compassion, for sanctity is sharing the mind and heart of the Christ who was able to feel for us in our infirmities (Heb. 4:15).

To regard others as persons, not indifferent to any man: this is the practical test of charity. What is our immediate reaction to a request from another (for a real test case, let us take someone for whom we feel little natural liking)? Do we think first about how much this is going to disturb us? Or do we think first of the other's need? When we are with a group, do we look around for those whose company we enjoy? Do we feel tempted to avoid someone because he gets on our nerves? At times, because of our own frailty, it may be best to do so, but we still have a long way to go. With others, how much do we think of what we can give them? Christ said, "It is better to give than to receive." Psychologists say that a necessity for maturity and equilibrium is "a giving, rather than a receiving attitude." In our discussions, how much is there of our wanting to get someone else to accept our opinion? How "impersonal" is our seeking after truth? In our conversation, how much is what we want to say and are determined to say anyway?

In religious communities and in the Church in general, I wonder if sufficient thought is given to true personal charity toward superiors. Those in authority are often apart and alone. Sometimes the fault may be theirs, but that is their care, not ours. Most frequently, the fault is ours. Bishops and superiors are there to command, to make decisions, and to see that they are carried out. The natural thing, then, is for us to think of them as those whose decisions we have to accept to our own self-renunciation. Because we see their authority as coming from God, we must think in terms of their "office," which we accept in faith, irrespective of the personal qualities of the man who bears the burden of office. But how often do we think of adding to faith that share of true fraternal charity to which the person is entitled in his personal dignity? Beneath every pectoral cross is a human heart, as there is beneath every badge of office. There is a personal worth and dignity with its demands for real personal charity. All of us are subject to authority. We respect the authority—which is only half of what we have to do. How many of us add our need of personal love? Yet we all should for the fullest sense of a living charity. "Bear ye one another's burdens" (Gal. 6:2). The greatest burden is that of authority over one's fellow men. Let us not add to it by steeling our hearts to a brother's need, by regarding him merely as the occupant of an office that restricts the expansion of our "self." To do so is to be far from the mind of Christ.

A further aspect of charity, the "social dimension," will be treated in Chapter 16.

3. Obedience

"What I do is always what pleases him" (John 8:29). Doing always the things that please God, seeking His will and not our own, is, after the example of Christ and according to His repeated teaching, the norm of holiness and the test of true charity. Giving ourselves to God means renouncing self, losing our life to find it. This is not something special to charity—it is the common law of any personal love. Even the human love which brings a man to natural perfection does so by demanding successive and repeated self-renunciation. A life of celibacy will be lived on a higher or lower level than married life—even from the viewpoint of human personality. It will be on a lower level if it is not filled with personal love. It will be on a lower level if our love for God is not a constant self-giving and self-renunciation.

If . . . it is remembered that nuptial love is itself a process of ineffable renunciation, it will without doubt be perceived that virginity manifests the dialectic immanent in love. By a voluntary choice it takes its point of departure where the other love should reach its culmination. That which in normal love is realized little by little, which matures slowly, is achieved sorrowfully, this donation of self spread over the years, is imposed upon conjugal love more by circumstances, by necessary metamorphoses than by the conscious will of man and wife; whereas virginity realizes all this in a kind of timeless moment repeated through time. From this aspect, between nuptial love and virginity, there would be the relation which exists between thought and speech, theorem and demonstration, or, to use a metaphor, between a gold coin and its copper change: virginity would be given the whole of love at a stroke while the other way of life parcels it out in successive installments.[4]

This is a layman's view of virginity and religious life. It is true, but with the same truth as the view of marriage as "marrying and living happily ever after." Religious life or vocation to the priesthood, in the initial experience of a personal call and its full acceptance, is a complete self-giving to God, and a complete self-renunciation, gladly made. But here—to continue the metaphor—the initial contract is more easily made than the protracted, faithful payment of installments over the years. What was given in a moment has to be given again daily as life unfolds. Charity is a human love, although God-given. It has a double law of growth—assimilation to the divine and perfecting of the human. It must follow the law of its own inner human logic. Like all human love in its great moments, especially in that deep personal experience which is its beginning, it will be carried along by an emotional current— a current which will flow less strongly, more calmly, through the years. Like all human love, it must undergo a transformation.

Love opens with an emotional phase; it is only after long duration that it can be transformed into sensibility. This sensibility is a kind of habit of the soul, but it must be remembered that there are two kinds of habit, one which is simply mechanical and automatic, the other which is a quality always alert, a disposition ever more constant, a kind of ever-increasing awareness of spirit, an awakening of obscure potentialities in the soul. This quality is not far from being a definition of sensibility. Sensibility exists in us without our always being conscious of it; but at the least provocation, it shows itself in the guise of a tender emotion, at once very gentle and poignant. Instead of sweeping our personality beyond itself . . . it restores it to itself.[5]

In a very true sense, in the beginning of religious life, or any call to closer intimacy with God, the personal attraction of grace swept our personality beyond itself. When the strong sweep of grace in the initial emotional reaction is less felt, we find ourselves very much with our own personalities again. A usual reaction is to wonder whether things have gone wrong. Rhetorical exhortations, such as "remember your first fervor," turn the wondering into a conviction. But of course the conviction is wrong, and the exhortations are more directed to feelings (uneasy feelings) than to sound reason. If that "first fervor," were to continue throughout life, it would be a protracted spiritual adolescence and a substitute for true spiritual maturity. Hence, any repining for this "first fervor" is akin to the nostalgic longing for the carefree days of childhood.

For the true test of fervor retained, we must look not back to what it was, but to what it ought to be as it develops. We are constantly reminded of the danger of doing things merely out of routine, from habit. "But, it must be remembered that there are two kinds of habit; one which is simply mechanical and automatic (which is a deadening of all personal spiritual life), the other which is a quality always alert, a disposition ever more constant, a kind of ever-increasing awareness of spirit . . . ."

These lines were written of human love; and since they are true of it, they will be true of the highest of human loves—charity. They are the psychologist's expression of the Psalmist's words: "My eyes are ever toward the Lord" (Ps. 24:15), and of the attitude of Christ, looking in all things to the Father.

Alertness, awareness of spirit, waiting on the indications of His will, prompt readiness to do His will—these are the qualities of charity, of any real spirituality as it progresses. This is the attitude of religious obedience. The gift of self to God, the renunciation of self, is not made once and for all; it is lived through all our days and all our life. It does not consist of initially taking a set course, and settling down into that. This would lead to routine, to habit in the mechanical sense, reattachment to our own way of doing things, a hardening of personality, an obtruding of nature or "self" into what should be our personal life for God. This means, in practice, a readiness to change our occupations, our way of doing things, at the least sign of God's will. It is an attentiveness to the demands of God's love. It is, in anything approaching real perfection (or definitely on the way to real perfection), incompatible with habitual not-noticing, not-remembering what is expected of us. For these things indicate that we are moving along our own path. Our first movement, our first thought is of what we want. Our next is to see if we can get our own plans approved by authority. This is not real self-renunciation, real self-giving. It is not, first of all, having our eyes lifted to the Lord. Our eyes are lifted only (if at all) after we see clearly what we want. First of all must be the question: "Lord, what will you have me do?"

If this is the attitude in which we live, then we do not need to fear whether what we have begun for God is still truly given to Him. But if there is no alertness, no increasing awareness of spirit, then the love of God has certainly not reached its full growth in our life, and there is still a lot of self-love mixed with it. If so, we have reason to worry about how much of our life is "supernatural," given to God, personally lived for Him. And while that is so, all efforts we make in other directions, if we make none in this, are a waste of time.

NOTES

[1] M. Flick, S.J. and Z. Alzeghy, S.J., "L'Opzione fondamentale della vita morale e la grazia," *Gregorianum*, 41 (1960) 593 ff.

[2] J. Mouroux, *The Christian Experience* (New York: Sheed and Ward, 1954) gives a good exposition of St. Thomas's doctrine, pp. 255 ff.

[3] G. Klubertanz: "Vertus morales 'naturelles' et 'surnaturelles'" in *Revue Thomiste*, 59 (1959), 565 ff.

[4] J. Guitton, *Essay on Human Love*, pp. 141–142.

[5] *Ibid.*, pp. 111–112.

Chapter 8

SANCTITY PROPERLY SO-CALLED

―――――――

Every religious experience of encounter with God is followed by the question: "Lord, what will you have me do?" (Acts 9:6). Initially, especially if one is given a vocation in the stricter sense, finding an answer to the question is easy enough. There are very definite courses of action for the young religious and priest. Also, in the Church's life and liturgy, and the general guidance all priests can give, the first part of a layman's more generous living for God is sufficiently catered for. Later, especially if one feels called to a "life of perfection," one wonders about the worth of what one is doing for God, and if one is really doing all that is required for sanctity. This and the following two chapters are aimed at giving the doctrine which is most helpful for a solution of these practical difficulties; doctrine that helps contribute to the peace of soul which should be the lot of all who are called to serve God.

Various definitions of Christian perfection are given. The most common ways of expressing its essence are:

(a) "The perfection of the Christian life consists principally and essentially in charity" (Pope John XXIII, "*Ad Conditorem*").

(b) "The high state of perfection which here we call

the union of the soul with God" (St. John of the Cross in *proemium* of *The Ascent of Mount Carmel*). In the doctrine of the saint, since this union is effected by the theological virtues, especially charity, this definition differs little from the first.

(c) "The goal of the spiritual life is the union of the soul with God by incessant conformity to the divine will" (St. Francis de Sales).[1]

In practice, union with God and conformity to His will cannot exist separately. "The two explanations are not different; they strengthen and complete each other. . . . There is no true conformity without habitual union of mind and heart with God. Nor is there any union with God without perfect conformity to his will."[2] Nor is there any true charity without conformity to God's will. If we love God, we will keep His commandments; if we follow Christ, we will make it our aim to do in all things that which pleases the Father.[3] Conformity to the divine will has, of course, always been insisted on by the masters of the spiritual life. Here, because of the practical import for many whose lives seem to consist of a daily round of unimportant duties that may not seem very "spiritual," it should be useful to consider the importance the Church has given, in recent years, to this conformity as a norm of sanctity.

1. The Will of God

In 1916, Pope Benedict XV, in promulgating the heroic sanctity of Jean-Baptiste de Bourgogne of the Friars Minor, declared: "Sanctity properly so-called consists in simple conformity to the Divine Will expressed in the exact and constant fulfillment of the duties of one's proper state."[4] Again in 1922, the decree on the heroic virtue of John

[103]

Nepomucene Neumann, Redemptorist, says that heroic sanctity consists in "the faithful and constant accomplishment of the individual's personal duties and office."[5] Father Gabriel of Mary-Magdalene, O.C.D., well known authority on spiritual matters, writing as a Consultor of the Congregation of Rites, said that the above expression could be regarded as "the quasi-official formula of the Church."[6]

There is, of course, no need to stress that all sanctity is God's gift; that it is He who unites us to Himself, and that all sanctity comes to us through God's grace and Christ's life in us. The above formula gives a practical norm for judging whether a person has co-operated with the grace of God and has allowed himself to be transformed by the inflow of Christ-life. It also gives a practical norm to those who are trying to live for God. What should they do in order to advance in perfection? What should they strive for to make their lives an expression of their love answering the call of God's love to them? The answer is simple: an exact, constant, and faithful accomplishment of the duties of their state in life, seen as the embracing of God's will and as the expression of their personal dedication to Christ.

It may be as well to draw out some of the implications of this norm of sanctity. Conformity to God's will is, of course, much more than a lifeless acceptance of whatever happens; it is more than natural indifference. It is, as St. Francis de Sales said, an attitude of readiness to accept whatever God might choose, readiness to accept His will— and in this sense an indifference to all things. But as soon as the will of God is made known, we must will it with all the power of which we are capable. This is what is meant by "Abandonment to Divine Providence," a spiritual doctrine admirably developed by St. Francis de Sales, Father de Caussade, S.J., and repeated by Dom Lehodey, Garrigou-Lagrange, and other spiritual writers.

This presupposes a living faith in the Providence of God, in His "holy and hallowing will," in His power to use all things to bring about our sanctification; a belief that, "to them that love God all things work together unto good" (Rom. 8:28). It sees the manifestation of God's will in the circumstances of life, and especially in the guidance of the Church; and sees that sanctity has to be worked out according to the laws of human nature and not in an abstract "spiritual" order.

Sanctity in its practical demands "will vary according to the circumstances and conditions created for each individual by his own duties, which are not the same for all. It has thousands of gradations according to the difficulties arising for each individual from his temperament, the obstacles he encounters, the work he undertakes, the form of life he embraces."[7]

"The duties of state" must be understood in the full sense of this phrase: "the commandments of God, the rule of one's institute, the duties of one's profession, the duties which arise from personal circumstances, from the individual call of grace, from the necessities of those around us who ask for help, from particular circumstances which give special urgency to one form or another of charity or apostolate, etc. All of this has to be judged in the concrete."[8] Hence, the norm will be verified in different details in the lives of contemplative religious, priests engaged in the active apostolate, lay people in their families. Detailed application to the many varied conditions of life would obviously be impossible. The general principle is clear. And always our daily duties must be carried out "with attention, piety, and deep fervour," as Pope Pius XI wrote.

They must be carried out not just as "duties to be performed," but in the spirit of personal dedication to God in Christ. It must be noted once and for all that this "faithful" carrying out of our duties demands that we aim at complete generosity in doing them. It is far more than a question of having a certain set of duties neatly listed which we perform with regularity. There must be alertness to the demands of charity, alertness to the calls of God's grace, and a readiness to respond when the invitation to do more for God is made quite clear—according to the usual norms of judging whether inspirations, etc., really come from God.

St. Thomas wrote that endurance and constancy were very difficult things for human nature.[9] It is always easier to start an undertaking than to see it through to the end. It is easier to do our duty for one day, than day in and day out. Hence in judging sanctity, much attention is paid to constancy in the faithful carrying out of duty. On this point, Pope Pius XI, in proclaiming the heroic virtue of Benildus of the Christian Schools, said some things that should serve to give assurance and courage to all whose lives for God seem to be spent in doing very ordinary things. He says of Benildus that he was

. . . a humble servant of God, whose life consisted only of modesty and silence, entirely commonplace and ordinary. But how uncommon and un-ordinary is such ordinariness as this! The daily round, always the same, with the same weaknesses, the same troubles, might well be called the "terrible daily routine." What fortitude then, is needed to resist this terrible, crushing, monotonous, suffocating daily round! We need uncommon virtue to carry out with uncommon fidelity—or rather without that infidelity, negligence, and superficiality which are so common and everyday and ordinary—but rather with attention, piety, and deep fervor that mass of common things which fills our daily lives. Holy Church shows herself at her most just and most wise as a teacher of holiness when she exalts these humble lights, so often ignored by those who have been favored by seeing them shining before their very eyes. Extraordinary deeds, important events, great enterprises need only to be seen to awaken the highest instincts of all; but the commonplace, the ordinary, the daily round, with no relief and no splendour about it, has no power to excite or fascinate. And yet it is this which makes up the lives of most people—a life which is ordinarily woven only of common things and daily happenings . . . How often do extraordinary things arise in the course of a lifetime? They are rare indeed, and woe to us if sanctity were restricted to extraordinary circumstances! What then would the majority of men do? For we must declare the truth: to all without exception comes the call to sanctity![10]

These words should be well meditated by all those who dream of "doing great things for God." For, not uncommonly, religious and others fail to integrate their work with their "vocation ideal." This failure leads to discontent and at times to neurosis.[11] They begin with a desire to give their lives to God, to "live a spiritual life"; but the duties they are asked to do appear to them as "unspiritual" and not sanctifying. Unfortunately the will of God is not used as one of the basic elements on which spirituality is constructed. It is only invoked as an answer to (but not an explanation of) the difficulty encountered in doing things which they classify as "nonspiritual."

It is therefore necessary to begin with a true concept of God's will and holiness. This point is well treated by Yves Congar.[12] It is necessary to see "how the Bible understand things. . . . God's will is holy; not because it is good by reference to a right and good object, but because it is the Lord's will, He who is in Himself absolute holiness. Nothing is holy unless in dependence on and in conformity with God who alone is holy. And accordingly, spiritual men all declare obedience to His holy and hallowing will to be the content and final test of holiness." Because He is God, God's will sheds holiness on whatever He wills. In this sense, Congar quotes the Psalm *Iudicia Domini vera, iustificata in semetipsa* (18:10): God's will is justified because it is His will, and His will bestows sanctifying efficacy on all that He wills for man on his way to God.

In the light of this, it is easy to see why De Caussade (and after him many others) insisted on the value of what he called "the sacrament of the present moment." *Sacrament* he used in the general sense of a means of union with God. We are in fact united to God by uniting our wills to His. God's will comes to us, or "His love is given to us" in what He wills for us here and now. It is only in the present moment that we can be actually united to God. If, by faith in His Providence, we see His will under the external appearances of what His Providence brings us, and unite our wills to His by accepting what He wills for us, we have a "lived union with God." The present moment is the time to conform and unite our wills to the divine will, with all the love and generosity of which we are capable. Every moment of our lives should be a sort of "communion with the divine love." Sanctity is a lived union with God in the historic unrolling of our lives. It is not merely a static quality inhering in our souls; it is something dynamic and existential: a living communication and acceptance of the divine from moment to moment. "We must leave the past to the great mercy of God, the future to His loving providence, and give all the present to His love by fidelity to His grace."[13]

Since, as we have seen above,[14] one of the norms for

judging sanctity is the psychological balance of the person concerned, it will not be irrelevant here to give the following quotation from Dr. C. Nodet: "This abandonment of the past to the past is a vital necessity of psychological health. Deprived of its conscious and unconscious references to past fears, bitterness, and self-justification, the present then opens out to the future in a naturally conquering dynamism."[15]

2. The Virtue of Religion or "The Spirit of Faith"

In order to live fully this conformity there is evident need of a deep spirit of faith: of a conviction of the things we do not see, faith in the transcendence of God, in His power, in His Providence which leads all men to Himself in spite of seeming obstacles. Particularly today is it recognized that there is need for this spirit of faith, or this sense of God as God. It is not easy to say whether this spiritual reality is best expressed as a living attitude of the virtue of religion or a deep spirit of faith. The important thing, however, is to see the importance of this spiritual reality for any real sanctity. It has often been remarked that the spirit of the age makes it more than ever necessary to insist on this. "The persistent presence of an environment tending all the time towards materialism in thought and action" has been pointed out.[16] Frank Sheed writes of "the modern tendency to treat God as an equal or an extra."[17] Another writer says: "A more fundamental reason why people leave [religious life] after profession is that even in reputedly Christian families, life is not now based on faith as much as it used to be . . . the fact that religious profession has something sacred and definitive about it escapes them."[18] Again, Father Spicq writes: "The modern mentality of pious souls imbued with laicism finds it difficult to take in the idea of the subjection of man in relation to his Creator."[19]

We live in a democratic age. To some extent we have, quite unconsciously, tended to extend our democratic relations even to God. Being accustomed to criticize the policies of our governments and to have our own ideas on how our countries ought to be governed, we do not take for granted, as an initial postulate of faith, that God is making the best possible job of ruling the world. It is then, necessary for us to keep alive our faith in God's omnipotence, wisdom, power, and providence, and our relation of complete subjection and dependence as creatures. Father Spicq writes—in particular reference to priests, but in terms which apply to all:

If God commands, no one can escape His orders . . . the sentiments of confidence, love, and devotion give a new quality to a priest's relations to God. But they are in a sense secondary when compared with the accepting of our submission to a transcendent and omnipotent Master, who has every right to demand everything from His creature, without giving the least consideration to the desires and preferences of that creature.[20]

If, at times, we find it hard to accept the will of God, it is perhaps that we have lost our sense of the reality of our created selves before the reality of God, our Creator and Master. (I am multiplying authorities on this point, because of its importance.) De Guibert wrote that one of the reasons why many pious souls did not advance as much as they should was the neglect of the virtue of religion. Its practice is one of the remedies he proposed against mediocrity:

. . . the exercise of this virtue keeps before us our true

relationship to God, insofar as it marks out the relations of the creature to the Creator, and imbues our whole lives with reverence for his supreme Majesty. For, although charity makes us friends of God, and our adoption and elevation by grace makes us His children, yet we always remain his servants, because we are creatures. Hence, no matter how wonderful the kindliness with which God receives us, this essential relationship between him and us, which is fully expressed by the virtue of religion, can never be taken away . . . Hence the importance of performing acts of religion to express our subjection to God and to show our reverence for Him . . . there is no opposition between humblest reverence and filial love. Care should be taken that this sense of reverence does not vanish from the spiritual life . . . the special atmosphere imparted by the virtue of religion should pervade our whole life, just as filial reverence and love should inform all our dealings with our parents. The main source of this atmosphere is the spirit of faith, which gives us a deep knowledge and realization of what we are in the sight of God.[21]

Another writer, speaking of the maturity of faith demanded as a criterion of religious and priestly vocations, writes:

Has he understood that you do not bargain with God, that you do not treat with Him as equal with equal, that the unique alliance between God and man cannot be codified, because God freely gives all—and man only receives unconditionally? Does he realize that when God marks out one of His sons for a mission, the one called does not make any conditions—he accepts unconditionally, or he does not accept at all. He does not calculate what he can keep for himself of his own time, ease, leisure, desires, or natural inclinations.[22]

This sense of faith in the transcendence of God is one of the bases of a spiritual life lived in conformity with His will. Another is, of course, a belief in the love of God for us, which we have already mentioned and to which we will return. From this belief in God's love guiding us and His omnipotent Providence guarding us springs a confidence which enables us to devote ourselves to His will in peace of soul and a spirit of joy. Thus we realize another aspect of the virtue of religion—that in submitting self to God, a man finds himself and his true happiness. There is joy in religion, a deep happiness that can only come to those who have found themselves in all truth by finding their true relationship with God. This is well brought out in the spirituality of the French School in which one of the main stresses is placed upon the virtue of religion. Cardinal Bérulle, founder of the school, made "all his interior life, all his direction lead to this: to confess the greatness of the supreme being—joyously, lyrically, even unto folly." To those desirous of seeing a fuller development of the part the virtue of religion can play in a "spirituality," a study of the doctrine of the *Ecole française* would be most rewarding.[23]

3. The Law of the Incarnation

If we do not accept and embrace the will of God, it is because our faith is deficient in one way or another. Perhaps the way in which it is most commonly deficient, especially for those whose life is lived more fully under ecclesiastical or religious authority, is that we fail to recognize and accept as the will of God the decisions and commands of superiors. Perhaps it would be better to say that our conformity to the will of God would be more perfect if our faith were more perfect, faith especially in the will of God mediated through the Church and those of her members to whom authority has been given.

A mature faith is faith in the mystery of Christ prolonged in the mystery of the Church, belief in the transcendence of the Church—as of Christ, but as a divine institution incarnate in human weakness and human limitations. "The instinctive movement of heresy will always be to break the prodigious linkings of time and eternity. Certainly it will adore God in heaven, but it will fail to recognize Him when He draws ineffably close to us in the fragile and fleeting events of time . . . it will fail to recognize the true spiritual riches when they are presented to us through visible forms (i.e., in and through the Church)."[24] The faith of the Jews in God was not deep enough to extend to the acceptance of God come among them in the weakness of human nature. "Is not this the carpenter's son?"

We have been given faith in Christ and in His Church. We must see that it does not fail because of the necessary limitations and human weakness in which the power and authority of Christ is continued. The power of God to sanctify through the sacraments is not limited by the frailty of human ministers. This we accept. Nor are the power and Providence of God lessened by the limitations, lack of foresight and understanding in those who exercise authority in the Church. Yet how often do we find that faith is tested, and conformity to God's will weakened, by a failure to see beyond the human limitations, the appearances through which the reality of God's will is made known to us. "He who hears you hears me" will always hold good.

One element of maturity is facing reality and accepting the necessary limitations of others. An element of maturity of faith is accepting this reality of the authority of God mediated through His limited and imperfect members. It is not unusual that Alexander VI and Julian II create no obstacles since they do not effect the divinity of the

Church; yet they are troubled in faith because of the lesser limitations of those who exercise office in the Church. Here again, perhaps we are too democratic and not sufficiently ready to seek to know and do, in all things, the will of God in the way He has willed to manifest it and make it known.

Superiors do not expect all their decisions to be the best possible. What they should be able to expect is that, after they have considered before God the responsibility which He has laid on their shoulders and exercised their authority, the subjects then carry out their responsibility before God and accept these directives.

When you think of Him whom alone you obey, you see that obedience is an act of worship, and that it is explained only by a divine presence. Between superior and subject at the moment of obedience, there arises suddenly the figure of Jesus Christ. Faith tells us that it is He who speaks through the superior, it is He who acts through the will of the subject. Both then must consider one another with the same veneration in the Lord; they are—each in his own fashion—made equal in the same love of Christ, who, through men, communicates Himself to other men, to make them all like to Himself.[25]

4. Spiritual Activity or Apostolic Work

While it is all very well (and very necessary) to insist on the supernatural realities just treated—the will of God, faith, the law of the Incarnation—it is not sufficient to consider them as realities isolated from their psychological setting. By this I mean that insistence on these things will often produce a sense of frustration in some people because of real psychological difficulties. They have given their lives to God, and superiors have set them to washing dishes and doing the laundry, doing office work, looking after accounts, teaching arithmetic. You can appeal to the will of God, but that will not solve their inner conflict if they feel that they are called to an "apostolic vocation" or "the spiritual life." They have dreamed of "doing great things for God," and what they do amounts to very little. They have felt the call to "apostolic work," want to spend their lives "saving souls," bringing the Gospel to every creature. While millions are waiting for the Word of God, they are constrained to spend their days on duties that "anyone could do," with only an occasional opportunity for exercising their zeal. One or other of these difficulties: the "nonspiritual" or "nonapostolic" character of the greater part of what they do is encountered by most who give their lives to God. They are fortunate if they have resolved the resultant conflicts. Those who have not succeeded in resolving such conflicts are not few in number—they are probably far more numerous than is often realized.[26]

When such difficulties are expressed, those who are consulted generally reply with an appeal to the will of God and an exhortation to be more supernatural. Their replies would be more helpful if they were more natural and appealed to common sense—their own and that of those who direct them. Spiritual theology and spiritual guidance cannot be content with only half the picture. At times it must have recourse to blind trust in God, but it does not encourage blindness when some light is possible. In these particular difficulties, some light can be had from the principles of common sense and the psychology of maturity.

First of all, there must of necessity be a certain quality of unreality about our youthful dreams of the spiritual life—as about all youthful dreams. This is to be expected. But it is to be expected that we grow out of it, and that those responsible for our guidance and enlightenment help us to do so. It is good that we be fired with enthusiasm to do "great things for God," to give "ourselves completely to God and the spiritual life," to help "cast fire upon the earth." But it is necessary to remember that the real will always falls far short of our ideal concept of life, that we must early face up to the realities of our own limitations. It is necessary to remind ourselves that "it is this which makes up the lives of most people—a life which is ordinarily woven of common things and daily happenings." The spiritual life does not mean that the one called to live it passes into the ranks of a spiritual aristocracy, leaving behind the necessities of human life, such as cooking, mending pipes, and paying bills. It cannot mean that in all these things we are waited on hand and foot while we say our prayers. We live our life for God in and according to our human nature. What makes our "ordinary" duties pass into the sphere of the supernatural is the personal dedication of which we spoke; just as the drudgery of household duties is transformed in worth, but not taken away, by the fact that they are done for personal love of others instead of from constraint. Hence it is necessary to give much thought to what has been said on personal dedication and duties of one's state in life.

A further necessary consideration—particularly with regard to the apostolic difficulty—is that the apostolate, or the work of saving souls, is the work of Christ. He wills to continue that work through men, of course, but through His continued Incarnation in the social structure of the Church, the Body of Christ. It is in her—the Church—and through her that each is assigned his mission from Christ. The divine power works through the limited means of a human society, using human means, constrained by human necessity: the necessities of organization, finance, office work, legislation, supervision, formation of members, etc. It must perform a human service for God, a human work for God. When an individual is called to the apostolic life, he is called to it within this framework of the work of the Church. He gives himself to Christ for the extension of the Kingdom of God and the salvation of souls. Carrying out this work and marshalling her forces to carry out the work is a commission given to the Church. She passes on the commission to individual members. Individuals can volunteer for special works to which they might feel themselves called. But the call from Christ comes through the Church, with the mark of her individual determination and selection. We can not all be in the front ranks, though we might all desire to be. Here we can ask ourselves: What is my chief longing? That fire be cast on earth, or that I be the one to cast it? We all work so that the love of Christ might be enkindled in the hearts of men. If that be so, we must be content. St. Paul's image of the various parts of the body all working to the good of the whole, all doing their necessary part for the success of the effort of the whole, is just as pertinent in our day as in his. We have given our lives to Christ for the extension of His cause. We are privileged to work for that cause. Do we surrender to Christ and His cause, or do we lay down our own conditions of service?[27]

It must be further borne in mind that it was by His passion and death that Christ won salvation for the world. We who are incorporated into Christ, to share in His work of redemption, will do so by sharing in His suffering and self-sacrifice. Often He may ask from us, as part of our sacrifice, the harder part of waiting and watching and working in obscurity without the satisfaction of seeing the fruits of our work.

5. Personal Witness

One of the causes which can contribute to a certain dissatisfaction with work that is not apostolic is a rather rare-
fied notion of grace, and of the apostolate which involves
this purely spiritual reality. Apostolic work is not just ad-
ministering the sacraments, preaching the Gospel, saying
Mass, giving spiritual instruction. We have seen that grace
is God's taking a human person into personal relationship
with Himself. It is God's free gift to man, but supposes
man's free response, man's full, unselfish surrender to the
demands of God. This response can only be made by a
human person who is prepared to renounce Himself to
submit to God; who is unselfish enough to make such a
renunciation and live it constantly. For this full personal
response a certain amount of intellectual enlightenment is
necessary. A person must see that it is good to submit to
God; that it is not in the possession of created goods, nor
in the possession of one's own complete autonomy that
one's greatest good is to be found. Preparing a human person for receptivity to grace is a complicated affair and far-
reaching. The grace of God is, of course, powerful
enough to compel rebel hearts, to break down the walls of
selfishness, to cut through the veils of ignorance, prejudice,
and pride. It can do this without the mediation of men.
But ordinarily that is not God's way. He brings men to
salvation through other men: He established a Church of
human beings to help in the work of leading all men to
God.

God alone gives grace and faith. But He asks men to dis-
pose and prepare others to receive them. All work that
brings a human person to accept this personal relationship
with God, which grace is, and to live it is apostolic work.
Anything which helps mould a human personality to un-

selfishness, maturity, acceptance of authority, facing reality, etc., helps to make a human person more fitted to receive the grace of God. All effort to dispel ignorance, prejudice, injustice, greed, materialism is an effort to prepare the soil for the seed of God's grace in the world. What use is it to sow the seed in rocky ground, if it will only wither away? What use is it to baptize someone, giving him grace, when there is no possibility of a Christian formation? The Church's legislation[28] presumes that it is probably no use at all. Who performs the most useful apostolic work: the priest who administers baptism on a passing visit, or the person who through the years patiently teaches virtue and truth and forms a Christian personality?

Grace is not just something that apostles put into people's souls; it is a life of personal dedication to God and demands a complete formation of personality. Forming a personality is a slow process and involves many human factors and influences. Seen in this light, the work of Christian education is seen as most eminently apostolic. And the work of parents, through the vital years of training their children, is an apostolic work whose importance can hardly be calculated. Education has been said to be the influence of one mature personality on another person. This personality influence is exercised in numerous ways; it is exercised in deep and lasting fashion, generally only with time. And since the time at our disposal is short and the number of people we can influence lastingly in that time is limited, this basic apostolic work must, of necessity, be limited. There are some who will preach rousing sermons and make a sudden impact. The majority of those who work for God will have to do the more drawn out, and more lasting work which is even more necessary. This limitation of the amount any one person can do is a necessary limitation of human nature. We must always do what we can. We must not be surprised if what we can do does not amount to much. God asks of us a co-operation that is according to the human natures on which He works and through which He works. He asks us to co-operate in any way we can. Teaching children fair play, teaching them to accept a defeat at sport in a good spirit, all contributes to the formation of character and personality—and all makes a human person more ready to enter into personal relationship with God.

Concerning this point, I think there is (for some) one unfortunate consequence of having St. Francis Xavier as patron of the missions. He is, of course, a model of untiring zeal, an inspiring example of the charity of Christ urging us on, and thus a wonderful patron for apostles. But, in practice, those who are inspired by his example often think that their work will be something the same: rapid conversion of thousands of souls. However, it is only in an exceptional combination of circumstances, which occurs rarely in the history of the Church, that such things can be. For the vast majority of apostolic workers, progress will be slow—the laborious advance by way of personal contact and personal witness; the slow work of gradually influencing and moulding a human personality to fit itself for the life of grace or for constancy in living the grace it has been given.

I would refer again to what has been said in Chapter 5 of this work on the harmony between internal and external graces. It follows from this that the chief apostolic work of men will be through their personal contact and personal witness. Hence their work will be more effective in proportion as they bear the mark of deep personal attachment to Christ; in proportion as their words and deeds and regard for other persons bear the stamp of a personal dedication to God and to all those who have their individual, personal worth in the eyes of God. The power of God is not limited by the imperfection of His created instruments. "God can enlighten with mud, as with the finest matter,"[29] but the mud can take no credit for contributing to the final result. God can work through us in spite of our limitations—and this must be our consolation after we have done our best. But normally God wills to use instruments adapted to His purpose; He wills that those who are to be instruments in bringing others to give their lives to Him should themselves be given wholly. Complete dedication to Christ will be the first and most powerful apostolic influence of all those who want to bring others to God. Mouroux expresses this well in the following passage:

Normally Christian truth must make itself known through a Christian person; and we can describe the process by which it comes to be acknowledged. Personal commitment is the very foundation of faith and is, in fact, faith itself. It tends by its own energy to become purer and more profound, and issues in full faith, becoming daily more personal and richer in lucidity, reality, and efficacy. The Christian then experiences the power, the life, and the joy which God gives him through faith, and naturally, this shines forth in his life. That intense spiritual *élan*, which is what self-giving is, raises the entire human material, informs, moulds, orientates, and unifies it by its mighty form. It confers on it a significance which becomes more and more marked. Acts and thought, charity and fidelity, reveal a person wholly given to God; and thus the action and the presence of God is revealed through this person. Moreover, since man is in a state of tension and desirous of communion, he will be stirred to the depths of his being when he comes into contact with another wholly given to God. . . . The self-surrender which is seen and experienced will tend to evoke its like. The role of the witness is thus to realize a presence and transmit a call. . . . Testimony is not primarily a question of doing, but of being. It manifests the profound richness of the person who has given himself. It expresses the sovereign efficacy of a faith which ennobles and transforms the person, because it is itself ennobled and transformed by the Holy Spirit.[30]

This was St. Peter's idea in his exhortations to the early Christians: "It is yours to proclaim the exploits of the God who has called you out of darkness into his marvellous light. . . . Your life amidst the Gentiles must be beyond reproach . . . you must let them see, from your honourable behaviour, what you are; they will praise God for you, when his time comes to have mercy on them" (I Pet. 2:9–13).

These truths are rich in consequences for all those who give their lives to God, for all who desire to bear effective witness to Christ and His Church, for priests, religious (active or contemplative), and laity alike.

There is another important practical consequence for all those whose responsibility it is to take on work for their subjects, i.e., for superiors, religious and ecclesiastical. De Guibert, treating of the fact that many people called to perfection cease to advance in perfection, says that, in some cases, this is "due to the pressure of many undertakings (even though they are done for God)."[31] Superiors have a duty to see that their subjects are not subjected to pressure of work which would be an obstacle to their progress in perfection. Since also they have a duty in charity and zeal to work for the good of souls, they find themselves facing the problem of having to decide between the two demands. Frequently—particularly under pressure from those in pastoral office—they decide in favour of "the greater good," exhorting the subject to have trust in God and to accept His will. This is, of course, the easier way out. The subject who has promised to obey must accept his superior's decisions, even if he feels that too much is being asked of him. Even should he accept reluctantly, he will cause less unpleasantness than might result from a refusal to a higher official. The decision may not always be as purely motivated by "care for the greater good" as it is said to be. Even when it is so motivated, the reasoning is invalid.

There can never be any real clash between the spiritual good of the worker and the success of the work. There can never be a case in which the good of souls demands that some worker be overburdened with work. (N.B.: It is a question of being really overburdened, not just a question of hard work. Further, the amount of work which each one can reasonably manage varies according to individual capabilities.) A decision to sacrifice the spiritual good of the worker to the greater good of the work is a decision to sacrifice the greater, permanent good of the work itself. This follows from what we have just seen— the importance of the spiritual personality as a factor in apostolic work. If, through pressure of work, apostles become tense, impatient, discouraged, they then have ceased to be "witnesses" in the sense given above, the only true sense of the word.

It is well enough known that one meets with constant difficulties in one's life of prayer, and in consequence in the apostolate. It is equally well known that many worries gather in one's inmost heart, that a religious life can be degraded by this activity which absorbs the attention of the mind, commands the desires of the heart and the decisions of the will, uses up all physical and nervous energy. In one's work one can be capable and competent, but one is always less the worker of the Lord. In this matter subjects have their own responsibility; but superiors have, even more than their subjects, a heavy duty. . . . All work, all devotedness which, in the long run, tends to make of religious only women left to their own natural forces and worn out by their activity, and thereby deprived of their life of prayer, should be re-thought and better ordered.[32]

It is sometimes pleaded that this overwork is necessary because "the harvest is great and the laborers are few." Apart from the fact that it renders the laborers unfit to work effectively for the harvest, this line of reasoning runs full into a vicious circle. It is often precisely because laborers are overworked that they are so few. The grace of vocation is intimately bound up with the personal influence of those already living the vocation. And if those living a particular vocation are worn out and worried by their work, near-neurotic and impatient personalities or merely lackluster persons, they will mediate no attraction. On the contrary, they will repel prospective vocations.[33]

But what is the answer to our problems of mission work, Catholic education, etc.? I do not know; but this is clear: the answer does not consist in destroying the fullness and freshness of the vocations we have got. Faith in Him who, in a world in need of Him was "not sent but to the house of Israel," must be exercised not only by subjects.

This is a difficult and delicate problem. It must be faced by all: with a generous zeal and ready co-operation on the part of subjects, who will be wary of the human tendency to be satisfied with what is less than generous; and on the part of superiors with careful regard for the good of the subjects. The heart of the zealous Christian must always bleed for the sheep without a shepherd. In this he will share the compassion of His Master. But he will also know that if he desires that all men be saved and come to the knowledge of truth, his Lord and Savior desires it even more. He must pray and work for the spread of the Kingdom, knowing that this is what God wants of him. But he must know and believe that God saves the world, not he; that God demands of him an effort, which though continued and generous, needing his full energy and inventiveness, remains still a human effort and hence limited. He must know that though his arm is shortened, the arm of the Lord is not; and he must learn to trust in the Lord alone for the salvation of others, even as he trusts in the Lord for his own.

If any modern apostle, solicitous for the salvation of souls, had had charge of organizing Our Lord's earthly campaign, he would certainly have arranged it differently. The need was urgent, and the need was world wide. Yet Christ limited His apostolic campaign to a short period and a small territory. He was urged to do more and to go out to others, but to them He "was not sent." These thoughts should not lessen our zeal; but they can sometimes lessen the acuteness of our concern for the salvation of those we cannot reach by our own efforts, and lessen the feverishness which some people bring to their work, thus lessening their own effectiveness within their sphere of labor, hindering the work of God in them and through them, or in and through those under them.

NOTES

[1] P. Pernin, "S. François de Sales" in *D.T.C.*

[2] A. Saudreau, *La Vie d'Union à Dieu* (Paris: Apmat, 1909), pp. 10–11.

[3] John 8:29; 14:21.

[4] *Acta Apostolicae Sedis*, 12 (1920), p. 173.

[5] *A.A.S.* 14 (1922), p. 23.

[6] "Present Norms of Holiness" in *Conflict and Light* (New York: Sheed and Ward, 1953). (A translation of "Trouble et Lumiére," *Etudes Carmélitaines*.)

[7] Gabriel of Mary Magdalene, *art. cit.*

[8] *Ibid.*

[9] For a treatment of St. Thomas's concept of perfection, see O.

Marchetti, S.J., "La Perfezione della vita secondo S. Tommaso," *Gregorianum*, 1 (1920), 41 ff.

[10] Quoted by Gabriel of Mary Magdalene, *art. cit.*, from *Osservatore Romano*.

[11] See *Spiritual and Intellectual Elements in the Formation of Sisters* (New York: Fordham University Press, 1957), pp. 32 ff.

[12] *Lay People in the Church* (Westminster, Md.: Newman, 1957), p. 403 f.

[13] J. P. de Caussade, S.J., *Self-Abandonment to Divine Providence* (London: Burns, Oates, 1952).

[14] Ch. I.

[15] *Direction Spirituelle et Psychologie*, p. 309.

[16] "Christian Asceticism and Modern Man," *Blackfriars* (London, 1955).

[17] *Theology and Sanity* (New York: Sheed and Ward, 1946), p. 23.

[18] "Vocation," *Blackfriars* (London, 1952), p. 71.

[19] *Piété Sacerdotale* (Paris: Ed. du Cerf, 1949).

[20] *Ibid.*

[21] *The Theology of the Spiritual Life*, p. 278.

[22] M. Devis, "Y-a-t'il une methode de discernement des vocations?" in *Supplément de la Vie Spirituelle*, n. 49 (1958), 131–132.

[23] P. Pourrat, *Christian Spirituality* (Westminster, Md.: Newman Press, 1953), Vol. III.

[24] C. Journet, *L'Eglise du Verbe Incarné*, Vol. II.

[25] E. Mersch, S.J., *Morality and the Mystical Body* (New York: Kenedy, 1939).

[26] "Spiritual and Intellectual Formation of Sisters," *supra cit.*

[27] The "Church" aspect of apostolic spirituality is well developed by L. Lochet, S.J. in *Son of the Church* (Chicago: Fides Publishers, 1956).

[28] *Code of Canon Law*, Canons 750 and 751.

[29] De Caussade, *op. cit.* Vol. I, 125.

[30] J. Mouroux, *I Believe*, pp. 91 ff.

[31] *The Theology of the Spiritual Life*, n. 341.

[32] A. Delchard, S.J., *La Prière* (Paris: Ed. du Cerf, 1959), pp. 300–301.

[33] This fact is evident, if one gives the matter a little thought. Dr. J. Wain, e.g., writes: "The price of retaining one such maladjusted person in the community without giving him the proper care and attention [he is writing of neurotics] might be the loss of twenty vocations from among successive classes of pupils and the estrangement of an equal number of tentative converts." *Review for Religious*, 20 (1961), 81.

Chapter 9

THE LIGHT OF THE CROSS

---

1. Positive-Negative

Among the tensions inherent in Christianity is that between so-called negative and positive elements. In all attempts to blend two seemingly different movements, it is easy to err on one side or the other and a delicate matter to strike an exact balance. At various times through the history of spirituality (and at different stages of each person's spiritual development the same may be true) there has been an overstressing of the negative aspect, which cannot be viewed aright merely in isolation. Reactions usually swing too far in the opposite direction. In the opinion of many, we live in an age which, if it errs, will err in the direction of being over-optimistic.

"We can say that the present renewal in the Church is essentially a rediscovery of the Resurrection."[1] While the Church could never forget the Resurrection, it is certain that in biblical and dogmatic theology, and consequently in devotion, more attention has been given in recent years to the place of the Resurrection. Any age which regards itself as "rediscovering the Resurrection," and which regards ages which preceded it as having concentrated on the Passion and the Cross in too exclusive a fashion, is of necessity in danger of swinging too far in the opposite direction and of not giving enough importance to the Passion and the Cross.

In close connection with this is the fact that today there is insistence on "constructive, positive" spirituality, and on the truth that the supernatural perfects the natural in man. There has been so much insistence, in fact, that it has frequently been stressed that we cannot concentrate exclusively on this side of things. Bouyer writes of "the illusion that, side by side with the negative, crucifying asceticism of past centuries, there was room for a constructive, positive asceticism which would reject nothing in the world but would consecrate all in it to the glory of God. . . . If this book succeeds in convincing some that there is no such thing as a Christianity without tears, it will have fulfilled all the author's desires."[2] Another author writes of "the unreality of certain spiritualities (not lived, but taught more or less artifically),"[3] of which one is this neglect of the negative aspect. But if there is "no Christianity without tears," Christianity is more than tears, and, as we shall see, the tears belong in Christianity because they first belonged to mankind.

In this matter, possibly more than others, it is necessary to see things in their right perspective; it is essential not to think in terms of "positive *or* negative," "Passion *or* Resurrection." It was through the Passion and death that Christ came to the glory of His Resurrection. We are not baptized into His resurrection alone, but into His death and Resurrection; and it is by losing our life that we find it, by dying to self that we live to Christ. It is an error to stress either side to the exclusion of the other. In general, the more natural error (if error there be) will be to put too little insistence on the death to self. *Mortification, self-*

denial, renunciation are not words that evoke an immediate response, attracting us toward them. As a matter of fact, it would be unnatural to be attracted toward them in themselves; and death or denial can only be willed as a way to a fuller life. They are a necessary part of the way: "There can be no higher life except on a foundation of renunciation and death, no renewal in which there is not something old that has to disappear. The rightful order between nature and grace is certainly a harmony, the order which the Creator has willed and the Saviour will re-establish. But the rightful order is obstructed by a factual order, the order of sin and redemption by the Cross."[4]

All things that God has made are good. But sin has brought disorder into the universe. And Christ has redeemed us from sin by His death and Resurrection. These are truths which we must fit harmoniously into our whole view of the spiritual life—truths according to which we must live.

2. The Cross

We know that Christ died on the cross to save us. He suffered for us, and we must suffer for Him. That is true, and fairly generally, I think, it is understood in the following sense: It would have been so much easier for us if Christ had chosen some other way to redeem us, but since He did choose the way of the cross, that must be our way, too; we must, to some extent, expect our way to be a hard way, for it is a following of Christ. The shadow of the cross falls across our lives, as it fell on His. These thoughts are variously expressed. We find them in our songs and poems: "The shadow of a cross arose, upon a lonely hill." Francis Thompson, English Catholic poet, wrote:

The salt tears in our life's dark wine
Have fallen on it from the saving cross.

Swinburne, a non-Christian poet, wrote:

Thou hast conquered, O pale Galilean,
The world has grown grey with thy breath.

As Christians we reject the last statement. Many of us fail to see that the other statements are equally, if not so obviously, untrue. The tears did not come into our life from the saving cross. They were already there, for they are the lot of fallen humanity. The cross casts no shadow over the life of man. To men already living in "darkness and the shadow of death," Christ came to bring not suffering but hope and love. The shadow of the cross fell across His life from ours. His cross is only light—the light of God's love come into the world to save the world and suffer with it. Suffering was already there and the necessity of death. We had to suffer and die. But Christ did not; however, He willed to do so to lead us back to God. He took the cross from our lives; we must learn to take the love from His. It is very important to see these things in their right perspective. There is a prayer often said during the stations of the cross:

O Jesus who for love of me didst bear thy cross to Calvary,
In thy sweet mercy grant to me to suffer and to die with thee.

These and similar prayers must be rightly understood. We do not pray that we may suffer and die. That we must do whether we like it or not. Our prayer is that we may support our suffering and embrace our death in union with

THE LIGHT OF THE CROSS

Christ, and that through them, His love may lift us to eternal life. Christ did not tell us to take up His cross—He told us to take up our own and follow Him: "If anyone wishes to come after me, let him deny himself, and take up *his* cross daily, and follow me" (Luke 9:23). The cross of Christ is not laid on our shoulders; but ours was laid on His. "God laid on his shoulders our guilt, the guilt of us all" (Isa. 53:6). Our cross was laid on His shoulders, and because it weighed so heavily on Him, it rests more lightly on us. The "self-denial" of which Our Lord speaks was always a necessity if sinful man was to regain friendship with God. Again, it came before the cross of Christ; it is not its consequence. This is no more than one aspect of the doctrine of original sin.

As we have seen, God created man for eternal personal union with Himself. In the beginning Adam was taken into a personal union with God. Living a life in which the love of God possessed him, he was open to the inflow of divine life and love, the creating, strengthening love of God which kept his whole will directed to God and his whole life lived easily in loving loyalty. Consequent upon this was the harmony of all the forces of his nature that helped him serve God in ease and delight, and to live in loving dependence on God, receiving from Him all that he was and had. God's providence guarded His children, saving them from suffering and planning to lift them to eternal life without the necessity of dying. If this happy state of things had continued, each child who was born into the family of Adam would have been born into the "household of God," or, as we say "born in the state of grace." The object of God's creating love, each child would have received the same gifts as our first parents had.

Adam's sin was a declaration of his own autonomy and

independence—a decision to center his life around himself, to seek first his own good and own glory, to be only what he could make himself.

In Adam we all have sinned (Rom. 5:12), in that we are born outside the household of God, without His grace and friendship, and in that, with the self-centered nature Adam passed on to us, it was impossible for man not to seek himself instead of seeking God. For he was without the grace of God which alone could lift him out of his own self-centered world. Hence humanity was imprisoned in its own closed circle, in which it lived and from which death was no deliverance, for even death was not a surrender into the hands of God. Human nature had chosen to be what it could make itself. The long years of its history before the coming of Christ had shown just what that was—for a world of self-centered beings could not but clash with one another, seeking themselves in all sorts of self-centered ways.

Christ came into the world, taking a human nature to lead men back to God, to take humanity where it could not go, of itself. "He emptied himself, taking the nature of a slave" (Phil. 2:7), taking a human nature with physical weakness and able to die and taking upon Himself the mission of dying for the salvation of men. His human nature shrank from death, for it wanted to cling to its own life. "His freely-willed submission to the weakness of the flesh, even to their consecration in death, represented the most intense effort to come to God, for it was a submission of obedience, dragging man away from the autonomy of his flesh, and carrying him towards God in a renunciation of self which became, in death, a total renunciation."[5] In His passion and death, Christ, against all the natural shrinking from death of His human nature, wrestled that human nature, in agony, to its own self-renunciation as a gift to

God. The Father accepted His offering which He made on behalf of us all. And now, if we are "born anew," baptized into Christ, we become through Him what we could never have been without Him—members of God's household and again children of God. We are baptized into Christ's death and Resurrection, passing, through death to self, to life in God (Rom. 6). The necessity of death to self was there before the death of Christ. But the grace of Christ makes it possible, and His love now gives it value.

3. Losing Life to Find It

This note is proper to the personal life of man—quite apart from religious considerations. As we have seen, a man comes to the full development of his personality by forgetting himself, by denying the "self" in him, by dying to self. This is a continuing process, constantly demanded by love and respect for other persons. Progress toward maturity of personality is progress in denial of self. Let us recall the steps in the development of personality. The child who awakens to a consciousness of others—parents, brothers, and sisters—as persons, gradually becomes aware of the fact that they do not exist just to give him all he wants, to answer all his demands, cater for all his needs, satisfy all his whims. Such awareness is usually a painful process.

This personal development in all its stages demands self-renunciation—giving up our own desires, our own wants and preferences, restraining our urges, mastering our emotions, overcoming our fears and anxieties to accept responsibilities, and so on. A little reflection shows how much this self-denial is a necessary part of human development. Any failure to see this is a refusal to face the reality of human nature in its necessary limitations. Man cannot even develop all his possibilities—in choosing one, he must reject or renounce another.

The perfection of love of others is again a self-renunciation for it means that we think first of them and what they want or need. Altruistic love is a surrender of self.

If a man wants to be miserable, he will see all the hard things in life, all that he cannot have. But he sees only the negative side of things. Seeing things truly he will see all renunciation as directed to positive realities. "Nothing lives but something dies, and nothing dies but something lives." As Benjamin Franklin used to say, "Most folks are about as happy as they make up their minds to be." People who want to make of religion an unhappy affair can find hard things in it. But, as G. K. Chesterton said, here again it is a matter of deciding whether one is going to say: "Why should I have to live in such a hard way to get to heaven?" or—with an appreciation of how much has been given us— "Why should I have been allowed to live and get to heaven at all?"

The sacrifice and self-denial which are present in every life are not something which the Christian religion has added. They are necessary steps for sinful, self-centered humanity to fight its way back to God. The death to self which religion asks is only the death to self that is necessary if any man is to reach the fullness of his human personality—losing his selfish life to find the fullness of personal relationships. Religion is the further interpersonal steps of self-denial a man must make to find himself: all that self-renunciation which is demanded by human interpersonal relationships. Religion is the further interpersonal relationship between man and God. Any further self-renunciation, or losing of the life of self, is a further finding and a further perfecting of the human personality. Christian asceticism is not directed toward making a man a naturally well-balanced and controlled person; it is directed toward personal union with God. But in accord with the general harmony between nature and grace, it will include all that is part of human self-discipline and will take its supernatural character from its personal orientation toward God.[6] But its material will be the same: emotional control, assuming responsibilities, regard for others as persons,[7] accepting reality, etc.

It is Christian asceticism if it is directed toward a relation of personal friendship with God. If it is not that, it can be very self-centered and tainted with a deeper pride than is surrender to human weakness. Tennyson wrote:

> Self-knowledge, self-reverence, self-control,
> These three alone lead life to sovereign power.

With his characteristic perception, G. K. Chesterton later retorted: "These three, *alone*, will make a man a prig!" They will, for alone, and directed toward self, they are a subtler form of pride and self-glorification. When they are done to live a life of loyal friendship with Another, they are self-surrender and self-denial, and thus only do we lose our life to find it.

4. Love and Sacrifice

"Love and sacrifice go together": a sentence commonly uttered and quite true. But it is not always rightly understood, at least by beginners in the spiritual life. Some conclude from it that, if they love Christ, they must take on extra penance and mortification to prove their love. As it stands, such an interpretation will almost always be misunderstood. Hence it needs to be analyzed and the different aspects of it well thought out.

[135]

First of all, let us consider a human parallel. Suppose I love a human person and go to him and say that, to show my love, I have gone without food and have walked home from work instead of riding in the tram; I have endured this hardship just to show I love. Normally, he might be touched by my devotion, but he would think I was somewhat unbalanced—and he would be right. Love does not, cannot desire that the loved person suffer just for the sake of suffering, or even just to prove the worth of love. As a matter of fact, it is a very dubious proof of love and a fairly definite proof of lack of common sense. But suppose I were to say: "Look, I've bought you a present which I knew you would like. I had to go without lunch to do it, and had to walk home to save the extra money, but I managed it." Then the sacrifice would have some meaning and would be a proof of love (although love would not want to stress very much its own self-denial, attending more to what it had given rather than to what it had given up). The love of God demands sacrifice, but not in the unbalanced sense given above. In what sense it does demand sacrifice we shall now proceed to explain. But first of all, let us learn from the above example that suffering and self-denial are never demanded by God for their own sake. In themselves they are negative and meaningless—their meaning and value come only from their positive direction to something higher.

The whole of the Christian life is a living surrender to the love of God. Surrender to and acceptance of the personal love of another is necessarily a surrender of self, of any preferring of one's own desires and inclinations which would clash with the demands of the personal love for that other. The love of God demands that we keep the commandments, which are only guides for directing our lives toward Him. Centering our lives on God demands then that we deny ourselves in our inclination to seek natural satisfaction which is in any way opposed to God's will expressed in the commandments. This will entail an effort at self-mastery, subjugating our instincts, passions, and desires to the rule of reason enlightened by God's grace. Our going to God, is not, since original sin, a purely positive thing: It is first an overcoming of something negative—the unreasoned inclination to seek ourselves and to use all things in a selfish way. There is an initial lack of balance and harmony in all our human drives; directing them toward God means first of all their rectification. To straighten a warped board, it is not enough just to bring it straight again; it must be bent in the opposite direction and held there for some time. Hence, ascetical efforts to achieve equilibrium and mastery will not be limited merely to avoiding what is wrong. They will include a renunciation of what is lawful in order that we might strengthen what is weak and warped within us. Fasts and other penitential practices are directed to submitting the inclinations of nature to reason enlightened by faith so that, in all our activity, we will not—as children do—move without reflection toward what attracts us naturally. We aim at achieving an enlightened judgment and mastery over natural inclinations, so that our first thought will be for the God whom we love, in whose light we judge and act. When our natural inclinations are stronger in certain directions, our efforts to submit these inclinations to the love of God will need to be more determined and constant. Thus will each individual have to measure his own mortification: The man for whom alcoholic drink is no danger will use it with moderation; the man who has alcoholic tendencies will renounce it completely. In this, as in other renunciations, there is no condemnation of the things that God has made. There is a recognition of one's own weakness and a resistance to the disorder of natural passions, which tend to abuse the good that God has created.

Asceticism is thus characterized by watchfulness against the things in us that could lead to separation from God. Since this watchfulness is inspired by love, it will not limit itself to the bare essentials. True love does not calculate carefully what it can keep of selfishness, what is the necessary minimum of generosity. A man does not ask himself how far he can go in certain matters without seriously offending his wife. If he wants to keep his love alive and lived strongly, he will avoid all things which could develop into selfishness and anything which could dull the keenness of his love. It is not the last step that causes the death of human love, but all the small preceding steps which are the beginnings of self-seeking. And so, in man's love for God, there will be carefulness to avoid all things which could dull the edge of his love for God. He will not ask whether a thing is allowed by the commandments without sin, but he will seek to know whether its renunciation will help him live his love for God more deeply. And of course, whenever he does without something that it would be lawful for him to have, if he does it in order to be careful to retain the freshness of his personal love for Christ, then so often will he grow in the tenderness of his love. Love goes further than logic—or rather love is more logical than mere reason: "We may have all sorts of plausible reasons for not doing things and yet perhaps it would be finer to do them. . . . I have all sorts of excuses for doing what is dangerous, and yet I know in the heart of me that I had better put them aside."[8]

A life of closer union with Christ is a life of greater self-renunciation. This, too, has to be seen as a law of love. If you give more, you must give up more; the more you give, the more you renounce. But if you give out of love, you do not think, mournfully, of the fact that you are giving up something. Renunciation will not be faithfully made unless it be gladly made. A person does not get married thinking about all the things he or she is giving up, for that would be condemnation to misery. A religious or priest gives up much, makes a sacrifice of many things. But it is useful to recall that the word "sacrifice" comes from the Latin words *sacrum facere*, to make something sacred by giving it to God. The word has come to denote first and foremost a giving up. But if what we do for God is lived mainly as a giving up, it will not be lived in fully human fashion. All that is given to God must be regarded as a gift that is gladly made out of love. At times, of course, it will be felt as a giving up; but if one lives in the constant thought of what one has renounced, that is not real sacrifice, and it is doomed to be a very dismal affair resulting in a lackluster existence. The one who has given more to God will find in the demands of duty, obedience, and fraternal charity[9] constant material for self-sacrifice or a constant means of generously giving oneself to the love of God.

There is, too, for the Christian, over and above the question of his own life for Christ, the fact of his union with Christ in the work of the salvation of the world. "I am glad of my sufferings on your behalf, as, in this mortal frame of mine, I help to pay off the debt which the afflictions of Christ still leave to be paid, for the sake of his body, the Church" (Col. 1:24). We do not need to find a completely rational explanation of all that is sacrifice and suffering, for, beyond the reaches of mere reason, we enter into the redemptive mystery of Christ. In union with Him we can offer our sufferings for the redemption of the world, helping by our own self-sacrifice to draw others

from their sin and self-seeking back to their self-renunciation in a gift to God.

5. Personal Asceticism

"It looks as though Christians today feel somewhat ill
at ease when confronted with the classical program of
asceticism . . . . There seems to be the keen awareness of
the danger of formalism inherent in all methods."[10]

From the point of view of the spiritual life, it is useless
to take on ascetical practices just because we "feel we
should be doing something in the way of penance." This
sort of thing can spring from several motivations—a sort
of guilt complex, a mistaken notion that there is value in
pain for its own sake, or seeking a feeling of security in
that we "are doing something." A primary necessity is an
enlightened understanding of the place of self-denial in the
spiritual life, an enlightened understanding of the basic
principles of the spiritual life in general. Wherever this
enlightened understanding is lacking, there will be danger
of error in one of two directions. Either there will be an
overoptimistic insistence on "all is good that God has
made," with a forgetfulness of the effects of sin on human
nature; or, you will find something of a recurrence of the
attitude of the fifteenth century when "people began to
externalize and objectivize their vague inner awareness that
all was not well, by making pain as such an integral part
of their system . . . an absolute value bestowed upon
pain . . . the idea that suffering is something noble, almost
sacred. . . ."[11] In our days, we are more inclined to fall
into the first of these errors. But because it is an error, it
usually takes with it, in those who want to live for God,
a certain uneasiness about lack of generosity. From this

they can be rescued only by the personal view of the spiritual life, with love's demand for self-forgetfulness and personal dedication in the demands of duty and fraternal charity, with self-discipline the safeguard of a life of personal love, and devotedness to duty a spending oneself with Christ.

A proper method of asceticism cannot be imposed from above. It cannot consist in doing things just because saints or holy persons did them. It must be a personal asceticism, properly integrated into one's efforts to live a life of personal love for Christ and dedication to Him. It will aim first of all at avoiding sin, which separates from the love of Christ, and at mastering all tendencies that lead to sin, as well as avoiding those things which are occasions of sin.

From what we have seen, it will be evident that conquering inclinations to sin is the same as overcoming selfishness in favor of surrendering to God. To this end are all the practices in early religious formation directed. Many things that are good in themselves are renounced, not because it is thought that there is virtue in the mere fact of depriving oneself of such things, but because the only effective way to achieve detachment from all things and to build up an internal strength is in this renunciation. Although "the aim of asceticism is not to produce decent, well-balanced citizens, but to make saints," nevertheless, in this formation "what we must put first is not respect for methods in themselves, even if they are traditional, but the acquisition of physical and psychological balance, which is normally the essential condition of moral balance."[12] This will be first in the order of time, not in the order of intention, for Christian asceticism is aimed always first at union with Christ the Redeemer. However, as we have seen, all that perfects the human personality prepares a

[141]

man to live more perfectly his personal relationship with God, and while he looks to God for grace, he must make every effort in the human, personal sphere.

While in many things human nature and human weakness do not change with the centuries—hence certain ascetical practices will always be necessary—some of the practices of former times can lose their efficacy, and some of the older methods employed in religious orders are of doubtful efficacy, so that many have been revised. This is the result of a healthy reaction against formalism, which means to attach more importance to outward forms than to the essence or purpose for which they are adopted, or to do things just because "they are always done this way." This reaction against formalism can sometimes degenerate into an unhealthy tendency to brand as "out of date" anything which is not in accord with our personal preferences, as Pope Pius XII recently warned in his address to the Jesuit General Chapter of 1957. With young people today, who are so inclined to be attached to their own judgment in all things, a very salutary ascetical practice is to accept without question whatever is proposed by those in charge of their formation. They thus strike most directly against one of their chief forms of attachment to self. On the other hand, those responsible for their formation have to cast a critical eye over certain practices and in the light of psychology and the history of asceticism ask: "Why was this practice introduced? What did it aim at? Is it still efficacious in achieving such an aim, or are other means better adapted to the purpose? If the reason for its introduction is not still valid, is there some other reason why it should be retained?"

The general direction of asceticism is toward shaping the human personality to be possessed by the personal love of Christ. As well as the general lines given above, each individual, taking stock of his own character and his own particular inclination to pride and selfishness,[13] will adapt his effort to his personal needs. What is a helpful ascetical practice for one could foster selfishness in another, according to his natural inclinations. To this choice, each individual must bring a clear self-knowledge and sincerity before God. Then, also, there is a further stage in which his personal liberty and individuality must assert themselves—the transition stage from the first period of asceticism to the later period of acquired detachment and liberty. This transition stage—as all transition stages—must avoid a twofold danger. The first is that of leaving too soon the formative period, of judging too early and too rashly that one has achieved self-control and need not worry about what use one makes of creatures. The second is the danger of being attached to practices for their own sake, after they have outlived their usefulness: a sense of security in the things we have always done and an uneasy feeling if we give them up.

It should be observed that this determined fight against sense-enjoyment is a passing thing. Its object is to restore the perfect harmony nature once had. When the spirit has obtained complete mastery over the flesh, the ascetic may again make use of the joys of art and sense, as instruments now at every point responsive to the spirit . . . the phase of renunciation in Christian asceticism is there for the phase of later acceptance.[14]

The aim of these practices was to generate an inner strength, to be able to say in all things what St. Thérèse of Lisieux said of friendship, "I no longer feel that I must deny myself the consolation of the heart, for my heart has grown strong in God." It is this strength—which comes from real attachment to Christ—which enables the Christian to "reconcile in a living paradox two attitudes which appear incompatible"—attitudes expressed by St. Paul: "There is nothing I do not write down as loss compared to the high privilege of knowing Christ Jesus, my Lord; for love of him I have lost everything, treat everything else as refuse, if I may have Christ to my credit" (Phil. 3:8–9). "Everything is for you . . . the world, or life, or death, or the present or the future; it is all for you, and you for Christ, and Christ for God" (I Cor. 3:21–22). St. Paul thus reconciles

. . . two dispositions which seem to exclude each other, whose union however is necessary to the soul of an apostle: to mix with things and not to be bound by them, to give oneself and not to be held . . . to enjoy creatures, yet not be seduced by them. At one and the same time there is supreme detachment, yet love of all that is true and just, pure, lovable, virtuous, and worthy of praise. This means that in all creatures the purified soul sees only the gifts of Christ; but Christ is worth more than His gifts, and for His sake, if He is to be possessed more fully, the soul will abandon all things else, without taking an inventory and without regret, with a great and royal carefreeness: For me to live is Christ, to die is gain.[15]

This detachment, contrary to what some writers seem to indicate, does not mean that abandoning things "without regret" is a process which causes no deep feeling. At times, the feeling of loss can be very great, but because one is attached to the will of God, the loss is accepted without any regret of the will. St. Thérèse of Lisieux wrote that through loving God, one gave to others an "affection deeper beyond comparison" than any more selfish love. Obviously, loss of friends and separation from them will be as deeply felt as the affection for them; the renunciation of work to which one has given much of one's life will take pain with it. Detachment is not insensibility, but the readiness to leave all at the call of Christ. It may mean that, like Christ in Gethsemane, we too will pray: "Father, if it be possible let this chalice pass." If He could pray thus, it will be no imperfection in us—provided our prayer concludes even as His did: "Yet, not as I will, but as thou wilt."

The transition to the stage of later acceptance does not mean that man does not need thenceforth to exercise eternal vigilance, or that asceticism is over and done with. Henceforth he must guard against the general tendency to settle down into routine, must watch to see that he does not become attached again to what he detached himself from with effort. In particular will he guard against his predominant character tendency reasserting itself in different forms: "It seems inaccurate to say that we really do correct our faults, for to do that we would have to give an entirely new shape to our character structure. . . . Experience points to their reappearance even in people who practice asceticism most resolutely . . . . There will be victory only to the extent to which, through continual development, the personality gains ground."[16]

It is at this stage that there is value in concentrating on the personal character of asceticism, to make all that we do the expression of our personal dedication to Christ, with particular attention to the demands of charity and duty—not, however, seen as the impersonal "demands of duty."

This follows from the psychology of the development of the human personality. When a man has come to maturity he needs to redirect his ascetic efforts—at the risk of stagnating psychologically and spiritually. It is well to stress this, because most writers on this point envisage the formation stage and the asceticism to be practiced by the young, and the beginners to free themselves from selfishness and to channel the forces of youth. After this stage is passed, the danger is that the forces will remain forever in their rigidly fixed channels, that the personality will become set and hard, and selfish in adhering to what it has made its own. There can be just as much self-centeredness in the mature as in the young, and it will be so much harder in proportion as it has been justified by its possessor. The saying of Sainte-Beuve is, unfortunately, often true: "We do not really mature; we rot in some places and harden in others."

We must remember

. . . the undeniable egoism of the adult, especially male. Even if he remains generous, his generosity has not the same freshness as that of youth. It is less spontaneous, and less carried to extremes. It is also impregnated with prudence and calculation. This phenomenon manifests itself also in a woman, whose deepest tendency remains, however, that of altruism —with this difference that her egoism is less personal, more that of the family, and that she calculates not so much for herself as for the objects of her anxious love. . . . The inconvenience of this predominance of reason in the adult is a clouding over of the faculties of intuition and of sensibility, a characteristic dryness. Capacity for pity and enthusiasm, the ability to understand the other, divining his needs, and facility for communion also diminish. The adult accepts the other as a fact . . . rather than trying to go out to him in a sympathetic intuition. He regards the suffering of others as a fact, which must be appropriately remedied, rather than as an object of sympathy and compassion in the strong meaning of these words. Objective himself, the adult easily objectivizes. Being active, he easily falls into activism and pragmatism. He prefers external activity to immanent action . . . doing things. . . . As he tends to calculate all things, as he feels there is no great future ahead of him, he wishes to measure, in the present, the results of his action. The adult woman does not escape from this law; she remains more emotional than man and more capable of pity, but she loses her juvenile sentimentality. She becomes . . . characterized by the practical reason and "managing" activity.

By a curious consequence, this degradation of sentiment gives to the adult a more painful feeling of loneliness, for he does not have all the youthful means of fulfilling his need of union with others. . . . Solitude and self-sufficiency go together, the terrible self-sufficiency of the adult, which is conquered only by the approach of old age. Resigned to solitude, conscious of his importance in his family or profession, certain to count for something, proud of making his own decisions, jealous of his majority, his importance, his independence, closed to the intrusions of others, master of his sensibility whose exterior manifestations and inner disturbances he has learned to repress, finding it repugnant to express his inner sentiments, to confide in others, to ask help or counsel, and resolved to owe nothing to anyone, the adult has the impression that he is sufficient to himself, and that he can expect nothing from anyone, even from God. Whence the spiritual crisis of the adult, above all of the adult male, which has not yet been sufficiently studied. . . . The danger which strangles maturity is that of habit. The adult easily becomes a bundle of habits, waiting for old age to transform these into a knot of manias. These habits procure his ease, his security. But if they dominate him, he is lost. Adapted to a past which daily flees, they are inadapted to a present which changes with great rapidity. The asceticism of the young consists in forming habits; that of the adult obliges him to struggle continually against the tyranny of habits, even good ones. . . . It costs a person to arrive at this precarious perfection of personality which is the adult state. He does not reach it, nor does he maintain it except by the perpetual realization in suppleness and strength, of an equilibrium between external and internal, between his different tendencies, between autonomy and heteronomy, between egotism and centrifugal movements. It is, in fact, the equilibrium of the adult. . . ."[17]

I have given this quotation at length, because there is not a great deal in the general run of ascetical writings to include the main lines along which the efforts of the adult should tend. Grace works in harmony with the psychology of man's personal development. The grace that enabled him to conquer and direct the forces of youth will, in later years, keep him alert to the calls of God's love and save him from settling back into a limited, self-centered existence, the harder to break because the adult can be so sure that he has learned.

"When the adult has been able to keep some of the fire of youth, to recognize his insufficiency before the Absolute, and go beyond what is strictly obligatory, his religion is more solid because founded on reason, and more human than that of . . . the young man. . . ."[18]

As we grow, we must keep something of the freshness of our youthful eagerness and wonder at God's dealings with us, something of the ready generosity of youth. We must take a special care to retain a "personal spirituality."

Mortification is a word that is not pleasing to nature. It is natural that we would desire to take on a few definite "practices of mortification" once and for all, and have it over and done with. It is natural, but it is not much use— at least for those things over and above what is the formative and strengthening element in self-denial. To serve their purpose of keeping an edge on our selfless love for Christ, they cannot be only "things we do habitually." They must be things that we do as our self-renunciation out of personal love for God, things which we do as conscious acts of love. Devotion to duty and the practice of fraternal charity, as explained above, will give us countless opportunities to do this. But generally the masters of the spiritual life would agree with Father B. Kelly:

An occasional fast or abstinence, the voluntary acceptance of some lack of comfort in one's room, voluntary abstention from some amusement—these and similar practices never lose their value for the religious, no matter what his age or the progress he has made. There is much wisdom in choosing some one simple form of bodily self-denial to be performed daily or at regular intervals. Without a slight minimum of method, the life of a man, even a spiritual one, tends to become aimless. . . . True, God is the supreme Master of our spiritual life, and the best thing we can do is to commit ourselves to God, accepting trials when they come, and graces too, in their turn . . . but it is only reasonable that while leaving the initiative to Him, we should, by a minimum of practices, keep ourselves in continued preparedness for His action.[19]

As we indicated briefly above, there is in Christian penance, over and above all the efforts to live our life of personal dedication to Christ, the further element of living in union with Him as Redeemer of the world. Here we leave behind all merely psychological aids to the direction of self-denial and enter more fully into the mystery of the members of Christ being able to share by their suffering in His work of redeeming the world. This truth will help us, touched by the thought of the love which led Him to His passion and death, to offer our own sufferings in union with Him and out of love. Some will be called to give their lives as co-redeemers in something like what is called "the victim state." For these the signs of their vocation must be quite clear and their following of direction docile and humble. In a lesser way, we can all add something by way of penance, even though it be in small matters only, offered out of love for Christ and the world. In all cases, extra penance is of dubious spiritual worth if it springs only from the feeling that one should be "doing something," or from anything resembling a guilt complex or masochism. If such offerings are inspired by the spirit of God, they will be accompanied by detachment, humility, serenity, and peace.

NOTES

[1] C. Davis, Introduction to English edition of *The Resurrection* by F. X. Durrwell (London: Sheed and Ward, 1960), p. XIX.

[2] L. Bouyer, *The Meaning of the Monastic Life* (New York: Kenedy, 1955), Preface.

[3] A. Lefevre, "Ecole de Spiritualité," *Dictionnaire de Spiritualité.*

[4] Y. Congar, *Lay People in the Church*, p. 94.

[5] F. Durrwell, *op. cit.*, p. 55.

[6] Cf. Ch. 7.

[7] Cf. Ch. 4.

[8] Bede Jarrett, O.P.

[9] Cf. Ch. 7.

[10] Cf. *Christian Asceticism and Modern Man*, pp. 110, 280.

[11] *Ibid.*, pp. 30 ff.

[12] *Ibid.*, pp. 110 and 260.

[13] Cf. Ch. 4.

[14] *Christian asceticism and Modern Man*, p. 101.

[15] J. Huby, S.J. in Epist. Philip., IV, 4 (*Verbum Salutis*).

[16] N. Mailloux, "Obstacles to the Realization of the Ascetic Ideal," in *Christian Asceticism and Modern Man.*

[17] "Devenir Adulte," *Convergences* Series (Paris: Ed. Spes, 1958), pp. 33ff.

[18] *Ibid.*

[19] *Progress in Religious Life* (Westminister, Md.: Newman, 1954), p. 69 f.

Chapter 10

SECURITY: THE VIRTUE OF HOPE

---

1. Security

One of man's basic psychological needs is the need of security. According to Adler, it is the most basic of all. Be that as it may, man's need for security inspires much of what he does. In the material sphere, he tries to insure himself against all possible risks. Millions of people in insurance companies, banks, etc., make their living by trading on this need to secure oneself against all sorts of possible dangers.

It would be strange if in the spiritual life man did not likewise want security in regard to his eternal salvation and in regard to his progress in the spiritual life. The virtue of hope consists in this, that we look to God alone for our security and trust that we will find it in Him. Simple as this may sound, to reach anything approximating to the perfection of hope is one of the most difficult things in the spiritual life. It would not be an exaggeration to say that more than half of the worries of people "striving for perfection" follow from the imperfection of their hope. Furthermore half the reasons for the necessity of passive purifications and trials is the necessity of purifying our hope.

It is natural for man to seek to bring himself to the perfection of which he is capable and to rely on his own powers to do this. But the supernatural order to which he has been raised by God is one in which he can achieve his goal only in dependence on God. All that he does is first God's gift to him, and is God acting in and through him. In his striving for salvation and sanctification, his *only motive* of hope, the only ground for his security, is the power of God and God's fidelity to His promises. In ourselves we have no reason at all for hope. "Without me you can do nothing" (John 15:5) was a truth we learned early in life; yet we take all our lives to learn it, and we can learn it only in the school of failure, in the consciousness of our own weakness, limitations, nothingness. We learn in the school of suffering.

We have a natural desire to be somebody, to get credit for what we are and for what we accomplish. But this natural desire must be superseded by the readiness to be only what God makes us and to give all the credit to Him. We have a natural desire to make our own efforts for security in spiritual matters and to rely on their worth for success. This desire to rely on our own efforts must give way to a trust that is only in God. Normally speaking, this is done in successive stages, as we shall see.

In this matter, the Christian has to live one of the many paradoxes of his faith. He can spare no effort for his own sanctification nor for the salvation of others. He must "work as if everything depended upon himself, and pray as if everything depended on God." He must make every effort, yet after he has done all he can, he must know that he is an "unprofitable servant" (Luke 17:10), and that it is God who gives the increase. In his own life, he must strive to be free from all failure before God. But even though he be certain that he has nothing on his conscience, it is not in this that he is justified (I Cor. 4:4). For his justification, he hopes in God alone, relies only on His merciful love, trusts in his Father and his Savior. The important thing is that he be justified before the divine tribunal. If he acquits himself, that is of no importance. It is divine acquittal, divine mercy and love that create a new heart within him.

This is easy enough to see in theory. It is not easy to live. We can know it only through the experience of our own weakness and failure. When we can accept our weakness and failure without discouragement, starting off again with a glad confidence in God, we have come a long way toward spiritual maturity. Any maturity demands a facing of reality and the acceptance of our own limitations and failures. Spiritual maturity demands the acceptance of the reality of God and the reality of self. Much of what St. John of the Cross wrote is a description of how a man comes to the realization and acceptance of these two fundamental realities. Acceptance of the reality of self is not a downcast attitude, but, with St. Paul, a glad glorying in our weakness that the power of Christ might dwell in us (I Cor. 12:9). This was, of course, one of the central points in the spirituality of St. Thérèse of Lisieux, whose doctrine has been summed up as "a restatement of the teaching of hope in all its fulness."[1] But hope in all its fulness means a man's death to self, his renunciation of wanting to be anything of himself and by himself, ceasing to rely on himself, with his reliance only on God. This comes about in successive stages.

Let us take the beginner in the spiritual life. He has made an initial self-renunciation—that of wanting to be something in the merely natural or worldly sense. He starts to practice the virtues. But before long, as St. John of the Cross pointed out with such clarity, he is conscious of and slightly proud of the fact that *he* is practicing virtue, *he* is striving for perfection. It is a long hard road to self-forgetfulness. For quite some time the one who tries to live for God, to live a life of charity, is frequently finding that he has not forgotten himself. "The created self is possessive, not merely in the order of having, but in the order of being. What was, on a lower level, proprietorship of having, then of self, becomes proprietorship of one's own spiritual progress. . . . The soul is not satisfied with loving God, but wants to be assured that it is loving . . . to regard itself loving, and therein to be satisfied."[2] It tends to put its security in itself, its own spiritual practices; to rely on what it does in the way of good works, spiritual exercises, and prayers. It does not rely on God alone, but on what it does for God. Then, says St. John, it is in for trouble. In order to bring it to rely on God alone, it must come to feel that it is not its own efforts, but only the power of God that lifts it up. Hence it must pass through something of the passive purifications of the night of senses and later of the spirit. It is a mistake to think of the night of sense as something far advanced along the way of perfection or as reserved for contemplatives. Its essence will find a place in the lives of all who make any real progress in the spiritual life. Some people have the erroneous notion that the night of the senses is like a tunnel on a mountain railway. You plunge suddenly into darkness on your upward journey toward perfection, and you emerge equally suddenly into higher regions of calm and peace. This is quite wrong. For most people, the night of the senses is more like clouds drifting across the sun, in varying degrees of darkness and duration. St. John of the Cross gives a vivid description, it is true. But he must be understood rightly. He gives a "typical case."[3] Or rather he describes in one vivid picture all the various ways which God uses to detach a soul from itself. Probably all the elements could seldom, if ever, be verified in one person—for different people are in need of different forms of detachment.[4] What would help one to overcome his particular form of self-attachment would not be helpful to another person who seeks self in a different way.

2. Passive Purifications

If left to himself, man will always seek to be somebody, want to have the credit for having achieved something, and want to rely on the security that he feels in the sense of his own achievement. The passive purifications in their various forms are God's way of making us look to Him alone and lean only on His strength—to purify us from the residue of self-seeking and self-reliance which remains even after we have determined to live entirely for God.

(a) THE NIGHT OF THE SENSES

It was in his teaching on the night of the senses that St. John of the Cross put forward his essential doctrine of passive purification. Naturally, since he was writing for contemplatives, he traces the action of God in the life of prayer and the interior life in general. In its essence the night of the senses is a simple concept. St. John refers to those who have been practicing mental prayer and who, in their meditation, find they get much light on the spiritual life from the "senses" of thought, imagination, memory. When these "senses" cease to give light, there is darkness, the "night of the senses." A more theological examination of the constituent elements of the "night" can be found in many authors.[5] For the moment this will be sufficient, for we wish to examine it not from the point of view of progress in prayer, but as a purification of hope.

At such a stage, the reaction of the soul is sufficient evidence of the need of further purification of hope, a freeing from "proprietorship." Typical remarks to directors or confessors at this stage are: "I don't seem to be doing anything at prayer. I can't pray as I used to. I don't feel I'm getting anywhere in the spiritual life. I'm only conscious of my faults, of the little I'm doing for God." All this is true; and all is as it ought to be. But what is also true, and what is not as it ought to be, is something else that is *not* said but which evidently underlies what is said. Behind statements such as the above is also this frame of mind: "And I want to feel that I'm getting somewhere in the spiritual life; I want to feel that I'm doing something in prayer. I want to have the comforting assurance that I am doing something for God, that what I have done has some value. I want to be able to lean on my own efforts, to feel, as I used to, the security these gave me. But now I've got nothing to lean on; I feel nothing but insecurity and anxiety."

Nothing to lean on? *Only God.* It is not just by way of comfort that all spiritual authorities say that in these circumstances three things are most important for the soul: humility, trust in God, and complete acceptance of what He wills for us. These are not temporary supports to help us over a time of trial. They are the very goals at which this purifying action of God, who lets us feel our own weakness, is aimed. It aims at getting us to face reality: the reality of God, and the reality of self; the reality of God who alone is infinite sanctity; the reality of self, of ourselves, incapable even of a good thought (II Cor. 3:5); the reality that all that we have is God's gift, and that all that we do is His power at work in us to bring to perfection what He has begun (Phil. 2:12). This is humility. From it follows the acceptance of God's will, the readiness to be only what He makes us, knowing that all is His gift. Trust in God alone, not in our efforts, will give us real security and make us lean on the power of God, which is our only motive of confidence. We must stop looking to ourselves, wanting to feel in our own efforts that we have some grounds for confidence. We must learn to trust in the love of God alone. This will be a "renewed hope, the hope of the child of God, his confidence in his Father whose love he shares, because He has given himself to this love and already shares it. This confidence, far from being shaken by trials, is nourished by them."[6]

(b) ACCOMPANYING TRIALS

Sinful man hopes for an ever-closer union with a transcendent God. If he is to live the virtue of hope fully, he must have a deep conviction of his need of God (i) as the only good which can fill the needs of his soul; (ii) as the only guarantee of his reaching that union. Hence, hope cannot flourish where a man is satisfied with what he is and has—even in the spiritual order—or where he is confident that he can make out all right by himself. He can only know his need by feeling his weakness and frailty and proneness to sin. He has to "fear" his weakness, as the Council of Trent says.[7] This can only be if he experiences his own need, the reality of his finite sinful nature. Yet, when such an experience comes to one who is trying to live the spiritual life, he is often afraid that something has gone wrong. Something may have gone wrong, and this he must check. But something is wrong, also, if a man expects to feel in himself, and of himself, the strength that is his only from the grace of God. To those who expect

[157]

such things, even subconsciously, God will send trials and temptations that they might *know* the reality of self, and lean on the only reality, looking to God alone, in whom they put their trust. They come to what Fénelon called the "despair of nature," that they might be lifted to true hope in God. It must be added that this hope is a joyous thing, "gladly glorying in our weakness." It is like the joyous hope and confidence which flooded the hearts of the apostles at the Resurrection. They had hoped, it is true (Luke 24:21), but their hopes had been imperfect; and with the death of Christ, their own hopes had died.

Then came the glad news of the Resurrection. With it would have gone the numbing realization of how utterly they, the apostles, had failed Christ; with this realization went the knowledge of their own unworthiness for renewed friendship with Christ. At His coming they waited in wordless longing for a sign of His continued love. Wait they must, for how could they, who had failed Him so utterly, presume to expect anything from Him? If they received only His scorn, that was what they deserved; and they knew it through and through. Yet, knowing their need of Him and what He had meant to them, they waited and looked to Him, not even daring to hope. As they waited, they heard His words of kindness and no reproach. Wordlessly, in the abundance of their gratitude, they took hope again. The hope that came flooding back, tremulously at first, and gradually in joy-filled torrents, was their glad response to a love that was infinitely tender, poured out in refashioning strength on undeserving hearts. Their response was total self-surrender: a love that was stronger and purer, for it was humble now, convinced of its own inadequacy unless constantly supported by the love of Christ.

For the spiritual life to flourish in the soul of any man in similar newness and humble purity, each must see something of his own hopes die. All of us start our way to God, to some extent sure of ourselves; hoping for great things, but hoping from ourselves, almost as much as from God; more endowed with self-assurance than with deep humility; leaning on ourselves, instead of waiting and looking only to God for a love and a strength which we know are undeserved. We are sure of ourselves and the way we will go to God. All of this must die to give way to humble trust in God and confidence in the way He leads us. The trust and confidence will flow forth fresh and strong only when to us who, like the apostles, have known our failure in bitterness of heart and despair of self, comes the glad realization of the love of God poured out on us, undeserving and all as we are. "The grace of God our Saviour has appeared to all men" (Tit. 2:11); it is the light which gives joy and confidence to our lives and sets them on the path of humble trust.

To some this realization of the great love of God in its uplifting power poured out on them, who in no way deserve it, comes as a gradual revelation over the years. To others it comes in an experience that shatters their old complacency and self-confidence. It comes in a soul-stirring experience which is like a lived rebirth, a death, and a resurrection. In its poignancy and spiritual import it will stay with them all the days of their lives, as a source of gratitude, sweetness, and strength. Either way, if we are to grow in the spiritual life, such a realization must come to us all. Our life begins at baptism. We are baptized into the death and Resurrection of Christ who, in the human failure and complete renunciation of His passion and death, gave Himself into the hands of the Father, abandoned Himself to the power of God that raised Him up. It is this mighty power which, according to St. Paul, is to be the measure of our confidence in God (Eph. 1:19–21). In other words, it is to be without measure.

Like all things in the spiritual life, this is not done once and for all. Our life is a progressive entry into the dual mystery of Christ's death and Resurrection. We find that over and over again we are asked to die to self, to face the reality of our own weakness, in order that we might cling more closely to the love of Christ.

The contemplative answers the call to a life of prayer, convinced of its value. He finds in his exercise of prayer a certain satisfaction, feeling that he is getting something out of it and that he is really doing something worthwhile in God's sight. Since the hidden life is his whole way to God, his whole work for God, it must be within this field that he undergoes his essential purification. This passive purification begins when he finds that his prayer has lost its fervor and no longer gives him any consolation. He feels that it is worthless, that he has not progressed, that all his efforts are of no avail. Naturally, he becomes anxious and troubled. Anxiety is one of the chief notes characteristic of this stage, for the security felt in one's former way of prayer and practice of virtue is gone. The soul has drawn security from the fact that in prayer and the practice of virtue, it had something worthwhile. In this, as St. John stresses, it was leaning on itself, relying on its own efforts. Its motive of confidence was in itself. Furthermore, if temptations and other trials are added to shatter even more all confidence in self, all its hopes for union with God seem to die.

It is then, of course, as St. John of the Cross taught, that it must turn to God, look to Him alone, attentive to His presence in the darkness of faith. Thus it comes to a purification of its faith, hope, and charity. It should be useful to recall here what we said above[8] about anxiety and the full development of freedom. At this stage the soul stands on the threshold of the unknown. It is called to leave behind the less perfect, less mature ways of prayer wherein it found much natural consolation to follow the leading of God. The psychological process is the same here as at all such stages of crisis. St. John warns that the soul must on no account seek consolation, nor must it try to return to the old ways of prayer. This would be seeking the comfort and security of less mature ways that it is asked to transcend. If it insists on trying to remain in the "shelter" and security of what it has grown used to, it is condemned to remain forever immature. It must take the risk, trusting in God who will lead it forth to wider horizons and to an appreciation of greater spiritual values.

It should be noted that many of the accompanying trials are either aspects or consequences of this anxiety in spiritual matters. Tanquerey[9] lists temptations against faith, hope, patience, and peace of soul. All these will follow by a sort of psychological necessity from the state of soul we have described. All will cease to have the same disturbing force when the soul has learned to trust in God alone, in a calmer, more mature, more purified way. Still, one or other can continue in more acute form. Other temptations can be permitted by God to bring the soul to a deeper knowledge of the reality of its weakness and need of God's strength. External trials are sometimes added: temporal losses, misunderstandings, and persecutions. These are obviously incidental. Older authors (Tanquerey among them) were inclined to add "strange ailments which baffle physicians." They did baffle older physicians. But most such things are regarded today as a consequence of the nervous and physical reactions resultant on a stage of continued emotional upset, particularly anxiety. The famous "mystic malady," once regarded as a necessary accompaniment of contemplation, is put down as digestive disorders resulting from nervous tension or from an unbalanced diet.[10]

Sometimes, too, the trials of faith are due to the imperfection of our hope in regard to what we expect from God. Because God does not hear our prayers in the way we expect, our faith is tried. Karl Rahner has written of the "despair" when we "think there is no God, because we confound the true God with what we take for God. We are right in what we think, for the God we imagine does not really exist: the God who establishes security on this earth, the God who saves from disillusionment, the God who does away with risks, the God who takes care to see that His children do not cry and makes justice reign upon the earth, the God who wards off all scourges and sees to it that the love of man is never disenchanted. . . ."[11]

For contemplative and apostle alike, there is need of mature faith and hope in a God who wills to bring us to mature spirituality through facing reality, shouldering responsibility, without looking to Him to make our tasks easy and our prayer consoling. At times, of course, trials of faith concern objects of faith—the infallibility of the Church, real presence, etc. Although not the result of the imperfection mentioned above, these trials, too, are meant to perfect our faith even further.

(c) THE APOSTOLATE

St. John of the Cross, in his treatment of the night of the senses, considers more the life of prayer and the practice of the interior life. This was in accord with his purpose, which was to write for contemplatives. Some wrongly have thought that what he says does not therefore have any application to the active life. Others, also wrongly, have tried to apply it without any modification to the life of the apostle. The truth is that the underlying principle of the necessity of passive purification applies to all, but the way it will be effected will be in accord with the circumstances of life in which God has placed them.

The contemplative gives his whole life to prayer and the interior life. In the imperfect beginnings of his spiritual life, he will seek security and satisfaction in his own efforts within this sphere. In consequence it is within this sphere that he will be purified by the action of God. The apostle and the active religious will not be exempt from the general law of passive purification. But their purification, their night, will of necessity be within the whole sphere in which they try to give themselves to God and do something for Him. In the field of prayer, it will be less acute, although it will be there. For them this is not the whole field of their spiritual effort. Neither will it be the whole sphere of their purification.

It will be in the active life that they "feel they are doing things for God." It is there they will tend to rely on their own efforts and expect to achieve great things. They will seek security in what they achieve, relying on the things they have done, the successes that have come their way. Hence their trials will be the setbacks they meet in this sphere, the little success, the contrast between what they manage to do and all that there is to be done for God. There is a world to convert; millions of souls need the grace of God; the true apostle, especially in his early years, will endure anguish of soul when he sees how little he can do. He will feel that others do not share his zeal, his vision. He will feel his own powerlessness as he meets with hardened sinners and as he sees the failure of those for whom he worked and for whom he prayed. Then he, too, will be tempted against faith, against hope, patience, and peace of soul. He will wonder what is the use of prayer and what is the use of his efforts. He will have entered upon his night. He is called upon to grow to maturity as an apostle, to relinquish the idealism and dreams of youth, to face the reality of human limitations, and to face, too, the reality of God and His power and His will for the world; to persevere in prayer and devoted effort, to trust in God who gives the increase, who wills that all men be saved and come to the knowledge of truth.

It is in the exercise of his ministry that the apostle will find, his whole life long, the means which God uses to detach him from the natural desire to achieve something, with the credit going to himself instead of to God who gives the increase. In that same ministry he will also be provided with many opportunities to learn to lean on God.

It is a well-known fact that the big danger for the young apostle is that of discouragement.

In every flame, there is sufficient impurity to leave a residue of ash; in every life there is enough meanness to leave a taint of sin; in every action there is enough powerlessness to leave a feeling of failure; in every meeting there is enough incomprehension to leave a consciousness of loneliness. Therefore, for anyone who lives his life in the truth of his being and his action before God, the great temptation is not to vanity but to discouragement. The great danger is not to think that we will succeed by our own strength, but to doubt that even God can succeed with such a poor instrument. . . . The priestly ministry is at bottom a purification of hope.[12]

Apostles begin their mission with high hopes of achieving great things for God. They find that, in reality, men resist grace, fail to respond with generosity, and are unenthusiastic about the things of God. They meet with opposition, misunderstanding—and this on the part of those who work with them and over them. The hardest part is that many of these things which the apostle must accept from superiors or confreres can seem to him a hindrance to the work of God—as the cross seemed to be to the work of Christ. Thus is the apostle early brought to face reality: the reality of human limitations—his own and those of others. He will have to live through disappointment and failure. But facing reality is not merely a philosophical acceptance of these limitations. It includes an acceptance of the reality of God and His power and His plan for the redemption of the world through the efforts of human instruments. The apostle must see, too, that this experience of his own powerlessness is not meant to make him resign himself to little effort, but to work his purification, to make him lean on God alone, knowing that in all success it is God who gives the increase. Discouragement or bitterness, becoming soured or cynical, an apathetic "what's the use?" attitude, or limiting one's efforts to "chosen souls"—all these things are witness to the fact that the apostle has, to some extent, failed in his own personal spiritual life. He has failed to see that failures and setbacks are, in the plan of God, meant to be there as instruments of his own sanctification, as part of his agony in the garden, as part of his failure of the passion and cross, which will be transformed by God into victory.

There is a dynamism in faith, a confidence that God can convert the world, no matter how much we might fail. This is the *erectio animi* which gives rise to persevering effort, never daunted by failure, although never surprised at human failure. "We will fight and God will give the victory." So spoke Joan of Arc, a soldier of Christ and a saint. Every apostle must have something of her spirit of confident dynamic trust; every apostle must be strong in hope. The strength will come only through living an experience of weakness, only through fighting and overcoming temptations to discouragement and apathy, only through leaning on God.

(d) THE NIGHT OF THE SPIRIT

According to St. John of the Cross,[13] in the soul's progress toward more perfect union with God, a second period of purification is needed, which he calls the "Dark Night of the Spirit." Other authors speak of it as a "second Mystic Death."[14] In St. John of the Cross it fits into his general scheme of the contemplative life. But it has its universal application from the point of view of necessary passive purification. It is from this point of view we shall consider it here, bearing in mind also that, similar to the night of the senses, it has its varying degrees of intensity and duration. It can be explained from the theological approach of the influence of the gifts of the Holy Ghost. We shall see it more from the point of view of human psychology in relation to grace and progress in living the virtue of hope. One of the reasons why St. John says that further purification is necessary is that souls who have made some progress beyond the stage of proficients seek their security too much in what *they* do in spiritual matters.[15]

The nature and need of such purification is more easily understood from the point of view of man than from God's activity. God does not delight in inflicting trials: their necessity springs from man's imperfection. The first period of trial, as we saw, parallels a man's coming to maturity in the psychological order; its purpose is to bring him to spiritual maturity. Hence he passes through many trials which are much more easily understood in the light of his psychological development. There is a parallel between his personal crisis in coming to adulthood and his spiritual crisis in coming to maturity. Since grace perfects the human person, this must normally be. Similarly, the necessity of the night of the spirit, due to man's imperfection, finds its cause in those defects into which an adult is naturally inclined to fall. This second spiritual crisis parallels the "crisis of the adult." It will be greater in proportion as a man has yielded to the "natural" inclination, to

. . . the terrible self-sufficiency of the adult . . . conscious of his importance in his family or profession (we might apply it to his priesthood, religious family, or apostolate) certain to count for something, proud of making his own decisions, jealous of his majority, his importance, his independence . . . the adult has the impression that he is sufficient to himself, and that he can expect nothing from anyone, even from God. Whence the spiritual crisis of the adult . . .[16]

It is exactly against these defects in the spiritual life that the trials described by St. John are directed. In the Night of the Spirit, a man has the feeling that he is abandoned by God, that he does not deserve God's love or concern, that all that he has done is useless, that his life and life's work have been wasted; he feels abandoned, lost, and alone in "a more painful feeling of loneliness." Through all this, of course, his whole effort must be to cling to God in darkness, in faith, and in hope, in a charity which will seem to him no real love at all. Thus will he be brought to a fuller leaning on God alone, a deeper faith and trust, a fuller self-renunciation which is a fuller acceptance of his own nothingness.

Again, for the contemplative who has seen the whole "value" of his life in his prayer, the trials will be in that same field. For the apostle and the active religious who dreamed of "doing great things for God" in the apostolate, the trials will come in the "failure" of their apostolic work for others, or in the conviction that they themselves have failed to work for God and their own sanctification. For both contemplative and active, the trials will be greater if they have not known what to expect. They will be greater, too, if they are destined to higher union, or to a more intimate association with Christ in His redemptive suffering. They will normally be less if, after the initial crisis, the adult has grown in maturity, trust in God, realization of the reality of God and the reality of self and has avoided the mistake of settling down into the "natural" self-sufficiency of the adult.

3. Stop "Striving for Perfection"

Many spiritual authors cause more heartburn than they know. They cause not a few to resign themselves to mediocrity against which, ironically enough, they frequently warn. Much damage is done by the frequent use of phrases such as "striving for perfection," "striving for sanctity," "trying to be a saint," "aiming at the higher ways of sanctity." If anyone starts on the spiritual life with one of these things as his conscious aim, he is doomed to disappointment; or, if not disappointed, he becomes a victim of illusions. These may seem surprising statements, but a little reflection shows how true they are. Sanctity, perfection, holiness—these are abstract terms, and one cannot go on for long aiming at an abstraction. Furthermore (and this is the most important point) they give the beginner the impression that he ought to be able to know that he is becoming more perfect, travelling the higher ways of sanctity, becoming a saint. Unless he is a theologian he cannot but think this. But if he does think he is becoming a saint, if he is convinced that he is on the higher ways of sanctity— then, by that very conviction, he proves that he is not. As he grows in sanctity he must grow in hope in the reali- zation of his own weakness and imperfection before a God of infinite holiness. As he draws nearer to God, he will become convinced of the truth of the infinite transcend- ence of the holiness of God compared with his own. And as he becomes conscious of his imperfection and reflects on the exhortations "to be a saint, to travel the higher ways of sanctity," he concludes regretfully that the higher ways are not for him. The ones who have issued the exhortations are instrumental in making him resign himself, regretfully, with uneasy conscience, to what he considers "a lower way." They also contribute to the lack of real peace that is to be found in some whose joy should be full because they have given their lives to God.

Let them all reflect on the implications of the virtue of hope; on the necessity of knowing the reality of self, of accepting their weakness, and looking in loving confidence to the power of God. Our journey toward God is like a voyage on the open sea. Each day, the horizon seems just as far away; each day it seems that we have made little progress. It is not until our journey's end that we will see how close we have come to God.

Another unfortunate consequence of such expressions is that they tend to center attention upon oneself. *I* will be a saint; *I* work at *my* perfection. Very well; as long as you do that, your life will be self-centered. We will start to get somewhere in the spiritual life as soon as we begin to forget ourselves. Christ did exhort us to be perfect as our heavenly Father is perfect. He did not, however, stop with the exhortation to perfection. He immediately got us to look to the Father, out from ourselves toward God. The perfection of which He speaks is the perfection of love, a love which, in the context, is completely self-forgetful. The spiritual life is not thinking of our own perfection—at least not when we have made any progress. This should be evident enough from previous chapters.

If we want to live the spiritual life more fully, we must aim at living a personal devotion to Christ, our life centered on Him in a personal faith, love, and hope; receiving the gifts of His love and grace, and making our lives the joyful response of our self-giving. And if you do want to know whether you have drawn closer to Christ, the one true test is—gratitude. If, looking back over the years, you can thank God for all that He has given you, for His love lavished on you, and His guidance and strength and care in leading you, then you have got somewhere in the spiritual life. You will not see that you have done much for God. You will know rather that God has done much for you; and it is that which matters after all. We should not strive for "the higher ways of sanctity," but for a more intimate personal union with Christ, living in His love, gladly giving Him the little we can. Then, although we might express it in humbler fashion, we will find someday that our "lower" way was higher than we knew.

Growth in perfection means growth in self-forgetfulness. Positively it means growing more alert to the calls of God's grace and the indications of His will, growing in personal intimacy with Him and in personal dedication to Him. These must be our conscious aims, for these turn our attention habitually away from ourselves.

It is hope in its dynamism that urges us on in our continued search for a deeper knowledge of Christ, a closer union, a more generous dedication. This means that hope

always gives something of that vitality which was characteristic of St. Teresa of Avila, of whom Claudel wrote:
"Each day younger, each day stronger, each day more
sure in faith; each day more ardent, each day less satisfied
yet more joyful, carried on, when bodily strength fails, by
the strength of our desire."

In its dynamism hope is purified and perfected in time.
Beginning with the confident enthusiasm of youth, it can
be combative and impatient, brooking no delays. As the
years go by, while losing nothing of its persevering effort,
hope does lose something of its impatience and becomes a
peaceful aspiration toward union with God and the full
coming of His Kingdom. The soul knows that this will all
be in God's good time; it is content to strive, to endure,
and to wait. And so, in all its aspects, hope takes on the
calm and confident character which breathes through the
Psalms: our eyes lifted to the Lord, whence help will come
to us, the Lord, our Rock, our Deliverer, in whom alone
we trust.

NOTES

[1] J. Walsh, "A New Thérèse," *Month*, 20 (1958), pp. 150 ff.

[2] "L'Homme devant l'Echec," *Convergences* Series (Paris: Ed. Spes,
1958), pp. 210 ff.

[3] Gabriel of Mary Magdalene, *St. John of the Cross* (Westminster,
Md.: Newman, 1956), p. 46.

[4] See, Ch. 4.

[5] R. Garrigou-Lagrange, *The Three Ages of the Spiritual Life* (St.
Louis: Herder, 1948), pp. 47 ff.

[6] Lacan, "Les trois qui demeurent," *Rescherches de Sciences Religieuses*, 46 (1958), 321 ff.

[7] Sess. VI, c. 13., D.B. 806.

[8] Ch. 4.

[9] *The Spiritual Life*, Book 3, Ch. 2.

[10] Biot and Galimard, *Medical Guide to Vocations* (Westminster,
Md.: Newman, 1955).

[11] Quoted in *L'Homme devant l'Echec,* p. 219.

[12] L. Lochet, "Sainteté et renouvellement du sacerdoce," *Vie Spirituelle,* 100 (1959), 461–481.

[13] *Dark Night,* Book II.

[14] J. de Caussade, *Self-Abandonment to Divine Providence,* Vol. II.

[15] *Dark Night,* Book II, c. 2., n. 4.

[16] "Devenir Adulte." The quotation is more fully given in Ch. 9.

Chapter 11

PERSONAL SPIRITUALITY

---

1. Conscious Thought Control

As the world is threatened by herd-instinct and action for action's sake, these must be countered by the building of individual worlds of silence and recollection so as to allow of thought and prayer, for, as Lacordaire says, silence is the homeland of the strong. . . . Taking into account the needs of men today, the best way to cultivate the spirit of renunciation which the Gospels declare to be essential, seems to be to make religion more and more personal, to put more and more thought into it . . .[1]

This is the best way, in our age, to cultivate the whole of the spiritual life. We live in an "environment tending all the while towards materialism in thought and action,"[2] in an age of feverish activity, of radio and TV, of much writing and much spreading of news, theories, etc. Man is conscious of the massed forces of the world, of great movements, and of the fact that he, as an isolated individual, can do nothing to stem the various tides that flow around him. In theological and scriptural studies, there are "new" lines of thought, "new" movements, and in these fields and in his own spiritual life man can be always seeking new things, looking for new spiritual lights. Bewildered by all this, there are those who advocate a return to the simplicity of the Gospels, who endeavor to withdraw from the flow of life and progress in one or other of those regressive movements that may satisfy a few, but which are no solution for most members of the Church, that is for all times and can adapt her life to all ages. Others never quite succeed in establishing a steady and strong spiritual life that grows constantly, adapting itself to what is good in the new, resisting what is not, with a sureness springing from its own vitality.

A basic necessity of vital spirituality is to live consciously the realities of our personal relationship with God in Christ. Making this part of our conscious, constant living requires an effort. Some may even think that, in our preoccupied age, it is impossible. That is to admit defeat before making an effort, an effort which is possible to all. It is instructive, in this context, to see how doctors in their treatment of neuroses demand from their patients "conscious thought control." It is a well-known fact that much illness is emotionally induced, i.e., the result of the influence of emotional states, through the nervous system and glands, on the physical and mental health of the whole person. As one of the necessities of healthy living, these patients are told to make an effort at conscious thought control, not letting their worries prey constantly on their mind, but making a determined effort to keep their thoughts in more pleasant and contented channels. Now many of these people are temporarily and partially unbalanced—yet doctors ask and expect this of them. The possibility of "recollection" or "conscious thought control" for the allegedly balanced person should be obvious.

Recollection is like an atmosphere in which we live, like a backdrop to the stage on which we move. We have to think about what we are doing for God if we are to do it well. He does not expect us to work out complicated problems for Him, giving only half our thought to them. But in ordinary life there are two emotional levels: the fundamental and the superficial; it is the fundamental one which has most influence. To illustrate this let us think of someone whose mother is very seriously ill, during the critical period of her illness, with a strong probability that she will die. During this period of his mother's illness, a man will live his life, reacting to things more or less normally, taking an interest in things, laughing, etc. But all this is on the superficial emotional level. He lives more deeply the fundamental emotion of anxiety, which is the constant background of his life. In the spiritual life, the constant background to all that we do should be the glad consciousness of our personal dedication to God. This means that the various truths we have seen must really sink into our souls.

2. Faith

The starting point, as we have seen, is faith, "the root of all justification," not just accepting truth, but accepting the truth of God's love. We have seen that one of man's basic psychological needs is to love and be loved. One of his most basic spiritual needs is to live in the consciousness of God's love for him, as the person he is. This is the acceptance of a truth, but it is the most momentous truth in our lives. We all make our daily act of faith—but I sometimes think we make the wrong one: "I believe all Thou hast taught"—an assent to a general body of doctrine. Should we not add to it an act of deep faith in God's personal love for us?

Unfortunately even this becomes only a phrase for

many of us. "God loves us," *le bon Dieu nous aime:* it is written and said so often that it has no more effect on us than the statement that "our aunt loves us." It does not displease us, but it moves us very little. So, let us rethink it and examine it from any new angles that may help us get away from our dispassionate acceptance of the fact that God loves us. Let us recall the example, given earlier,[3] of Robinson Crusoe on his desert island, lost, hopeless, alone, with no future, condemned to live out a dull existence. Then he hears a voice, the revelation first and foremost of a personal presence; and he thrills to the sound of the voice of a person who comes to him in friendship. If the person said: "I have just dropped in to pay you a visit. It was nice seeing you. Good-by." Would that be love or friendship? God's love is benevolent and beneficent—which means that it wishes all the good possible for us and does us all the good we will let it do. Such is the love of God that has come to us. If to Robinson Crusoe a friend came who had spent long years seeking him, who had sacrificed all just to find and help him, then at that personal meeting and at the first word uttered, his heart would have thrilled in that strange mixture of emotions which makes you laugh and cry at once. There is something similar in the lives of all those to whom the love of God comes. We see it in the lives of the disciples of Christ, the early Christians; we see it in every real conversion. But for us it has become a commonplace: "God loves us. And why shouldn't He?" Why should God love us?

> Wherefore should any set thee love apart,
> of all man's clotted clay, the dingiest clot?

"Human love needs human meriting": The goodness in us attracts the love of others—if they are human. If he who loves us is divine, it is the other way round. If He had not loved us, we would not exist; if He had not loved us more, through the Incarnation of Christ, redemption, and the gifts of grace, we would not exist but with empty heart and an empty life, weighed down by the knowledge of our own weakness and sin. We have only to think of the slums of our cities and their thugs, tough girls, and hard men and women—as hard as hell, and as hopeless, unless the finger of God touches them. That we would have been, or worse, had the circumstances of our life been the same as theirs. Everything we are—in the order of nature or grace—is what someone else has made us, and God, in His love, acting through them.

God's love is worlds removed from a human "I like you"; it is the mighty power of God taking and lifting and cleansing us, and, in spite of ourselves and our ignoble qualities, bearing us in His arms to the eternal sharing of His intimate life and love, which will fill our heart and put an end to the pain and frustration and fearfulness of human existence.

We "have learned to believe in the love which God has in our regard." Let us vary the accent: It is the love that GOD has for us in which we believe. It is GOD who loves us, the Lord of life and death, the King of tremendous majesty, the God whom the Jews feared to see lest they die; God, needing nothing for His happiness, needing us not at all! And we need Him with every fiber of our being. Have we really learned to believe in the love God has in our regard, accepting it with all its implications? Until we do, there can be no question of real spiritual life.

3. Humility

Humility is the foundation of the spiritual life. This is

frequently stressed, and so we set about "learning humility"; we take the last place and accept humiliations, make acts of humility—and often succeed in getting no nearer to real humility than did Uriah Heep. It has been wisely said that for beginners to be formed in humility, it is probably best not to think about humility at all, but to concentrate on developing a sense of gratitude to God for all that he has done for us.[4] We cannot grow in humility if we think mainly about ourselves, but only if we see God and ourselves in right perspective.

"Towers are not tall unless we look up at them, and giants are not giants unless they are larger than we."[5] With a little more looking out and looking up, some day we will see ourselves in true perspective, with a deep gratitude to God whose love has been lavished on us, and a realization of our own need of God's help. Our need of God's help—if we do not know this deep down, we will never appreciate what it means to "believe in God's love." The prayer "Jesus meek and humble of heart, make my heart like unto thine" is not as innocent as it looks. We are, in effect, praying that we might know our own weakness and our need of God's help; and the weakness and the need go very deep indeed. If the Lord lets us feel them in their reality, we will come close to despair—which will not be a bad thing after all, if we then look to the love and the power of God.[6]

4. "Things to Be Done"

Many people are at least vaguely disturbed by two different yet connected worries: the feeling that they "ought to be doing more for God," and a doubt about the worth of the things they do. The root cause of both troubles is that their minds are too conditioned by repeated commendable exhortations toward an attitude of "things to be done." They thus like to take stock at the end of the day or the year and to be able to say: "I've done all these things for you today, Lord." Whereas what they should say is: "Lord, I've lived another day or year in your love, and I thank you."

This attitude extends to quite a few things: (a) *Duties to be performed*, which, as was said above[7] should be the living of our personal dedication. (b) *Works of self-denial.*[8] (c) *Spiritual exercises.*

Spiritual exercises, exercises of piety, are well-worn phrases, but the sooner we stop thinking of them in such terms, the sooner will they be part of our life for God. We "say" our rosary, office, and prayers; we "make" our meditation, our examinations of conscience, our spiritual reading. If, at the end of the day, our "spiritual exercises" have all been faithfully performed, especially if we have made an extra visit, we feel that we have chalked up a credit with the Lord. We have done something. These are all necessities of language. But a necessity of spiritual living is that they flow forth from a living, personal self-giving to God and are its expression.

There are two fairly common attitudes with regard to these exercises. After some time spent in the pursuit of perfection, many people settle into one or the other. The first is that of carefulness about all the "things to be done," with an accompanying feeling of satisfaction that all things have been done or a vague feeling of unease when something has been omitted. The second is the attitude that it does not matter much if one is not over-careful about them: Do them if you can; if you can't without some special effort, don't bother about the effort. They don't make that much difference. These are both dead ends; the one as dead as the other. The first is that which, as St. John of the Cross repeatedly stressed, we must transcend if we are to advance. The second is resignation to mediocrity; but at least it usually recognizes that it is such. The first is self-condemnation to mediocrity, accompanied by the mistaken notion that it is pretty well on the way to perfection. We have treated of this in detail in our chapter on hope.

The only way out of either impasse is to realize that the spiritual life is not first and foremost (even second or third) a set of things to be done. It is the flowing forth of a personal surrender to the demands of God's personal love. Our personal love will express itself in prayer or action or both. But unless both are consciously lived as our personal response, we shall never have any real spiritual depth. Faith is belief in God's love, undeserved, yet lavishly bestowed, taking us into intimate friendship with Himself; our life is our grateful and glad reply to the Persons who have lifted us to their level, taken us into their family. "Spiritual exercises," forsooth! Prayer is a withdrawing into the presence of God, "loving conversation with God who we know loves us," as St. Teresa said. We go to each time of prayer as to a personal meeting. We have to make sure that we do. Recollection is constant care to live on the personal level of our relationship with God. "Saying our rosary" should be our seeking to know our Lord in the mysteries of His life, death, and glorification. This, with spiritual reading, is a living of the *faciem tuam quaero semper*, a striving for more initimate personal knowledge of Christ. Our examination of conscience is not directed chiefly at making an exact catalogue of failings, but at putting ourselves again (if necessary) into personal contact with Christ, so that we may go forth again to do His will in more dedicated personal devotedness.[9] This will transform our lives. It won't transform them into extended high spots of felt enthusiasm and exaltation. But it will stop them stagnating, because through them will run the steady stream of personal dedication that will transfuse them with a deep peace.

For, as life goes on, personal love loses its edge of exaltation and flows more strongly on a deeper level. It flows on in spite of surface obstacles. The wife who visits her sick husband, invalided and irritable, does not go because she gets a thrill out of the visit. But she goes; and she goes with unwavering fidelity. The mother who gives years of her life to looking after her children through all the nerve-rasping stages gets anything but constant, unbroken thrills from her devotedness. But, in both cases, this is personal dedication at its best and strongest and most mature. It is personal love at its deepest and most constant. It does not feel that it is doing much—it is only doing what it must. It does not need to feel satisfied, for real love is always self-forgetful.

The man who does not care about his "spiritual exercises" because he does not feel that he gets anything out of them, or because he cannot see that they are very important, is not doing them from personal love and dedication. The man who must do them at all costs, who can never omit them, on any pretext without a feeling of having failed, is not doing them from a sense of personal dedication either. For the personal love which takes a man to his meeting with God at prayer can take him to do other things as well. The important thing is that his life is a personal dedication; as long as it is that, consciously lived, he will not worry where it takes him.

If it is that, it will take him to prayer, even when many cares make it almost impossible to "pray." It will take him even more strongly then, for he will know that he needs this personal contact with God. His prayer may be no

more than his going to make his tribute of personal dedication. But it can always be that; and it should be that.
His recollection and his "constant thought control" must
bring him back to that, when he "feels" that many things
make it impossible to spend time in calm and peaceful
prayer. Let us think of human examples of personal dedication. They can help us in our dedication to God.

If you want to grow in the spirit of prayer, forget about
"spiritual exercises" as things to be done. Think of them as
personal tributes of love and loyalty, a personal tribute of
love and gratitude and praise—a seeking for a more intimate personal knowledge of Father, Son, and Spirit. If you
want an ascetical exercise that can give new color to
your whole life: before you make a visit, say your rosary,
make your spiritual reading, perform an exercise of piety
or a spiritual duty, pause. What are you doing? Why?
When all these things are impregnated with the consciously lived personal note and when something extra,
which is not of obligation, is habitually done in the way of
prayer—not just for the sake of "doing something" but as
a human need to keep alive the "personal" note in our relations with God—then you can look around profitably for
something else to do. But, by then, you will have found so
much to do for God, and so much deep content in the
doing of it, so much sureness under the leading of God's
love, that you will neither be wondering nor worrying any
more.

5. Personal and Institutional

As is indicated in various places in this book, stress on the
personal character of the spiritual life in no way indicates
a rejection of external authority, practice, or any of the
institutional forms in which life for Christ is lived in the

Church. Any idea of living for God merely in the privacy of one's own soul without any outward expression and practice has always ended in heresy which the Church has had to condemn. However, it is a well-known fact that, when much insistence must be placed on one aspect of religion, there is a danger of regarding that aspect—important and all as it may be—as sufficient and complete in itself. Against Protestant errors, the Church had to insist on the value of the external, social aspect of the Church; her power and duty to make laws and to rule the faithful; the value of the sacraments as causes of grace; the duties of Catholics; laws for attendance at Mass and reception of the sacraments.

It would be strange if, as a result of this necessary insistence, no opposite tendency resulted, namely, to regard the externals as sanctifying almost apart from internal, personal dispositions, from the reality of personal contact with God and dedication to Him. I do not say that such a judgment is explicitly formulated, but it is implicit in many attitudes and practices influencing many Catholics more than they realize, and influencing the more fervent in ways we have already indicated in the earlier sections of this chapter. How many think they are good Catholics just because they go to Mass and keep the laws of the Church, even though these things may have little meaning in their personal life for God? Do we not tend to set more store on the numbers who attend Mass than on making sure they do so in an interior spirit of worship in spirit and in truth? To regard a layman as better than another if he joins a sodality? To be more concerned with getting children into Catholic schools than with examining whether, in the conditions in which they are taught, they really learn to live a life of personal dedication to God?

Our life with God and the life of God in us can only be personal. . . . There is no divine life except in men, and all things—organizations, buildings and the rest—serve only as instruments to develop the life of the Christian. . . . Nothing counts in the Church of God except the development of the divine life in souls. . . . No institution or framework confers the divine life automatically; no organization, no institution, no practice; everything, absolutely everything, must be measured solely according to its relations with supernatural development, and that supernatural development can take place only in souls. This applies to everything—to the relations of Church and state, to ecclesiastical institutions, to the rules of Canon Law, to religious practice, to the religious order, the clergy, laity. . . . Indeed this applies even to the sacrifice of the Mass . . .[10]

In recent years, much thought and study has been given to the personal aspect of the sacraments, insisting on the attention to be given to the right dispositions to profit by them.[11] Here I should like to point out how the concept of grace as a reality in the order of personal relationship with God must influence our approach to the sacraments. As long as grace is thought of as "something given to us," and the sacraments as "channels of grace" making "grace flow into our souls," many people will automatically tend to think of the sacraments as automatically giving them a certain "measure of grace." Hence, many can frequent the sacraments while their personal love for God seems to remain far from being intimate friendship, and they remain caught in their own selfishness. They must be taught to see the reception of every sacrament as a very personal act. In each Confession they renew their surrender to God, asking Him to help them conquer the selfishness that separates them from Him; and each Communion is Christ coming to them to make their love for Him a more deeply personal reality.

6. Mystical or Personal

The word *mystical* is used in a variety of ways. In its stricter sense, it is applied to the state of infused contemplation strictly so-called, of which an essential and distinctive note is the experimental perception of the presence of God and His activity in the soul, while the soul remains passive under His action. It was with this stricter connotation in mind that older authors distinguished between ascetical theology, which studied man's effort in the spiritual life, and mystical theology. However, nowadays the term "spiritual theology" is preferred for the study of the whole process of man's attaining perfection under the influence of, and in co-operation with, the sanctifying activity of God. This preference is due, to a large extent, to insistence on the fact that the whole of a man's progress toward perfection is entirely dependent on the action of God—it is His grace first and last, whether it be perceived as such or not. Growing in perfection means entering into a more intimate friendship with the Three Divine Persons; and this is done under the influence of the grace of personal attraction, sharing in the divine knowledge and love which God gives us. We grow in grace only by more complete surrender to God, by allowing ourselves to be taken into closer intimacy with Him, by submitting ourselves to His influence, and by being more alert to the leading of the Holy Spirit. The term *mystical* is applied by many authors to all this activity of God in the spiritual life (which is, of course, its essence) without restricting it to what is "perceived as the activity of God." In this broader sense, many writers insist, all our spiritual life is essentially *mystical*.

My reason for the above paragraph is not one of academic interest. It can have some practical consequences. All of us *hunger and thirst after justice;* we dream of more intimate union with God. Quite frequently, I think, we tend to suppose that a really close union with God is identified with the mystical in the strict sense of infused contemplation. But contemplation, in this sense, is not union with God. It is a means to that union; "it is not the only means."[12] "Seen from afar, it is a means which may readily appear delightful and easy."[13] Hence we assume, many of us, that if we could obtain this gift of contemplation, we would reach a delightful, satisfying union with God that would give rest to our souls.

But let us get two things quite straight. First—as the contemplatives have insisted—from the natural point of view, progress in contemplation is progress in suffering and in self-renunciation; union with God is an entry into the life of Christ by entering more fully into the mystery of His death. Secondly, no degree of intimate union with God, outside the beatific vision, can sate our hunger or thirst. "He who eats me will hunger still," until the possession of God in eternal ecstasy fills the heart at last. To live on earth is, in St. Paul's phrase, to be "absent from the Lord." Our longing for a delightful, satisfying union with God will receive its full answer only in the next life. A desire for "mystical graces" is permitted by spiritual masters only if they are desired as means of intimacy with God— not if they are, in any way, a desire that *we* might have greater and more consoling gifts.[14] Now it is important to note that the real content of the desire is not the means but the end. What we really long for is closer intimacy with God. Now—as we have insisted so much—this intimacy is possible to us all if we live the realities of grace and faith. We should live what we have, instead of dreaming vaguely about what we think it would be good for us to have. Instead of envying the mystics, let us live the reality of our personal union with God; for, in one sense, the mystical life is the life of personal intimacy with God.

The mystic loves for love's sake. He is caught up by God and can think of nothing else . . . The love the Christian soul finds in God, and which it yearns to respond to . . . such love is a part of the whole pattern of Christian sentiment, and is to be found also in the body of the Church. . . . We meet it again, for instance, in the missionary spirit. What decides so many men and women to devote their lives to the conversion of non-believers, solely for their good, to announce Christ to them, without any thought of self-interest, is the gratuitous love of God to which they want to make some response, to which they wish to give themselves as instruments. It is true that in the day to day routine of life many missionaries who set out with no other thought in mind fall back into the sluggishness of their ego; but the starting point was love and the objective is love. . . . The fervour of all apostles . . . all that is disinterested and seeks solely the Kingdom of God for that Kingdom's sake—and the Kingdom of God is the reign of love—all these are gestures, glimmers, sparks of pure love.[15]

We shall develop further the implications of this point when treating of "prayer and action." Here we wish only to stress the point that the *mystical*, in its truest sense, is identical with the personal: with the deeply personal conviction of God's love gratuitously bestowed on us and on all men, drawing us to personal intimacy with Himself; with our response a personal dedication in disinterested and gratuitous love.

[187]

NOTES

[1] *Christian Asceticism and Modern Man,* pp. 262, 260; G. Philips, *The Role of the Laity in the Church* (Chicago: Fides, 1956), p. 153.

[2] *Ibid.*

[3] Ch. 2.

[4] *Supplément de la Vie Spirituelle,* n. 52 (1960).

[5] G. K. Chesterton.

[6] See Ch. X.

[7] See Ch. VII.

[8] See Ch. IX.

[9] F. Charmot, S.J., *La Doctrine spirituelle des hommes d'action* (Paris: Ed. Spes, 1958), pp. 308–313.

[10] J. Leclercq, *Christians in the World* (New York: Sheed and Ward, 1961), pp. 106–115.

[11] J. Gaillard, "Les Sacrements de la foi," *Revue Thomiste,* 59 (1959).

[12] J. de Guibert, *The Theology of the Spiritual Life,* p. 359.

[13] *Ibid.*

[14] J. Lecercq, *op. cit.,* p. 129.

[15] J. Leclercq, *op. cit.*

Chapter 12

PERSONAL PRAYER

Prayer can be considered from various aspects. In line with the whole tenor of this work, it will be regarded from two closely allied angles. Prayer is the expression of our personal dedication to God. As we have seen, the encounter with a personal God in faith and in vocation is followed by a personal dedication to the God in whose love we have learned to believe. This personal dedication is practically identified with the term *devotion* of St. Thomas, which makes us give ourselves with ready eagerness to the things that belong to the service of God. And so it expresses itself in prayer, in adoration of God, in recognition of His place in our life and of our need of Him, in thanksgiving; in short, in an expression of all things that make up our personal relationship with God.

Prayer is also, as St. Teresa of Avila said, personal "conversation with God, who we know loves us." This implies the basic convictions of faith in God's love, trust in His power, and some knowledge of what God is and what we are. Then prayer is the conversation that spontaneously follows between ourselves and the God in whose love we have learned to believe. It will be the expression of all that is involved in our interpersonal relationship with the Three Divine Persons.

In its beginnings our prayer will need the help of some method, or some book which teaches us how to converse with God. Here there is usually no great difficulty. Many books are available.[1] It is simple enough to find one or other which will help us think about God and what He means to us, help us to make acts of love for Him, sorrow for sin, gratitude for His gifts, determination to serve Him better, with prayers for His light, guidance, and strength. They all help us to raise our minds and hearts to God, as do the prayers we all know—prayers of the Church and private prayers—which we pray over, slowly and repeatedly. Making a beginning at prayer, if we faithfully assign some definite time to it, is not usually a difficult task for one who has felt the call to closer intimacy with God. However, progress in prayer is a different matter. There are many good people—religious, priests, and laity alike— who wonder whether they are making any progress in prayer, who often feel that they are not doing so, and who either worry that they are not or resign themselves to the fact that they will make no progress.

1. Progress in Prayer

Let us begin with the outline of progress in prayer as described by Tanquerey in his widely known work *The Spiritual Life*. The quotation will be somewhat lengthy, but it is well worthwhile, even necessary, to see it at some length:

Beginners, as we have said, need to acquire convictions; therefore they insist upon reasoning and give little time to affections. But in proportion as these convictions grow and take root in the soul, less time is required to renew them and greater play is allowed to the affections. Smitten with love for God and charmed by the beauty of virtue, we rise with greater ease in loving aspirations towards the Author of all good in order to worship Him, to praise Him, to thank Him, to love Him; towards Our Lord Jesus Christ, our Saviour, Exemplar, Master, Friend, Brother, in order to offer Him the tenderest sentiments of love; towards the Most Blessed Virgin, the Mother of God and our Mother, the dispenser of God's gifts, in order to express to her our filial, trustful and unselfish love.

Other sentiments arise spontaneously in the soul: sentiments of shame, confusion, and humiliation at the sight of our miseries; ardent desires to become better, and confident petitions to obtain the necessary grace. . . .[2]

This, according to Tanquerey, is the prayer of those who have progressed beyond the way of beginners: the prayer of proficients, or those in the illuminative way. There are various effects of this kind of prayer:

. . . we realize all the better the worth of the divine attributes, once we experience the charming tenderness of God's love . . . desire of frequent communion, for we want to possess as perfectly as we can the object of our love, to welcome Him joyfully into our hearts and joyfully abide with Him all the day long. . . . In affective prayer we often find spiritual consolation. There is no purer, no sweeter joy than that found in the companionship of a friend, and Jesus, being the tenderest and most generous of friends, we relish in His presence a taste of heaven's joys: to be with Jesus is a sweet paradise. True, side by side with these joys, there are at times trials, such as aridity, but we accept these with a sweet resignation and we tell God again and again that in spite of all this we wish to love and serve Him. The thought that we suffer for God's sake alleviates our sufferings and becomes a source of consolation. . . . If we let our hearts produce sentiments of love, of gratitude, of praise, the soul experiences a sweet rest. . . .[3]

The next step in progress in prayer is, as Tanquerey explains, to the prayer of simplicity, which comes to one who has entered into the unitive way:

. . . reflection is replaced by an intuitive intellectual gaze. We thereby come to understand first principles without effort, as by an intuition . . . we grasp them with ease and delight. Thus the idea of father applied to God, which at the outset required lengthy reflections before we could grasp its meaning, now appears to us at a glance so rich and so fruitful that we linger with it lovingly in order to relish its manifold elements. It even happens at times that the soul rests content with but a vague vision of God or of divine things, which view, however, keeps it sweetly and affectionately in God's presence, and renders it more and more docile to the action of the Holy Ghost . . .

The affections undergo a similar simplification . . . soon one and the same affection is prolonged during five or ten minutes: the idea of God our Father, for example, excites in the heart an ardent love which, without expressing itself in a multiplicity of words, completely absorbs the soul for several minutes. . . .

When the soul considers that not only is she privileged to be in the presence of God, but that it is her happiness to possess that presence within her, such thought pierces her to the quick and causes her to enter into a deep state of recollection. . . . She beholds the Godhead with the keenest joy, and she delights in the bliss of her possession, and she finds therein an unspeakable rest, seeing all her longings fulfilled in so far as they can be on earth.[4]

The soul having thus entered the unitive way is prepared for infused contemplation, a still higher type of prayer. Before receiving this gift, however, the soul must, after the prayer of simplicity just described, pass through the night of the senses.[5] Tanquerey's exposition of the progress in prayer is simple and easy to understand. Similar explanations are given by Poulain[6] and by other authors who follow faithfully these two authorities. Can many of us, even those of us who have faithfully practiced prayer over the years, say that we have followed this path of progress? In all honesty most of us must admit that we have failed to do so. What is the reason for our failure—infidelity to grace? Wrong methods in prayer? The reason is simpler and quite different. It is that Tanquerey and Poulain and their followers are wrong—hopelessly and utterly wrong. They paint a beautiful picture, but it is the beauty of fantasy; it is unreal and untrue, and the perspective is quite false—at least for the majority of people. Because the works of Tanquerey and Poulain have been regarded (rightly) as of value, what they wrote about prayer has been widely accepted as quite correct. The necessary consequence is, for those who read them (or hear preachers and retreat-givers repeat their doctrine), that we note the difference between their picture (which we take as the ideal) and the reality of our prayer. The normal conclusion then is that something is wrong with our prayer; we either worry about it or resign ourselves to lack of progress. For real progress in prayer, and for the peace of mind of many, it is important to stress the fact that this teaching is not correct. Various authorities will be brought forward to prove this point. Here I will be content to state the fact that for progress in prayer, you must not expect your habitual state of prayer to be one in which you can sincerely say that you are "smitten with love for God, charmed by the beauty of virtue . . . relishing in the presence of Christ a taste of heaven's joys . . . at *times* trials such as aridity, but we accept these with a sweet resignation . . . touched to the quick by the presence of God . . . beholding the Godhead with the sweetest joy, she delights in the bliss of her possession, and she finds therein an unspeakable rest."

"At times, trials, such as aridity . . ." It will be aridity most of the time, when you begin to pass from the prayer of beginners to the prayer of proficients, and it can't be anything else. The above way of speaking fails to take into account one very enlightening fact: all prayer is the conversation of a human person with God. In its progress it will normally follow the usual psychological development of the human person. Grace develops the human person; the grace of prayer will not keep us in a stage of juvenile emotionalism while in all things else we develop along maturer lines where feelings, emotions, and youthful enthusiasm give way to a calmer, deeper, more willed exercise of personal dedication to God and His will. Prayer is conversation with God who we know loves us. It will have many of the characteristics of human conversation, for it is *human* conversation with God. The beginnings of any love and friendship (following on the discovery which a personal encounter is) manifest certain qualities that normally do not last as friendship grows and develops. This will hold good also of our prayer, conversation with God. In the beginning there will be the newness of discovery, or rediscovery on a deeper level of the truths of what we can know about God. There will be a certain intellectual delight in this discovery of God in knowledge. But as our friendship with God progresses, a lot of the newness will vanish, as will the early delight in discovery. God is infinite, of course, and there will always be fresh things to discover about the divine Persons. But our knowledge of God is finite and limited, and grow as it will over the years, the growth will be more gradual: a steady growth resulting from intimacy; a rewarding growth, but one which can no longer be described as a "delighted discovery" of what God is. It is now more the old truths that we have long known, which we see in greater depth. In a way we no longer search for new aspects, for the old ones have come to mean much to us, the simple yet momentous realities of grace and our divine sonship, our union with Christ and the Spirit of love. We do not need to think about these things at great length in order to make them mean something to us. Human friendship and human love in its beginnings need to find more words to express themselves than they do later as friendship grows and develops. If we return home after a long absence, our reunion begins with much conversation. There is a lot to talk about, there are all the joys of reunion to be relieved. But if our stay is prolonged, our living together in love and friendship does not continue its same outward expression, its same animation. We live in one another's presence, conscious of love and friendship, glad of it, but with less need, less inclination to find new or sparkling topics of conversation. It is something the same with our love for God and our prayer; we are more inclined to live contentedly in the knowledge of His love and our need of Him than to find all sorts of varied topics about which to talk to Him.

Thus, after mental prayer has been practiced for some time, the "considerations," i.e., the necessary thinking about God, His goodness to us and love for us in Christ, are lessened. We know these things now and they mean something to us; and because they do, when we think of them, we pass naturally to acts of gratitude, love, sorrow for sin, etc., that are the real heart of prayer.

Such prayer is called affective. Then just as when friendship has developed between two men, mutual understanding and community of purpose ripen, and words begin to carry a whole wealth of meaning—so, too, as intimacy with God increases and virtues advance accordingly, we may find that our affections (i.e., our acts of the will and other virtues) need fewer and fewer words for their expression, and it may sometimes happen that we are content to kneel in silent adoration, or mute sorrow, or in some such "affection" without using words. Thus our prayer simplifies itself. This simplified prayer . . . may be called the prayer of simplified affections.[7]

Now this all happens within the first stage of prayer, the prayer of beginners, or what is called "meditation." It is misleading to divide this prayer into three clearly distinct stages: discursive prayer where the reason—thinking about God and the truths of faith—predominates; then affective prayer, and thirdly the prayer of simplified affections (which some wrongly call the prayer of simplicity). They are not three clearly distinct stages (and even more important, they are not the three types of prayer proper to beginners, proficient, advanced). They are all gradual modifications, almost imperceptibly made, in the one type of prayer: discursive-affective meditation.

Just thinking about God is not prayer. Prayer is "the raising of the mind *and* the heart to God" or "the raising of the heart through the mind." "There is no prayer . . . in merely tabulating our knowledge of God, and describing it accurately and remembering it in great detail. All that would be possible without prayer; prayer means that the heart, too, has been touched."[8] From the beginning our considerations, our thoughts about the truths of faith are in order to move our hearts to love for God, sorrow for sin, etc. In the very first stages we will need to use our minds more, then less as the truths gradually become part of ourselves and affections more readily predominate. "Gradually and imperceptibly and spontaneously, the soul lessens the reasonings, because now it sees immediately what before it had to seek and so it gives more time to the affective part which gradually almost occupies the whole of prayer. The affections, likewise, when they begin to move the soul more deeply and habitually, become less frequent and varied and more frequent and long-drawn-out."[9] For some people, those of a very intellectual or affective nature, this type of prayer—with meditative or affective character—may continue for most of their lives. More generally, people pass now under the action of God's grace to a different stage of prayer. This generally is coincident with the passage from the stage of beginners to that of the proficient. The coincidence is usually quite evident in the life of contemplatives, often less so in those given to the active life.

The second stage of prayer begins with the "night of the senses"—at least with some form of it (as explained in a previous chapter). It is a very definite transition in prayer and differs markedly from Tanquerey's description of a passing into a prayer of simplicity with ease and delight. Its most marked characteristic is absence of ease and delight—it is darkness and difficulty in thought and aridity in the will.

The essence of the night of the senses is that it is the passage from meditation to simple prayer. It is that, and it isn't anything else but that. The essence of the night of the senses is that the senses get into a night, in which they can't be used. St. John of the Cross means by "senses" all that satisfies the sensual and sensitive part of man; that is the imagination (by the help of which the intellect works in this life) and the emotions and feelings that come from it. So long as these work, a man can meditate and ought to; the moment they cease to act (and you can't make them act, and the harder you try, the less you do) you must do without them—there is no other course possible—and take to simple prayer which St. John of the Cross defines as a "loving attention to the presence of God." There are no other possibilities. Either the imagination works or it does not. If it does, you can meditate; if it won't, you can't. The stoppage is the night of the senses, and the night of the senses is nothing more than this stoppage, and nothing else.[10]

Some writers, mistakenly, put the night of the senses far on in the spiritual life—after one has entered the unitive way. It may be necessary to insist that this is not correct. The night of the senses—and this passage to a more simple kind of prayer—comes normally to one who has, for a few years, given himself generously to the practice of prayer and the spiritual life. St. John of the Cross wrote: "The night of the senses is common, and the lot of many: these are the beginners."[11]

Souls begin to enter the dark night when God is drawing them out of the state of beginners, which is that of those who meditate on the spiritual road, and is leading them into that of proficients, the state of contemplatives, that having passed through it, they may arrive at the state of the perfect, which is that of divine union.[12]

Let no one be put off by that expression "the state of contemplatives" as something altogether too high for them. It is

. . . a mistake to regard it [this initial contemplation] as a very high form of mental prayer. It is a grace and a precious one, and the soul to which it is granted should be most grateful to

God, but I would say that it is a grace which God grants easily, frequently, even *normally* to souls which show sufficient generosity in preparing themselves for it. Here there is a question of only the lower degrees of supernatural contemplation.[13]

The real cause of this change, through the night of the senses, to a simpler form of prayer is that God infuses supernatural knowledge and love into the soul—higher than the field of emotions and imaginations—and the gifts of the Holy Spirit play a greater part in the soul's spiritual life. However, here we are more concerned with the practical side of things and have no wish to bring in detailed theological considerations that some might find too technical.

Approaching the matter from a different point of view, we can say that this transition period is one of passing to a greater spiritual and psychological maturity in our prayer and relations with God. In the earlier stages of the spiritual life, the person who prayed felt that he was getting somewhere, and was, to a certain extent, carried along by feeling and emotion, and the "sensible" joys which he got from prayer and from this living relation of personal friendship with God. As we have pointed out before, he felt that he was getting somewhere and could feel pleased with himself in the spiritual life. St. John of the Cross calls this "attachment to spiritual pleasures," from which, he says, the soul is to be purified. We have also pointed out how a personal love between two persons begins with emotional overtones, delighting in giving itself, hardly conscious of the fact that it is renouncing itself. Later, becoming more conscious of the self-renunciation which all true love implies, it is asked to advance to a deeper, more unselfish, more dedicated love. If a person is selfish and immature, he will regret the passing of the easier, **more** pleasant aspects, try to conserve them, and thus fail to grow into the perfection of pure and selfless love.

The same thing happens in the maturing of his love for God and in prayer which is the expression of that love. He comes to the stage where he "gets nothing out of prayer," "cannot pray as he used to," "does not feel that he is getting anywhere." St. John of the Cross is most insistent that if he now persists in trying to pray as he used to, to feel that he is getting somewhere, he is really seeking himself, his own spiritual satisfaction. He should, the Saint insists, accept the fact that he is being called to maturity in the way of prayer and in his love for God; he should accept the renunciation of the more immature spiritual pleasures, accept a more complete self-renunciation in the gift of himself to God. What then should he do in prayer? St. John of the Cross answers: "Let it [the soul] lovingly fix its attention upon God without specific acts."[14] Here again let us remember that prayer is a matter of personal conversation with a Friend in whose presence we live. Between friends, between, for example, a mother and her adult child, there is more in the way of understanding, love, and mutual regard than is—or needs to be—expressed in words. There is that underlying reality of mutual love and understanding which is lived habitually—and to some extent actually—just by being together and wanting to be together. With God, too, our prayer becomes more an attention in love—not felt much, but deeply lived—to a Person who is present.

Thus prayer simplifies itself into what might be called a lived attitude of soul that finds little variety of expression. It is, generally, the same thing day in and day out for people who have reached this stage of prayer. They go to prayer out of personal dedication to God, knowing their need of God, wanting Him, looking to Him. This is about all they do. It does not appear much, but it is all they can do and all God expects them to do, for it is more than it appears: it is a constant, humble, and trustful looking to God in faith, hope, and charity.

As we grow in the spiritual life, we grow in self-forget-fulness, with our thoughts and will and plans more and more centered on God and directed away from ourselves. Our prayer, as it progresses, will reflect this centering of our life on God. It will simplify itself along lines that are forgetful of self and thoughtful of God, His will, and the coming of His Kingdom. Our petitions will be less for ourselves and more that God may be glorified, that His Kingdom come, and that His will be done in all men and in the whole wide world. In mental prayer, as prayer simplifies itself, it will be along lines that look to God. Hence it is easy to understand why authors say that the prayer of simplicity, or the prayer of the advanced or spiritually mature, will usually be marked by one of three keynotes. It will be (i) loving attention to the presence of God in faith; or (ii) wanting God and His will; or (iii) an attitude of the virtue of religion—praise or adoration. At times, of course, other notes will predominate, such as gratitude, but more habitually it will be one of these three:

(i) Faith—the prayer of loving attention. This is what St. John of the Cross says: "The soul is pleased to find itself alone with God, to look at Him with love, without occupying itself with any particular consideration."[15] Here we have no more than the fuller living of faith in the sense explained in Chapter 2. Faith is awareness of God as a personal God, with our personal response to the love in which we have come to believe. It is a personal encounter, a contact with the divine Persons into which we are taken by the grace of God. As this personal contact becomes greater, we are less content with thoughts about God; we are drawn to closer personal union with Him. We live in His presence and for His presence, content to be united to Him, looking in trust to Him. Since God is three in Person, this prayer in its higher stages (the stages of infused contemplation) generally takes on a Trinitarian character.[16]

(ii) Wanting God and His Will. "The principal stage consists of this: O God, I want thee, and I do not want anything else. All our spiritual life is unified into this one desire of union with God and his will."[17] This, obviously, will harmonize with what we said in a previous chapter on the will of God.

(iii) The third line along which this prayer tends to simplify itself is that of praise, or adoration. "What do all my acts thread on? One thing only—adoration of God. I hold myself simply before Him in a silent attitude of adoration . . . our prayer changes into what is simply an "awareness of God" . . . in which the immensity, the majesty of God become so obvious that no actions of our own are called for."[18] In the same line, "praise or exaltation may be the chief or sole act."[19] "Praise is the most elevated form of prayer, and how agreeable to God! It alone would suffice, it replaces all the other forms of prayer."[20] This will be the characteristic note of the prayer of those who are inspired by the spirit of the liturgy, the "eucharistic" aspect of prayer which is a combination of wondering awe before the wonders God has worked, especially in and through Christ, by manifesting His power and His loving benevolence toward men. Man's reaction to the wonders of God's ways is grateful and adoring praise, confident looking to God. Those who learn to pray in the school of Saint Sulpice will also normally find their prayer developing along this particular line.

However, these three chief lines of simplification do not constitute three different types or classes of prayer. They are very akin to one another, and all spring from a deep realization of the reality of God and the reality of self. The Night of the Senses brings us to this realization. From the profound conviction of our own weakness and need of God's uplifting grace, of the grandeur and majesty and sanctity of God, and from wonder at His love poured out on us, prayer will flow forth along one of the three lines we have indicated. Or rather, our prayer will be a living of one of those attitudes. Once these convictions have possessed us, our prayer cannot be anything else. Psychologically, the prayer of simplicity must follow on this profound conviction and acceptance of the reality of God and the reality of self. Theologically, it is explained by the greater activity of the gifts of the Holy Ghost, especially the gift of knowledge and the gift of understanding. But, of course, as everyone knows, the gift of knowledge gives us a deeper knowledge of creatures in their relation with God (the reality of created things, and self), while the gift of understanding gives us a more penetrating knowledge of the truths of faith (the reality of God).[21]

Hence, it is not difficult to see why St. John of the Cross says that at this stage of the spiritual life we receive in our prayer infused knowledge and love. Hence the Thomists call this prayer "initial infused contemplation." The Carmelite School prefers to call it "acquired contemplation." Neither St. Teresa nor John of the Cross uses this term. But since St. John calls it simply "contemplation," while St. Teresa reserved the term "contemplation" for yet higher ways of prayer, the Carmelites have—for reasons of convenience—judged it advisable to use a different term. The important thing to remember, however, is that both Carmelites and Thomists agree on the reality of this type of prayer, called by different names, and on its place in the spiritual life.

This type of prayer will be the lot of many for most of their life, even after they have entered the unitive way. Their prayer, and their effort in prayer will not alter essentially once they have entered this phase,[22] i.e., once they have passed the more troubled period of the night of the senses in its beginnings, and have accepted the reality of self and the reality of God in a humble and selfless looking to Him, wanting Him and His will in love and abandonment to Him. In the practice of this prayer, there may be many distractions—on a superficial level—for it "is darkness to imagination and intellect," but underneath there is that constant current of wanting God and His will, looking to Him. The time of initial crisis will pass. But it will not be succeeded by a period of calm and consolation (at least not on the more superficial level of old), although there will be deep peace in our gift of self to God, accepting to *be* what He *makes* us. "We must not think that distraction, dryness, desolation, is merely a state of trial that we pass through on our way to perfection. Perfection in this world is not a calm union with God unless God so wishes. Our Lord suffered temptation and desolation to show us that they are not incompatible with perfection, but *are* perfection."[23]

2. Tests of Progress in Prayer

St. John of the Cross gives three signs that the time has come to pass from the prayer of beginners to the prayer of the advanced:

1. Impossibility of meditating, no pleasure in using the imagination in prayer, inclination to remain in God's presence.[24]

2. Dryness, without comfort either in God or in His

creatures, painful anxiety as to fervor and one's inability to meditate.[25]

3. Keen desire to serve God, thirst for justice, fear of sin, and a resistance to temptation.[26]

Dryness, with a distaste for meditation, is not of itself a sign that one has come to the night of the senses. For dryness—lack of sensible fervor—can result from the absence of real fervor of the will and can be caused by one's lack of generosity. Hence the real tests of prayer are taken from outside prayer, in the proof of one's generosity in the service of God and real detachment from self. This, however, must not be exaggerated. Complete detachment is the effect of the nights and of advanced prayer, not a necessary condition for them. We are detached from self by being more closely united to God. We do not have to be first completely detached from self, and then as a distinct step, more closely united to God. Real generosity and effort is required, but not in a heroic degree at this stage of the spiritual life. Hence, it should be useful to give the following quotation from Dom Chapman:

Many persons pass long years in this night, when they cannot meditate and yet are afraid to contemplate; and the signs may be less easy to recognise. They have tried methods one after another; they have tried reading and pondering and then reading again (a good way to keep off distractions); alas, perhaps they have almost given up mental prayer in despair. They find it hard to believe that they are in the mystical "obscure night." They do not feel urged by a frequent thought of God, nor do they dare to say they have a disgust of creatures. On the contrary, they have found the spiritual life so dry that they have felt thrown upon creatures for consolation. They have often taken in distractions which are not sinful, because recollectedness seems impossible. They have imagined themselves to be going back, because they have no devotion, no "feelings"; and perhaps they really are going back, since they have not learnt the right path forward.

But they have the essential marks of the obscure night, for they cannot meditate—it is a physical impossibility. (When they attempt it, either they cannot fix their thoughts on the subject at all, or else they fall into distractions at once, in spite of themselves.) Nor do they wish to meditate. They are as able to think out a subject, to work out a sermon as anyone else is; but they feel that such considerations are not prayer. They want to unite themselves to God, not to reason about what He has done for them nor what they have to do for Him. This they can do at any time and all day long. They can examine themselves and make good resolutions; they can think of the mysteries of Christ's life and death, of the words of Holy Scripture, of heaven and hell; but when they come to prayer, all this vanishes, and they feel that if they think, they put themselves out of prayer. They do not want thoughts about God, but God.[27]

If we remember that prayer is the expression of friendship with God, we will find an easy norm for judging whether the aridity is a sign of progress or not. "Everything that will make or mar friendship in its intimacy will make or mar prayer."[28] If, outside of prayer, we deliberately refuse to do something that we know a generous love would ask of us; if we deliberately persist in doing something which we know should be renounced in favor of love for God, then that is the cause of aridity in prayer and must be put in order before we can make progress. We cannot come before God in prayer, making prayer the expression of a completely devoted friendship, if such a friendship does not exist in the rest of our lives. Hence, a traditional norm given by which we may test our prayer is a striving for the four purities:

(a) Purity of conscience: renunciation of all deliberate sin, or deliberate imperfection, for these things would be a deliberate withdrawal of part of our heart from God.

(b) Purity of heart: an effort to keep all the affections of the heart for God, permitting no attachments except those in accord with God's will.

(c) Purity of mind: the effort at recollection and control of the emotions, thoughts, and memories.

(d) Purity of action: a constant watch over the motives that animate our actions, a constant guard against self-seeking.

If we grow in prayer, our prayer becomes more self-forgetful, more centered on God. Whence it is clear that, if outside of prayer we are self-seeking, we cannot be the opposite in prayer. Hence, two of the acid tests of prayer are fraternal charity and obedience, in the sense explained above.[29] If all these things are aimed at, if outside prayer we want only God and His will, we will pray in one of the ways mentioned above. It is all we are expected to do. We trust in God, remain in His presence, and look to Him.

3. The Right Perspective

It is of the utmost practical importance to have the right perspective on the normal development in prayer; hence, too, because of the widespread influence of the writings of Tanquerey, one of the best known "complete" ascetical works in English, and one at times used as a textbook in seminaries, it is important to make it quite clear that his perspective is wrong. The usual and correct grading of the stages of prayer is:[30]

1. The initial stage of discursive-affective meditation, which naturally and without difficulty sees a lessening of the "reasoning" and "thinking out" element, with more

time given to affections and acts of the will. These latter gradually become more simplified and less numerous.

2. The prayer of simplicity, or "acquired" or "initial infused" contemplation as we have described it above. At the transition stage this is the night of the senses with its notes of anxiety, worry, etc. Later it is the more peaceful attention to the presence of God, wanting God and His will, adoration and praise, etc. For those not called to contemplation in its higher stages, this will be their prayer for their whole life as a habitual thing. There will be minor and temporary variations.

3. Infused contemplation strictly so-called, whose beginnings will be the night of the spirit for contemplatives. A study of the various grades of infused contemplation is apart from the scope of this work.

Furthermore, it is a general teaching that the second grade of prayer is "the lot of many" as St. John of the Cross taught,[31] the normal thing for generous souls, coming relatively early in the spiritual life. Father Gabriel of Mary Magdalene gives as a typical example a seminarian after a few years in the major seminary[32]; Dom Chapman speaks of "most religious"; Poulain of "most nuns"; St. Ignatius of "Scholastics"; B. Butler of "many lay people."[33]

Tanquerey's picture is quite different. For him the stages are as follows:

1. Discursive meditation, where the reasonings predominate. This is the prayer of beginners.

2. Affective prayer, with less use of reasoning and more affections. This, the prayer of the advanced, entails passing trials of aridity.

3. Prayer of simplified affections with ease and delight, the prayer of those in the first stages of the unitive way, the beginnings of contemplation.

4. Then, after the beginning of the unitive way, the

night of the senses. After this come the various grades of infused contemplation.

The difference is enormous. The consequences of Tanquerey's distorted picture, for those who regard it as the true one, are most unfortunate. Those who come to the beginning of the night of the senses will think that this is only passing aridity. (They must think this, if they follow Tanquerey.) They will make efforts to meditate as they did before and will wait for the aridity to pass. But it will not pass until they die. Then, seeing that they do not progress in prayer in the way they think they should, they will resign themselves to not progressing. "They have imagined themselves to be going back . . . and perhaps they really are going back, since they have not learnt the right path forward." If they go to a director to teach them, he, if he has been taught the same ideas, will be quite incapable of doing so. He will give them advice about prayer which would incur the strong condemnation of St. John of the Cross for putting "one's crude hand on the delicate work of God and arresting the soul's progress." These practical consequences are most harmful; but they follow necessarily from such teaching. People who come to this stage will obviously not be far beyond the stage of beginners. Since the night of the senses and acquired contemplation are thought to be for those who are in the unitive way, what they experience must seem to be something else: the trial of "passing aridity," or the result of lack of generosity. And if, in spite of Tanquerey and in spite of wrong direction, they find the right path, they will often have a lingering uneasiness, because they think that somehow they have missed the right road. From this the right doctrine of St. John of the Cross will deliver them and lead them into paths of peace: the way of maturity in prayer in its higher exercise of faith, hope, and charity.

4. Devotion to Our Lady

Marian devotion is an essential part of any true Christian piety or spirituality. Sometimes it is very much to the fore in certain "spiritualities." At first sight, this may seem an unlikely place to treat of such devotion. However, since we shall consider mainly progress in this devotion, the principles for progress in prayer in general apply to it and give the best norms for seeing how it should develop. As in the matter of prayer in general, it is common enough to hear people say that their devotion to Mary is not what it used to be, and that they are wondering if they have true devotion to her. Here again, the general principle applies: If their devotion has progressed, it will not be what it used to be. Like all parts of Christian prayer and devotion, devotion to our Lady will develop along the lines of simplicity, maturing from the more emotion-tinged, sensation-seeking, image-needing beginnings to a more personal and theological simplicity.

In our day much is being written on Mariology. Laurentin, in reviewing recent literature on the subject, says, in half-despairing fashion, that it has reached "almost pathological proportions." Influenced by the enthusiasts of the "Marian age," many repeat what has been called "that pious fiction 'de Maria nunquam satis,' "[34] and regard any question as to the value of much "Marian" devotion as disloyalty to our Lady. Such an attitude—that of not tolerating even constructive criticism—is itself a sign of unbalanced devotion to Mary. For mature devotion can always regard itself calmly and reasonably. St. John of the Cross (and every theologian after him) pointed out that there are necessary imperfections in our devotion to God that must gradually be purified. From a too-human devotion we must rise to a more mature and spiritual one. If that be true of our devotion to God, it will be even more true of devotion to our Lady which, more easily still, is mixed with much that is merely human and natural. It is a field in which, since Mary is woman and mother, there can remain more of the infantile and the sentimental than in other fields of piety. Sometimes this is not adverted to—or is cloaked over with the facile phrase that "we are all Mary's children." She is our Mother—true; and for that very reason she would want to see us grow up.

The whole matter of progress in Marian devotion can be fairly adequately treated by considering three different aspects of it:

1. The theological basis or core of all devotion to Mary. This, again, can be summed up under three main heads:

(a) Mary is the Mother of God, the Mother and associate of Christ, God-Man and Redeemer of the world. Whence comes Mary's sublime dignity and title to veneration; whence, too, her close association with Christ in the work of the redemption, and, through the Assumption, in the triumph of Christ's Resurrection and glorification.

(b) Mary is the Mother of Men, Mother of the whole Christ, who forms Christ in His members, and who, as mediatrix of grace, wins grace and blessing for us all.

(c) Mary is the Virgin Immaculate, free from all sin and imperfection, full of grace and holiness, heroic in the practice of faith, hope, charity, and all virtues. In this is she a model and inspiration to all men.

2. There are the "extra-theological" elements in devotion to Mary. Under this head I would class all those things which, while they can and should be connected with the theology of Mary in her relations with God and men, are yet not part of the deposit of faith, nor of the practice of faith, to which all Christians are bound. These would include: apparitions of our Lady, miraculous medals, special

[211]

titles, shrines and statues, scapulars, specially efficacious devotions, novenas, etc., and other Marian "devotions." Of this second class of elements in Marian devotion, it can be said that:

(i) Insofar as they are linked with the theological "core" of devotion, helping us to a deeper understanding and living of it, they are good, useful, and—in varying measure for different people—necessary.

(ii) If they are not so linked, then they bear the stamp of imperfection in devotion to Mary, and, at times, can be even worse than that. It must be remembered, too, that imperfection is always a necessity in human life and devotion. The more imperfect forms of prayer are not rejected just because they are less perfect. The prayer of beginners is necessarily less perfect than the prayer of the mature; but it would be wrong to try to get beginners to practice a more advanced form of prayer. So, too, with Marian devotion; it would be an error to reject all "imperfect" forms of such devotion. This would be a parallel to those art "purists" who want to smash all plaster statues! Here, as in all popular devotion, a careful distinction must be made between outward popular expressions, which could not be used in a scientific work of theology, and the inner content which, though imperfectly expressed, is often true and most theological.

However, it must be admitted that wrong attitudes, often bordering on superstition and "false messianism," can come into these things. Some people tend to attach more importance to the latest apparition or Marian revelation than to the deposit of faith. Others incline to regard Mary as being more merciful than Christ, obtaining favors from Him which His severer justice would not incline to give.[35] Again, there is the tendency to regard one novena as more efficacious than another, Our Lady of Guadaloupe as more powerful than Our Lady of La Salette, etc. With regard to these special devotions, I think that the title *The True Devotion* is somewhat unfortunate. It is not uncommon to meet with people who have no attraction toward it. Yet, since it is called *The True Devotion,* many of them feel—wrongly, of course, but quite understandably—that they have not true devotion to our Lady. But, fortunately, true devotion to our Lady is wider than any particular form of spirituality in which it is practiced.

3. *Devotion* to Mary in the subjective sense, as lived by the human person as part of his prayer and spiritual life. This devotion should follow the universal law, maturing from the more human and more "emotional," to the more spiritual and simpler forms.

(a) The first stage will be the equivalent of the first stage in prayer—with the same characteristics and the same defects. It will be more "natural," dependent on emotions, imagination, feeling. It will delight to "weave patterns of thought" about our Lady, to think out all the implications of her privileges, her relations with God and with men. It will love to sing "the glories of Mary," to think over her relations with Christ at Bethlehem and Nazareth. There will often be a lot of sentimentality mixed with this—as is evidenced by Marian hymns: "Lovely lady dressed in blue . . ." "O Mother, I could weep for mirth, joy fills my heart so fast," etc., with pleas to be taken under Mary's mantle and shielded from all that can hurt or harm us: pleas which often hide a wish to be saved from facing up to the responsibilities of life with its realities of hardship and struggle and battle.

(b) Then comes the stage which parallels that of the night of the senses, and in Marian devotion, too, there will be the necessary transition stage—with its inherent worries about loss of devotion, because of loss of delight in these older things, less inclination to multiplication of practices, novenas, medals, and so forth. This is an entering into the phase of deeper and more mature devotion. In it we will come closer to Mary in the depth of her faith: in her cleaving to God in darkness, in the renunciation of all that was "natural" in her relationship with Christ, a renunciation culminating in her standing beneath the cross. We will come closer to her in charity—in the depth of personal dedication to Christ and the Father's will; closer to her in hope, trusting in God when our world is shattered about us, and our looking to God only for spiritual realities, not for human consolation. We will now learn more of her true dignity and glory. Our devotion will be more theological and more true.

(c) Our devotion to her will thus be more deeply personal: as the devotion of an adult toward the mother whose wisdom, self-sacrifice, and understanding he has come to appreciate over the years. It is precisely because it is more deeply personal, because it is a more supernatural contact with the Mother of God in faith and charity, that we can no longer, in prayer to our Lady, go through all the old reasoning and emotional reactions to truths about her. "We cannot come into real contact with a person by the use of our critical faculty, by the sort of reasoning we use to solve problems; still less can we reach him by acts proceeding from blind impulse or animal appetite. A person is apprehended in a spiritual contact and by a phenomenon of communion."[36]

Our seeking after further knowledge of Mary will not be so much a search for new truths about her, but rather an effort to penetrate more deeply into the supernatural realities of her relationship with Christ and the Body of Christ. And this—since it is supernatural—can come only from the light of God's grace. Thus does our devotion grow more perfect, in its ontological reality and in its deeper personal level—simpler and more unified because more centrally contained in the simple reality of our union with God in Christ.

Not infrequently, there comes a stage in which a person reacts against his earlier use of all the accidentals of devotion; he rejects many of his old practices in honor of our Lady—novenas, kneeling before statues, medals, etc. (One of the main causes of this can be overzealous insistence by the devotees of Mary on the "value" of these things.) Later, he may resume some or many of these practices, as the simple expression of his deeper, more theological devotion. But his devotion to Mary can never be "what it used to be." He is still "Mary's child," but the child has become a man, and his devotion will have matured with him.

5. A Note on Infused Contemplation

It would be outside the scope of this work (whose concern is with the more ordinary ways of the spiritual life) to devote much space to a study of infused contemplation strictly so-called.[37] First of all, I do not consider that infused contemplation in the strict sense will as a rule be habitually given to those called to the active life nor that it is necessary for their perfection. Secondly—and this is a much more important—the general rules of conduct to be followed do not differ greatly for those who have passed beyond the stage of "acquired" contemplation. What differences there are will be easily indicated by St. John of the Cross and in practice by any spiritual director.

(a) NECESSITY OF INFUSED CONTEMPLATION

This question is disputed in theory. In practice it makes no difference to the mode of conduct of those who have not received the gift of contemplation. For, (a) it is not certain that it is necessary for perfection; (b) it is certain that if you carry out God's will generously, and pray as well as you can, God will give you all that is needed to attain perfection; (c) therefore, in practice, we must concentrate on generosity in doing God's will, forgetting ourselves, praying as well as we can. This is all that is needed *from us* for our perfection. If more is needed as a gift from God (in this case, infused contemplation) we can confidently expect it from Him.

In theory, there would not seem to be any sound argument to prove its necessity. Nor does there seem to be any reply to a very sound argument that proves it is not necessary. This argument is briefly: Theologians are agreed that certain conditions of life are normally needed if one is to receive the gift of habitual infused contemplation in the strict sense. They are also agreed that heroic sanctity consists in the faithful and constant carrying out of the duties of one's state in life.[38] But it is evident to all that for many, the will of God demands that they live and work in conditions which make impossible that calmness of mind and long hours of prayer which are normally needed for the gift of infused contemplation. God's will is that we come to perfection because of, and not in spite of, the duties of our state in life. Hence the logical conclusion must be that for most people, the normal way to sanctity cannot be that of infused contemplation.

One of the main exponents of the opposite opinion in our day is Garrigou-Lagrange, who argues mainly from the necessity of the higher exercise of the gifts of the Holy Spirit (especially that of wisdom) and from the necessity of purification. Neither of these arguments proves anything. St. Norbert showed long ago, against St. Bernard, that the trials of the apostolate could be just as purifying as the passive purifications of infused contemplation. (We have seen the main aspects of this in Chapter 10.) Also, St. Thomas is quite clear that the gifts of the Holy Spirit can be directed to action as well as to contemplation, the gift of wisdom among them.[39] Another Dominican author and master in theology writes:

It has not been sufficiently appreciated that the higher gifts of knowledge, understanding, and wisdom can be exercised in a manner that is essentially practical. These gifts will direct souls, as under the constant guidance of the Spirit of God, they spend themselves in the field of action. . . . The great spiritual masters of the past were men dedicated, most of them, to the cultivation of silence and solitude. . . . What should be done here is to study again the entire Christian doctrine of theological faith and charity against the background of the gifts of the Holy Spirit. The study should be made from the point of view of action, and the gifts considered as directed to action. . . .[40]

Also, as Dom C. Butler writes:

Fr. Garrigou-Lagrange admits that in the active life, without the gifts of contemplation, there may be a great generosity which merits the name of perfection, but it is not the full perfection of the Christian life. He has in view a piece of academic theological theory, for he admits too that many of these souls whose perfection is of the inferior grade may be more advanced in virtue and true charity than others who have received the highest kind of infused contemplation.[41]

A further consideration is that in this matter the difference of opinion between many authors is more apparent than real. We have already noted a difference of terminology between Dominicans and Carmelites with regard to what the latter call *acquired* contemplation. Dominicans and some others call it *infused* contemplation; and many of them, when asserting that infused contemplation is needed for perfection, have only this prayer in mind. Carmelites, denying the necessity of infused contemplation, assert the necessity of *acquired* contemplation, and so, in reality, there is agreement where there appears at first sight to be a real difference.

Moreover, others who assert the necessity of infused contemplation for perfection do not maintain that there is any necessity of habitual contemplation. They assert that there will be "flashes of the infinite," "mystical touches" or passing "mystical graces," not perceived as such. This, of course, is quite beside the point of the main discussion. For "infused contemplation" in the strict sense includes the note of infused knowledge and love, which is perceived by the soul to be the direct action of God, and this in an habitual way.

Hence, in conclusion it can be stated that the vast majority of authors assert that there is not only one "unitive way," or one way to the fullness of Christian perfection: the way of habitual infused contemplation in the strict sense. Furthermore, all sound theological arguments prove that it is not the only way. "Great discussion goes on whether there be two 'unitive ways' or only one. (And there is more agreement and less discussion than there used to be.) There is much to be said for the view that there are not one, nor two, but many, just as there are many mansions in Our Father's house."[42]

NOTES

[1] E. Leen, *Progress through Mental Prayer* (New York: Sheed and Ward, 1946); Cardinal Lercaro, *Methods of Mental Prayer* (Westminster, Md.: Newman, 1957).

[2] A. Tanquerey, *The Spiritual Life* (Westminster, Md.: Newman, 1945), p. 461.

[3] *Ibid.*, pp. 414 ff.

[4] *Ibid.*, pp. 638 ff.

[5] *Ibid.*, p. 667.

[6] A. Poulain, *Graces of Interior Prayer* (St. Louis: Herder, 1949).

[7] E. Boylan, *Difficulties in Mental Prayer* (Westminster, Md.: Newman, 1943).

[8] B. Jarrett O.P., *Meditations for Layfolk* (London: Catholic Truth Society, 1943).

[9] Boylan, *op. cit.*

[10] *The Spiritual Letters of Dom Chapman O.S.B*, ed. Huddleston (New York: Sheed and Ward, 1959), pp. 279 ff.

[11] *Dark Night*, Bk. I, c. 8.

[12] *Ibid.*, Bk. I, c. 1.

[13] Fr. Gabriel of Mary Magdalene, *St. John of the Cross*, p. 46.

[14] *Living Flame*, St. III, n. 33; cf. Fr. Gabriel, *op. cit.*, p. 157.

[15] *Ibid.*

[16] *Living Flame*. Cf. J. Mouroux, *I Believe*, pp. 86 ff.

[17] *The Spiritual Letters of Dom Chapman O.S.B*, p. 283 f.

[18] R. H. J. Steuart, S.J., *The Two Voices* (London: Burns & Oates, 1952). Cf. entire section "Map of Prayer."

[19] Dom Chapman, *loc. cit.*

[20] Dom Marmion, quoted by M. Philipon O.P. in *The Spiritual Doctrine of Dom Marmion* (Westminster, Md.: Newman, 1956).

[21] Garrigou-Lagrange, *The Three Ages of the Spiritual Life*, Vol. II, p. 192.

[22] Rules for the direction of the soul at prayer are much the same after the night of the senses.

[23] Dom Chapman, *loc. cit.*

[24] *Ascent of Mount Carmel*, Bk. II, c. 13.

[25] *Dark Night*, Book I, c. 9.

[26] *Living Flame*, St. III, n. 34 ff.

[27] *Op. cit.*, pp. 283 ff.

[28] E. Boylan, *op. cit.*

[29] Cf. Ch. VII.

[30] Dominicans, Carmelites, and the majority of spiritual writers.

[31] *Dark Night*, Bk. I, c. 9.

[32] *Op. cit.*

[33] B. Butler, "Mystical Prayer," *Clergy Review*, 38 (1953), 450 ff., is a good treatment of this subject.

[34] H. Holstein, S.J., *Finding God in All Things*, ed. Young (Chicago: Regnery, 1958).

[35] Y. Congar, O.P., writes strongly against this tendency in *Christ, Our Lady and the Church* (Westminster, Md.: Newman, 1957).

[36] Mouroux, *I Believe*, pp. 50–51.

[37] Infused contemplation strictly so-called is marked, as we have noted above, by the note of experiencing the activity of God or the presence of God.

[38] Ch. 8.

[39] *S.T.*, I–II, q. 68; cf. M. Philipon, O.P., "Les Dons du Saint-Esprit chez S. Thomas," *Revue Thomiste*, 59 (1959), 457 ff.

[40] M. Philipon, O.P., *The Eternal Purpose* (Westminster, Md.: Newman, 1952).

[41] *Western Mysticism* (London: Constable, 1926), "Afterthoughts."

[42] *Ibid.*

Chapter 13

PRAYER AND ACTION

---

1. The Problem

In the lives of most Christians who are trying to live a more perfect life there are two main elements that must be combined into harmonious unity: prayer to God and work for the spread of His Kingdom. There are few who have given serious thought to these matters who have not gone through at least a period of worry as to whether they have successfully combined these two elements in their lives. There are many who never succeed in reaching a solution that satisfies them and gives them peace of soul. The problem exists on two levels: that of doctrine, and that of practice.

(a) DOCTRINE

One of the chief factors contributing to the modern problem is the fact that "the great spiritual masters of the past were men dedicated, most of them, to the cultivation of silence and solitude."[1] One has only to think of St. John of the Cross, St. Thomas Aquinas, St. Teresa of Avila. Earlier still there were Cassian, St. Benedict, Denis, St. Bernard, the School of St. Victor, St. Bonaventure, the

Flemish Mystics, Catherine of Siena, Thomas a Kempis, Blosius, Baker. These are only a few names, but they were undoubtedly "great spiritual masters" who placed great stress on prayer and contemplation, giving relatively little thought to the spirituality of the apostolate. The apostolate itself was envisaged in conditions entirely different from those of today. This was no great problem while apostolic activity could be carried on with very little disturbance to the ordinary regularity of monastic life and prayer. Prayer continued; care was taken to see that activity did not disturb one's life of prayer. *Contemplare et contemplata aliis tradere* was an ideal not difficult to maintain.

In the more disturbing and exacting conditions of the modern apostolate, the problem became more acute. It was accentuated because many continued to speak an older language, to give admonitions and solutions, which just did not seem to fit in with the demands of the modern apostolate. Firstly there is the continued insistence on the sanctifying value of prayer and contemplation—in such a way that whoever reads these writers is left with the impression that perfection and contemplation (in the strict sense) are identified. If you are not a contemplative, you are not living the full Christian life. *In actione contemplativus* (a contemplative even during your activity) is a nice phrase, but the busy apostle, if he is honest with himself, will most likely regard it as a pious unreality. Secondly, there is the oft-repeated warning of the "dangers of action": "beware lest you lose contact with God, becoming sounding brass and tinkling cymbals; do not let the well of your spiritual life run dry, drained off by the exertions and dissipation of the ministry." "Without the interior life, action becomes mere agitation. We imagine we are doing wonders, but in reality we accomplish nothing. We drain our energies and often run the greatest personal dangers. Woe to action which does not spring from love."[2]

As a result of much writing along these lines, "the apostolate is not placed among the means of self-sanctification. It is a means of sanctifying others after we have sanctified ourselves. It is something to be sanctified, not something which sanctifies."[3] There is, as a result, a certain uneasiness in the hearts of many modern apostles. The demands of the apostolate seem to make it impossible for them to develop the spirit of prayer, or to give to prayer the time which these authors demand. Statements that prayer should flow over into our daily activity, making our life a continued prayer and us "contemplatives in action," seem to be pious flights of fancy.

Hence there is a tendency to reject such solutions and to seek one diametrically opposed: *Laborare est orare*. To work is to pray; make your work a prayer, the prayer of life offered to God out of motives of zeal and charity. The calls of zeal are many; refuge in prayer (and some even say in religious life) is shirking the real issue, ignoring the urgent demands of the apostolate, the call to action of Christ and the Church. Give yourself to the task out of love for Christ, trusting in Him for whom you work, saying what prayers you can, and thus will you sanctify yourself most effectively.

(b) PRACTICE

It is evident enough that for each individual (because of what has been written on the subject, and because, under the influence of grace he will feel the need of prayer and the call to action) there will be the practical problem of deciding, in his own life, what will be the relative measure of prayer and action. For religious, in other days, the problem was not very acute, for apostolic activity was more easily fitted into the regular routine of religious rule. Today, however, in hospitals, schools, parishes, and missions the demands are so many that regularity in religious life and exercises is achieved only with great difficulty. For the priests of dioceses all over the world, it is a personal problem.

From the very nature of the formation of apostles (priests and active religious), each must go through something of a personal crisis in this matter; for each must go through a period of transition. That transition is from the more recollected atmosphere of the training period in a seminary or novitiate to the more distracting field of the apostolate. During the first period of regular life of prayer and study, the exercise of prayer is easy enough. One builds up a certain habit of prayer and does not realize the difficulties that will later stand in the way of continuing a calm, regular life of prayer. Conditions change; the young apostle feels the conflict between the calls of action and all that he had come to take for granted about the need of prayer and the time to be given to it. What is he to do? Must he first of all ensure that nothing disturbs his practice of prayer and then undertake what activity he can? Is he first of all a man given to God, and an apostle "in overtime"? Or will he put his activity first, since it is a call to zeal, conserving what he can in the way of prayer, using the yearly retreat to conserve his spiritual energy?

2. Solution

(a) DOCTRINE

We have already seen two proposed solutions to the problem, as such solutions are put forward by various authors. As they stand, both of them are wrong. First of all, we must not reject the teaching of the great masters of the spiritual life as impractical, on the ground that they were contemplatives. But secondly, we must not apply indiscriminately to the active life all that they wrote for contemplatives. Being masters of the spiritual life, *they* would never have done so. It is obviously unreal and un-evangelical to begin with the assumption that the contemplative life is the fullness of Christian life, and thence to conclude that those who have to carry out works of the apostolate must save what they can from the wreckage by fitting into it whatever they can from contemplation. All Christians are called to love God and serve Christ as members of the Church. Some will be contemplatives, but they will be a small minority; others will be apostles who are sent to work for the spread of the Kingdom. All share in the work of Christ the Mediator with its twofold direction: glory to God and salvation to men; all share in the life of charity with its twofold object: God and man. Some will give glory to God and live in His love and intercede for the world in the silence of contemplative prayer. Others will be called by Christ to work for the spread of His Kingdom—before they have attained the stage of infused contemplation and in conditions in which it is naturally speaking impossible to attain it. As St. Paul said, head and hand are both part of the same body, but one does not try to be as like the other as possible. The strength of both comes from a common life principle.

There is a certain similarity between the various parts of the body and the various functions of the many members of the Body of Christ. The perfection of each function is not measured by its similarity to the function of a more perfect member, but by the vitality which flows into it from the common source, acting through it toward a common end. You cannot reach a satisfactory spirituality of the apostolate by trying to make the apostle as much like the contemplative as possible. Prayer and action must be combined in the life of the apostle. Many sought to find in prayer the source of sanctity, and have prayer flow over into action, sanctifying it and safeguarding it from "naturalism and activism." But this seems to be "a road without an exit." The two—prayer and action—are united and vivified by a third thing, the common source from which they spring, drawing their value, life, and strength from it. This must be so, for any spirituality of action must be consonant with the basic principles of spirituality and flow forth from them. Hence, in formulating such a spirituality, you must not start with prayer, particularly contemplative prayer, and its value for sanctification and then proceed from there. You must go back further to the source from which true prayer springs. St. Thomas says that this is *devotio,* an act of the virtue of religion, or an attitude of the will—a readiness to give oneself to all things pertaining to the service of God.[4] We shall not go into a speculative analysis of *devotio.* Suffice it to say that the living reality of *devotio* is that eager readiness to give oneself in love and generosity to whatever the will of God might ask of us.

Thus we come back to that personal dedication which springs forth in a living faith, hope, and charity from our personal encounter with God under the personal attraction of His grace of faith and vocation. We have seen how the heart of the supernatural life is this personal intimacy with God, how all our life can then be the living out of this personal dedication. Our lives will be more vigorous as they are more consciously lived in this light. This personal dedication will lead some to give their whole lives to God in prayer and contemplation, exercising the apostolate of prayer for the redemption of men, united with Christ in His continued intercession with the Father. It will send others out into the world to work with Christ and as His instrument for the sanctification of the world. But without this personal encounter and personal dedication, neither contemplation nor action has any meaning or any value. "It is not apostolic action itself which sanctifies the apostle. It is charity received from God and exercised in living faith, humility, and hope."[5] It is not the exercise of prayer, considered as an exercise performed, which sanctifies the contemplative but the living exercise of faith, charity, humility, and hope, which finds its expression in prayer.

The Apostle does not assign a certain time to prayer in order that God's blessing might be on his work and its success ensured. Nor does he pray in order that, in his work, he may not himself become a castaway. He is not, before all things, one who gives his life to work for the Kingdom of Christ. He gives his life first of all to Christ whom he has met in intimate personal friendship. It is that meeting which colors all his life and dictates all he does. If it is the real personal encounter that is the necessary source of any spiritual life, he will not ask whether action can take the place of prayer. For prayer is a time of personal intimacy with God to whom we are united in a living love of personal friendship. It will be the need of a man's soul to spend time in intimate converse with Christ, and he will not ask himself whether his prayer is wasting time that should be given to his work. For the work he does is done as his personal service, the expression of his personal dedication to the will of God; it is only thus that it has value either for God, himself, or others. He can not harm his work by deepening his personal intimacy with Christ; and if his work ever becomes more important to him than intimate friendship with Christ, then he is no longer a true apostle, no longer a witness to Christ. Nor will he, on the other hand, fear that his "interior life" is endangered if, from time to time, the pressing calls of duties undertaken for God make it necessary for him to lessen the time given to prayer. "The great prophetic vocations of the Old Testament all begin with a vision of God and all end with a mission to men. It is always the same. It is also that which constitutes the apostolate. It is by the adoration of God, the discovery of His transcendence, that man hands himself over to Him wholly. It is only in this surrender of his being into His hands that he can be sent and become an apostle . . . His mission binds him to God and to the world."[6]

The doctrine of the combination of prayer and action in the life of the apostle is a corollary following naturally and logically from the principles of the spiritual life expounded in previous chapters. These principles should be sufficiently clear and should not need to be repeated here.

(b) PRACTICE

Even with the doctrine of the union of prayer and action clearly formulated, there will still be the practical problem of making the personal decision of how prayer and action are to be combined in one's own life. It will not be easy to decide in practice whether my devotedness to action is purely the expression of my personal dedication to Christ or the expression of a natural desire to get things done. It will be hard to decide in certain cases whether my preferring prayer to further work is really from my need of personal converse with God or just shirking difficult duty. We are bound to err on one side or the other. But if, in all honesty and sincerity before God, we really try to make our whole lives the expression of our personal dedication to Christ and His cause, we will, with the help of His grace, succeed in doing so.

If we are to reach the right combination of prayer and

action in our lives, we who are called to the apostolate must keep certain things clearly in mind:

(i) First we must recognize the fact that in this matter we are certain to tend to deceive ourselves. If we are the normal active types (as most apostles are), we will tend to err on the side of not giving enough time to prayer and of not making our prayer sufficiently "prayerful," i.e., a tribute of real adoration and worship, of personal love and longing for God in a deep realization of our need of His grace and strength, a loving union of our wills with His. If we are by nature more "contemplative," or rather less inclined to effort, we will tend to use prayer as an excuse for not giving ourselves generously to work. (This will be a less common error, particularly if one really prays in the time not devoted to action.)

We avoid this second error by realizing that "the apostolic life can and does enrich the life of prayer. In the direct apostolic life, men and women find by action and works and deeds of devotedness the concrete and effective responsibilities that are necessary for the development of their personalities. Certain persons succeed in overcoming some difficulties, such as temptations to feelings of dissatisfaction and uselessness, only in a directly apostolic activity. Action helps many to attain to a certain equilibrium of physical and nervous energy. It is not rare to find religious who do not really discover the true gift of prayer, who do not enter into a life of prayer, except in and through an effective apostolate."[7]

(ii) It is more universally important not to forget that prayer enriches the apostolate and is a necessity for the success of apostolic work. The work of the apostolate is the work of personal witness. Our words and our work will be external graces insofar as they bear witness to our personal attachment to Christ.[8] "A religious (or priest) loaded with work, nervous, irritable, can give the example of wonderful devotedness but will not show to the world the features of a person 'saved' by Christ . . . will fail to be a real witness of the Resurrection." We may work, but it is God who gives the increase. "The apostolate is not truly such unless it is a working under God, in union with Christ for the Redemption of the world. It is prayer which gives us that living union."[9]

The truth of the apostolic life willed and lived for our brethren is authentic only if this life is, at the same time, a life of prayer in God and for God. It is then, at least of doubtful quality, if the religious (or priest) cannot or does not want to find, in and through prayer, that basic union with God. To leave our brethren to find God is not a denial of our duty as apostles, not even a reducing of that duty; for he who has the will, and at certain hours, the courage to go to God for God, finds his brethren in God, and finds again in God the true living strength which makes him go to others and devote himself to them without reserve.

(iii) Our apostolic activity is the fulfillment of our vocation and the means of our own sanctification if it is animated by charity, i.e., if in flows forth from our personal dedication to Christ and is the concrete expression of that dedication. We would all like to think that this is so, even if there is much to be desired in our life of prayer. However, this could be only wishful thinking. From what we have just seen, it follows that the sincere personal dedication to Christ, which is the soul of the apostolate, cannot be lived with habitual negligence in the matter of prayer. There must be habitual fidelity in safeguarding the times set aside (according to rule or direction) for prayer and spiritual reading (for spiritual reading is necessary nourishment for a life of prayer). We should, when the calls of the apostolate are many and urgent, be able to sacrifice some of this time for a period. But an apostolate truly exercised for Christ cannot demand that such a sacrifice be habitually or permanently made. We deceive ourselves if we neglect prayer habitually on the pretext of duty, saying that we would like to give more time to prayer. Time given to prayer is a condition of its truth, a test of the sincerity of our desire for union with God: a personal union with God in our own souls, a vital union with Christ in our activity, which is only co-operation with His action.

Authors say that over and above the exercise of prayer, we must have "the spirit of prayer." To remain within the lines of this book, the "spirit of prayer" can be identified with what we have written in previous chapters, notably those on "Personal Spirituality" and "Personal Dedication." For, as one author writes, "we pray according to what we are."[10] If the fundamental driving force in our life is our living personal dedication to Christ, then we have the spirit of prayer, which inspires our exercise of prayer, and which in turn is nourished by intimacy with God in prayer. Have we got this spirit of prayer? A good practical test is: "Nothing is more characteristic of the spiritual life of the soul than the level of the concerns, the centers of interest it finds spontaneously, as soon as the importunity of its cares loosens its bonds with the outside and leaves it to itself. The miser finds himself close to his treasure . . . the prayerful soul in the presence of God."[11] "When silence comes and activities cease, it is one's being that exists alone before God. What have you made yourself?"[12] How do you find yourself when you are alone? Or can't you bear to be alone with yourself before God? Do you need to be doing something, distracted or entertained by something? If so, then you have not found God on the deeply personal level, which is your need if you are to live for Christ and work for Christ and His Kingdom.

You pray according to what you are. And if you are an apostle burdened with solicitude for the Church and souls, you will take your burden with you to prayer. You bear the burden for God, and there is no reason why you should pretend not to bear it when you come before Him. Prayer as it progresses becomes less self-centered. The prayer of the devoted apostle will often be a prayer of petition, not for himself, not that *he* might succeed, but that those for whom Christ died might receive the graces of light and life and strength. The prayer of humble petition is not merely the prayer of the beginner; it is a prayer for all times, particularly for the apostle—not an impassioned plea for the success of our enterprises, but patient and confident pleading the cause of the world, entering into the intercession of Christ the High Priest. Thus too will we all, active or contemplative, carry on the apostolate of prayer for those whom our action cannot contact as well as for those for whom we work. It is the will of God to do many things through secondary causes. He uses us as His instruments in our direct apostolic work. And He who has commanded us to pray has willed that the increase which He gives should come about through our prayers.

You pray according to what you are. And, careful and troubled about many things, as the apostle must necessarily be, you cannot expect your prayer to be serene and care-free and without distraction. But you pray also as one completely surrendered to the personal love of Christ, and each exercise of prayer can at least be your personal tribute and the expression of your need of more intimate personal union. As an apostle you go out to do the will of God. It is His will that effects the conversion of human hearts, turning them from sin to Himself. Your effectiveness in the apostolate will be in proportion as your action is caught up in the effective current of the divine will. You come to prayer to renew your personal contact, to ensure that you are united to God, within the stream of His creating will which renews the face of the earth.

(iv) *In actione contemplativus:* contemplative even during activity. This phrase is meaningless and a pious fiction if we think of contemplation in the stricter sense of complete absorption of mind and will in divine things. But let us recall what we saw when treating of the simplification of prayer, that stage of it which is variously called the prayer of simplicity, acquired contemplation, or initial infused contemplation. The essence of it was an underlying awareness of personal union with God, or Christ, of union with His will, of wanting His will, or of an attitude of worship. This becomes a habitual state of soul, a backdrop to our various activities, and it is this which comes to the surface when preoccupation with present duties cease. The apostle who sees his whole life as his living personal dedication to Christ, his attachment to the will of God to which he unites his own, who looks to Christ to work through him, who lives in the assurance that Christ is with him—such a one will be *in actione contemplativus.* Obviously he cannot be that without the practice of prayer. And, over and above the ordinary prescribed prayers and times of prayer, he will find great help to this spirit of prayer in the practice of some small exercises of private devotion, particularly to Christ, the Holy Spirit, and our Blessed Lady.

NOTES

[1] M. Philipon, O.P., *The Eternal Purpose* (Westminster, Md.: Newman, 1952).

[2] *Ibid.*

[3] A. Plé, O.P., "L'Action apostolique, école de perfection," *Vie Spirituelle*, 95 (1956), 5–27.

[4] *S.T.*, II–II, q. 82.

[5] A. Delchard, S.J., *La Prière* (Paris: Ed. du Cerf, 1959), p. 290.

[6] L. Lochet, S.J., "Apostolic Prayer," in *Finding God in All Things*.

[7] Delchard., *loc. cit.*

[8] See Ch. 5.

[9] These and the following quotations are from Delchard.

[10] Elie de Jésus-Marie, O.C.D., "Les Principes de l'Oraison" in *La Prière*.

[11] L. Lochet, S.J., *loc. cit.*

[12] Elie de Jésus-Marie., *loc cit.*

Chapter 14

THE EVIL SPIRIT

There are angels good and bad, "pure spirits" who by evil influence or by incitement to good play some part in human affairs. Within man himself, there are conflicting forces, some of which urge him to do good, while others incline him to evil. Spiritual writers and teachers have always recognized that it is necessary in the spiritual life to give some thought to the spirit by which we are led. The "good spirit" is a general term under which they would include the Holy Spirit, God's angels, and natural inclinations to good. The classification regards less the immediate source of some inspiration, movement, or decision but looks rather to the goal toward which the movement takes us. Similarly, the category of "evil spirits" includes all the sources whence instigation to evil, or to the less good, comes to man. This point of view is the one which has most practical importance, and it is the one which unifies this chapter. However, we shall also indicate how there is a certain unity in the ultimate origin, at least, of the influences which obstruct our steady progress in our upward path to more intimate union with God and to a life lived in complete generosity of response to the calls of His love.

1. Our Adversary, the Devil

(a) IN THE APOSTOLATE

Into the personal drama of our life in Christ and our work for His Kingdom, the villain enters: the figure of Satan, whom many find it more convenient to forget. But, as St. Peter and St. Paul warned us,[1] we have to contend with him in our personal lives and in our apostolate. Christ established His Kingdom through struggle with and victory over the devil. We, who are called to work for the spread of the Kingdom, are called to share in the victory of Christ. We will have our part in the victory only if we have our part in the struggle against the forces of evil. In our struggle Christ continues His. In the early Church there were the monks and desert fathers who went out into the desert to spend their lives in prayer. They chose the desert not mainly because it was a place of silence with the absence of crowds, but because it was regarded as the dwelling-place of Satan. It was in the desert that Christ was tempted; it was in the desert places that Satan was regarded as having his chief dwelling. These holy men of the early Church chose to carry the fight to Satan, to combat him directly, in the front lines of the battle.

"The world also is a desert, the desert of the absence of God. The Church, sending her priests into the world, sends them forth to do battle, to carry the fight to Satan, to carry on the battle of Christ."[2] As apostles we are sent to carry on the battle of Christ. He, as a divine Person in human nature, did not have to fight the battle against any personal passion or weakness of soul. With us, it is not so; in us is all the inclination to evil that is the result of original sin. We will feel within ourselves the battle against evil which we fight for Christ. This is part of the price we must pay if we expect to extend the victory of Christ beyond our own souls. Extending the Kingdom of Christ, we will feel the force of the attacks of Satan. We will be tempted in those very things against which we strive and from which we fight to deliver others.

The priest engaged in the ministry cannot escape the spiritual combat, neither in himself nor in the world. It is well that he should know this. Perhaps we may be tempted to avoid the combat, not to believe in the activity of a spiritual adversary. . . . Perhaps we may be tempted to seek a ground on which we don't meet him too directly. That would be to flee from the very essence of the apostolic ministry. . . . (This combat) is necessary if we are to enter into the work of the Redemption.[3]

(b) IN THE INTERIOR LIFE

There was a time when all obstacles to the workings of grace were put down to the spirit of evil. In later years, the devil went out of fashion, and what were formerly put down as influences of the evil spirit were explained in psychological terms, subconscious urges, etc. In reality, the two explanations are not as opposed as might at first appear. For Satan is "the Father of lies," and all self-seeking and self-deceit are the result of original sin, of which Satan was the instigator. All pride and self-seeking which "are the result of sin, and incline to sin," in the phrase of the Council of Trent, are, indirectly at least, from the devil. If he continues his activity—as we know he does—it will be along the same lines, exciting or seconding all those movements of nature which prevent a man from giving himself wholly to God. The field of Satan's influence will be that field studied by psychology as illusion, flight from reality, lack of emotional control, etc. It will be particularly the field of pride and self-seeking. In all these matters, it is impossible, in the normal course of events, to say what is directly from the devil and what is from nature. It is impossible, yet not important. The important thing is that, whatever their source, they are obstacles to the grace of God and hence good material for Satan to use in obstructing the work of God. And, as we have seen, the whole lack of harmony in man's nature is originally from the devil.

According to St. John of the Cross, as we have said, the action of God on the soul is directed toward bringing us to realize and live the reality of God and the reality of self. This could be said to be based on two things: faith, the foundation of the theological life, and humility, the foundation of the moral life. Hence, says St. John, the devil's main attacks are launched against these two key points. He tries to make us fail in faith, to nourish ourselves on appearances, for which our sensibility can have quite a taste, keeping us back from attaining the reality of God in purity of faith and strength of hope. Humility means a just realization of the reality of self—needy and sinful creatures that we are. The devil tempts us to pride, to all sorts of false ideas about ourselves. Also, he leads by way of fear—fear of what we will lose; and by way of attraction—"you will be like gods." The least lack of humility, the least self-complacency is enough to open the door to the devil. His is a constant invitation to pride, even in our relations with God and what we do for God. Even as we advance in the spiritual life, the mode of attack of the devil is the same. "Radically, there is always a confidence in oneself, a rash sureness of one's own way, refusal to submit to the judgment of him who holds the place of God, or simply the sweet inebriation of pride in feeling that one is more favored by God than others are. From this starting point all possible intellectual derailments are possible."[4]

The safeguards which St. John gives are then, as we might expect: (a) a spirit of faith; (b) humility; and (c) obedience, for obedience to those over us in the Church is the concrete way of living a spirit of faith and true humility. Essential also is confidence in Christ who has won a victory over Satan and who will not let us be tempted beyond our strength. The rules for the discernment of spirits help us in this matter. There are certain artifices of the devil, who, after all, is a very intelligent being. These it is useful to note and remember.

(i) He takes the soul by its weak point (whence the need for self-knowledge),

(ii) in moments of negligence and distraction (hence the need of vigilance),

(iii) proposing good ends, but indiscreet (whence the usefulness of taking counsel),

(iv) in little things if the soul's resistance to grave falls is proved,

(v) dissimulating vice under the appearance of virtue, which is the same as making us fall victims to illusion.

(c) ILLUSIONS

As "the father of lies," Satan works through illusion and deceit. He finds plenty of scope within man to foster illusion and self-deceit. "Spiritual tradition is unanimous in declaring that illusions are one of the greatest evils that affect those who are tending to perfection." Anyone, then, who is completely confident that he does not deceive himself in anything, or that he is secure from that sort of error, is already victim of the greatest possible illusion. Faber gives an excellent treatment of illusions, the causes, roots, and varieties.[5] He lists seven varieties, which it may be useful to set out briefly:

1. The self-deceit that takes no advice.

2. The self-deceit that is always taking advice, and often takes advice from everybody. This is not uncom-

mon, and it really cloaks a desire to have one's own way. If one receives enough conflicting advice, one can conclude that, since authorities are divided, one can do what one thinks best—which is just what was wanted in the first place. Not infrequently, such a person really suspects himself of being in the wrong, and, in seeking advice, does not really seek counsel, but rather that someone else should tell him that what he wants to do is all right.

3. Complacent self-deceit, convinced that it is always right; any mistakes are never its fault, but are due to someone else.

4. Censoriousness. This is the fault of those who condemn all things different from their own way. These usually have a cynical disapproval of any enthusiasm.

5. Ambition, which in spiritual matters is impatient for quick advance, and, when such advance does not take place, regards oneself as excused from effort. Ambition can make one think that he has great qualities which are not recognized—whence come discontent, bitterness, and criticism.

6. The self-deceit that is scrupulous.

7. The self-deceit that is falsely humble. This makes a man say that he has not the capabilities to do certain tasks asked of him, or to attempt great things. Often this attitude hides a fear of failure—"too proud to be prominent."

As causes of these various forms of self-deceit, Faber lists vanity and taking ourselves too seriously ("an honest, humorous sense of ridicule is a great help to holiness"); dwelling on self, love of praise, and palliating what is acknowledgedly wrong.

2. Satan and Psychology

As we have seen, grace perfects the human person.

There is complete harmony between the working of grace and the development of the human personality. For a human person reaches his full stature by complete openness to the personal demands of God, by surrender to God's grace. And as God's grace leads a man to more perfect intimacy with God, to a deeper living of the divine life, it will lead him along the way of self-forgetfulness to seek only God and His will. All sound psychology that helps to the development of the human personality, says only, from a different approach, what the theology of grace and its action in man teaches, too.

Psychology studies the obstacles to the development of the human personality. As we have seen, these are, in the main, various forms of self-seeking, self-exaltation, or defense of the concept of the ego which one has formed. Further, these elements square with the biblical concept of sin and the effects of sin in man. They are from sin and incline to sin. From theology, we know that Satan is at work in the world; that he was the instigator of the first sin, and hence, at least indirectly, of all sin in the world, and that his active work will be along the same lines.

We tend to judge as a rather simple attitude the readiness, in former times, to regard all hindrances to good or to progress in the spiritual life as being from the devil. We think that we have explained many of those things by psychology. So we have; but we have not explained away their deeper origin. Whether all these entanglements which obstruct the growth of grace are directly from the devil, or only indirectly as the effects of sin, matters little to Satan. He is content that they are obstacles to the work of God. It should also be of small concern to us to know how directly they come from the forces of evil. It is even better for us not to try to find out. But just as sound psychology can help us in our understanding, and living, and teaching of the life of grace, so can it help us avoid self-deceit and self-entanglement, which are obstacles to our fuller living for God. Here too, the psychologists are mostly saying, in technical terms, what spiritual writers have been saying for centuries. It is interesting to see how little is said by modern psychologists that is not included in spiritual writings such as Faber's work from which we have taken a few brief points.

One of the most necessary means to save ourselves and those we guide from illusion is a knowledge of what is called "the mechanism of rationalization." Anyone who knows human nature knows something of this mechanism, although perhaps most of us use it ourselves more than we care to admit. As a matter of fact, there is no field in which it has more scope than in that of the spiritual life—as we shall shortly see. Suppose I were to tell you who read that there should be much more self-denial in your life, that you gave too much time to recreation, were too attached to this or that particular thing you do. You would immediately find reasons to say I was wrong. Your reasons might be right—but as someone once said: "There are two reasons why we do things: the good reason, and the real reason." It is extremely simple, when we want to do something, to find a "good" reason for it from spiritual theology: grace perfects nature, the liberty of the children of God, positive spirituality, etc. Since, in spiritual theology, there must be a delicate balance in harmonizing seemingly opposed principles, there is much scope for rationalization, the inventing or finding "of excuses or reasons for behavior and conduct that is inadequate, unacceptable, or damaging to personal integrity and status. By making such conduct appear rational, the person protects himself from the effects of self-criticism, as well as the criticism of others, and thus preserves his ego-integrity."[6] Rationalization is one of the most common ways in which man defends himself against the implications of inadequacy, guilt, inferiority, and failure. In all cases it conceals an inability to face up squarely to the real demands of a situation, to admit one's own weakness, or to accept responsibility.

Rationalization is, for one reason or another, one of the most common ways in which we excuse ourselves from greater effort in the spiritual life. There is fear in the heart of every man. We are afraid of what God might ask of us if we surrender fully to what He asks of us in the way of sanctity and sharing in the redemptive mystery of Christ, with its aspect of death as well as of life. All progress is a further entry into the mystery of Christ's death and Resurrection. All further life is a further death to self—and we do not want to die! All further perfection is further self-renunciation—and naturally we cling to what we are and and what we have. The prospective convert to the faith is afraid of what he might lose and finds reasons to justify his clinging to what he is and has. The same holds true of every step forward in the spiritual life. Every call of God to higher sanctity is a call to leave something of what we were, to go forth into the unknown. There is always the aspect of risk and the tendency to cling to the comfortable ways of old. Hence there is always the "natural" tendency to justify our caution, our "prudence," and really our fear of what we might lose, our attachment to "self."

Now it is evident that these two natural tendencies assist the devil in his work of hindering spiritual progress. As the spiritual masters insist, Satan leads by way of fear (fear of what we might lose), and of attraction to self-exaltation and self-satisfaction.

Devious and complicated as are the workings of self-deceit and deceit by the devil, the safeguard is simple, although because of our tendency to self-entanglement it is not easy. The safeguard is distrust of self and confident attentiveness to God. "The fundamental attitude of the soul must be to learn humility, confidence in God, distrust of self, opening one's conscience to a prudent director, obedience, care to avoid the occasions of sin."[7] More succinctly, St. John of the Cross insists on faith and humility as the best means of thwarting the influence of the devil—direct or indirect. St. Peter was even more summary: "Whom resist ye, strong in the faith." The strength of our faith (our belief in the love of God and our complete surrender to that love, our adhering to the First Truth) delivers us from the spirit of falsehood and self-deception.

3. Flight from Reality

The action of God and the workings of His grace are directed toward getting a man to live the reality of self before the reality of God and His demands. Since fallen man has a natural reluctance to accept these demands in their fullness, he will use some of the escape devices that human nature habitually employs. In this context, the spiritual theologian can profitably utilize the psychologist's expositions of the various types of "escape or withdrawal," which are "essentially a means of defense against the demands, stresses, or threats of the world in which the individual lives." All flight from reality constitutes some sort of obstacle to the full inflow of God's grace, with its inherent direction toward the perfection of the human personality. Daydreaming and fantasy thinking are common forms of such withdrawal. In its pathological form, this develops into schizophrenia. Another means of escape is flight into illness—which results in the various forms of neuroses. I do not wish to go into detailed treatment here. But it is obvious that those who are charged with the work of educating others in the spiritual life can profit by knowing the various types of neurotic disorders, the factors that foster them, and by being able to detect preneurotic tendencies which are extremely common. By helping to an early control of such tendencies, one can do much to foster a sane spirituality. Such control contributes much toward that peace of soul which all should find in their life for God.

4. Scruples

Although no detailed treatment of these matters will be attempted in this work, it may be of some practical utility to delay on one of the neuroses, which takes the form of scruples. The unenlightened sometimes think that scruples are a sign of fervor. They are not. They are a sign of neurosis. If this were clearly realized by all before they start giving themselves to the practice of the spiritual life, there would probably be fewer scrupulous persons to make the office of confessor more burdensome. It is unfortunate that even today we can find, in otherwise authoritative writings in good periodicals, statements such as this: "It is a paradox that the most fervent Christians are precisely those who are most tortured with that vice that has plagued the modern world, scruples."[8] This is no paradox. It is an erroneous statement. Grace and the fervor it fosters deliver from scruples, for grace brings a man to spiritual maturity. Scruples are a neurotic disorder. Some of the characteristics of neurosis are: immaturity and sensitivity; self-centeredness; unrealistic ego-ideal; rigidity and anxiety; isolation; lack of control; irresponsibility; morbid self-examination; self-pity; conflict. It is a travesty of the life of grace and its effects upon human persons to say that the most fervent Christians are immature, self-centered, lack-

ing control, irresponsible, etc. If it were true, how damn-
ing it would be! So let us get this matter of scruples
straight; for while it is bad enough to have a fairly common occurrence of this obstacle to the growth of the life
of grace, it is worse to have it regarded as the accompaniment of such growth.

Scruples, in the strict sense, must be distinguished from
(i) Delicate conscience, which is the fruit of a long
process of spiritual maturing and of patient education. This
is a question of an enlightened and supple will, with no
accompanying anguish nor deep disquiet.

(ii) Certain periods of disquietude, doubt, and passing
anxiety of restricted duration, which sometimes follow on
one of the various "conversions" in the spiritual life. Such
conversions, as decisions to lead a more perfect life, mean
that the "converted" person now sees most things in a different light and must go through the difficulty of adjusting
himself to this newness.

(iii) Disquiet which marks a lack of generosity. This is
called compensatory scruples and is the form of self-deceit
referred to above, occurring when people pick on trivial
details to worry about, when they are not facing up to the
real issue involved. This occurs, not infrequently, in one
who has thought he had a vocation to the religious life
and finds that there is more self-renunciation involved than
he had bargained for. He does not want to take the decision to give up his vocation, for that would be to admit
failure. Further, he is afraid of the responsibility of such a
step. But if someone else takes the decision for him, he is
freed from responsibility, and he, then, has not failed. He
has "been advised" to leave. Such a one then, often develops scruples in the hope that this will prove to others
that, because of his worries and anxiety, he should leave.
A blunt pointing out of the facts of the case usually helps

him to face up to the real issue and make his own decision with the maturity required of him.

Distinct from all these things are scruples properly so-called, which "are not a phenomenon of conscience, but an obstacle to responsibility."[9] They can be defined as "that form of psychasthenia characterized by worries of the moral and religious order." To understand scruples we must know what psychasthenic tendencies are. The psychasthenic

. . . has not mastered his own thought as much as it has mastered him. He is dominated by a multitude of involuntary thoughts, images, associations of ideas, imaginations, by all the throngings of the subconscious in the field of the conscious. He lacks the strength to free himself. As a consequence he feels quite powerless to face life; just as he can not direct his own reflection, he can not stick to a definite course of action. Rather he lets himself be buffeted about by circumstances, good or bad, and is influenced by those around him. . . . In face of all this, each feature assuming . . . the proportions of an almost insurmountable obstacle—his illness is one of uncertainty, of doubt. Submerged in a flood of contradictions, he can never come to a firm and definite decision. When he finally decides to act, he does it under the influence of unreasoning impulse . . . and in such a way that his obsessive doubt . . . now attaches itself to the action he has performed, the way it was done, and the consequences it will entail. The uncertainty becomes a real obsession which invades his consciousness and causes the most painful conflicts . . . Depending upon the individual in question this obsession of uncertainty (the essence of the illness) may reveal itself in different ways and in various domains.[10]

When this obsession of uncertainty reveals itself in the moral and religious fields, the illness (for such it is) is called scruples. The scrupulous person is obsessed with the fear of moral stain and guilt, is uncertain about many moral issues. The case is well illustrated by a comparison with people who are afraid of germs (which can be another form of psychasthenia). Obsessed by this fear, some people are always taking the most elaborate precautions to avoid infection and resort to frequent washing of their hands. Fear of germs becomes a real phobia. This illustrates well how their thought has mastered them. It is not hard to see the process of loss of control: They think of the countless germs—in the atmosphere, on food, left by the touch of some infected person on any object at all; germs are everywhere, all sorts of them; if you think about them long enough, you can almost feel them on your hands! Then there is the precaution of washing; but if you have a vivid imagination, you can go further: Perhaps the water you have used is contaminated; perhaps the towel was not clean, perhaps. . . . How can you be sure you are freed from all the terrible possibilities of contamination? It requires little thought to see how this can become an obsession and a fear-ridden uncertainty, which tries vainly, by all sorts of ways, to gain an impossible absolute certainty.

Scruples are a very close parallel: Concerned with the fear of moral stain and seeing possibilities of sin abounding, the scrupulous person also tries to make sure that he is free from all contamination. How can he be sure that he did not sin at least by carelessness, by self-deceit, by sinful motives? He seeks for an absolute certainty within himself. The more he seeks, the more egocentric he becomes, watching himself, analyzing sensations, impressions, different states of mind. He also resorts to the equivalent of handwashing, making frequent acts of contrition, going to confession. Then he doubts whether his act of contrition was sincere or effective enough, so he resorts to further prayers and builds up a whole series of them to ensure his

cleanness of conscience. Often they become too complicated to carry out, and their omission gives him further
cause for scruples.

Beneath all this, and the cause of it all, is a flight from
responsibility. The scrupulous person really wants to avoid
responsibility for the morality of his actions. As we saw,
the psychasthenic feels powerless to face life. He is faced
with many choices; there is always the possibility that he
may make wrong choices, and being responsible for the
choice, be judged guilty of fault. Basically there is pride at
the root of this. All fear of responsibility is fear of failure.
The scrupulous person is a perfectionist: he does not want
to admit that his actions can be imperfect. Since he attaches
a great power to thought, he sees clearly the "perfection"
of the ideal action he imagines. But the real order is one in
which we can never achieve the same perfection as we can
in thought and imagination. Hence, free choice and practical action make us enter the field of limitation and imperfection, with the consequent responsibility for the
limitation and imperfection of our actions. The scrupulous
person has an exaggerated fear of being judged as weak,
imperfect; of being criticized for his limitations; of accepting himself as limited and fallible in the field of action; of
committing himself to the acceptance of reality. He seeks
to avoid this responsibility and the possibility of being
judged culpable of sin in his action.

But *how* does his obsession of uncertainty deliver him
from responsibility? His is the excuse that is commonly
given: I was not ready for action; I did not have time for
full reflection, for deliberate decision. If a man is preoccupied with all the possibilities of moral stain to the point
of obsession, he spends so much time in hesitation and
doubt that the flow of life carries him into action "before
he was ready" for an action fully deliberated and con-

sented to as such. Therefore, he did not really act on the level of full moral responsibility. Then, looking back and worrying about his past action, he is prevented from facing up fully to further acts of deliberate choice. The more the preoccupation and the reasoning, the less the responsibility; and when responsibility has been avoided, so is the possibility of moral stain.

From his confessor, he then seeks assurance that he has not sinned; seeks, further, someone who will take the responsibility of the decision in these matters from his shoulders. The rules for the confessor's mode of action with penitents who are scrupulous are well known: It is useless trying to reason with the scrupulous, for they can always find pseudo-reasons for suggesting possibility of sin. Their view of the moral life is distorted and unnatural. Instead of seeing it as a movement of life, with decisions made after a moral estimate of reasons, they see each part as an isolated whole detached from the living context and, therefore, falsified. As one author says, they see, instead of a moving picture, a series of still photographs which, "frozen" into immobility and considered in isolation, always appear unnatural.

It is evident that from the point of view of spiritual theology and the education of the person to full Christian living, the full answer to scruples is not the confessor's taking the responsibilities upon his shoulders. This is a necessary step, but it can only be a temporary expedient if the scrupulous person is to develop any real spiritual life. For this, the burden of responsibility must, gradually, be placed back on the shoulders of the scrupulous person. He must first, of course, be educated to assume his responsibilities. This work of education will be a more or less lengthy process.

Here the general rule of direction holds good: [11]

Obviously, the direction to be given to these people is in the first place to obstruct their self-contemplation, to suppress their preoccupation with self so that they can develop a salutary exterior activity. . . . The director must insist above all, upon the positive character of the Christian life; he will know how to appeal to the healthy elements of the person's moral and spiritual personality to express the will to live in conformity with Christ . . .

He must be taught to live all the positive realities of the Christian life that we have set forth in previous chapters, for he lives none of them. He knows nothing of what surrender to the love of God means. He is morbidly intent on justifying himself. He wants to be sure that he did not sin. In an attempt to reach this security, he sets up all sorts of subjective norms:

True culpability is transcendent; false culpability is interior before false positions one has taken up. There is a sort of short-circuit: one aspect of the personality imagines itself culpable before some other aspect of the same. The subject never leaves his interiority, and a solution on this level is impossible. No fault is resolved except in a meeting with the love that recreates, restores, and gives new life. A true sense of culpability makes one abandon oneself with love unlimited to Him by whom one knows oneself loved with love unlimited. A false sense of culpability is a sterile caricature of this attitude, for it comes from a de-vitalized personality fundamentally lacking in courage.[12]

What does it matter if he does succeed in deciding before his own internal tribunal that he is free from sin? The only thing that does matter is that, whether he has sinned or not, he surrenders himself to the love of God and His mercy, whence alone life flows into his soul.

If the scrupulous person is to shed his scruples and to

enter into real life, he must be brought to see his life as a vocation, a call to live in the love of God; to live it with confidence in the Fatherly care and understanding of the God who loves him; to live it as a man, with courage, accepting the responsibility of his own decisions. He must learn to accept the reality of self: of a created self, imperfect, limited, suffering the effects of sin. He must live the virtue of hope, seeking for security not in any pretended strength or merit of his own, but in the grace of God. He must learn to see the commandments and all law as the paths tracing out his way of love lived for God. Above all, he must free himself from a rigid, literal interpretation of law, realizing that positive laws have excusing causes; that cases of conflicting laws have to be solved in a human way. On this point, it is interesting to note that it is claimed that scruples are a phenomenon of the Western world, with the concept of law built into its civilization and into its approach to morality in a way which does not exist in the Greek Church. If the observance of the law—to the letter—is your justification, that can give you security; but only until the complicated issues of life are not covered by the law. Then further prescriptions are necessary, and still further ones, until you have the equivalent of the Pharisaic conglomeration of legal rules, impossible to observe. The scrupulous person builds up such a mass within his own mind and succeeds only in condemning himself. From this captivity, he can be freed to the wider liberty of the children of God only by surrender to the love of God, opening his heart to the outpouring of this love.

5. Aggression

It is not only the defensive or introspective person who

has not fully mastered his emotions, submitting them to reason and through his mind and will to God. The same lack of self-mastery can be evident in an exaggerated aggressiveness or self-assertion through action which is demanding, overpowering, or possessive. A certain amount of aggressiveness is normal and constitutes strength of character. Exaggerated and unreasonable, it is called aggression. Such a form of reaction often results from frustration and is an angry reaction against what is regarded as the cause of frustration; it is also a form of self-defense—a reaction against implications of inferiority or failure; it can, furthermore, cloak a feeling of guilt, often in a field different from that in which the aggression manifests itself.

The ways in which aggression are expressed are many. In words it results in rudeness, biting sarcasm, and strong criticism. Other signs of it are resistance to authority, harboring grudges, excessive disagreement with others, and excessive irritability, sullenness, "getting even," and dominating others. In positions of authority, it manifests itself in harshness, jealousy of one's authority, and dictatorship or possessiveness.

Aggression can be a serious obstacle to the expanding of the life of grace, for it can be strong self-assertion and pride. Like all self-assertion, of course, it can find some specious justifying reason—righteous anger, reaction against oppression, etc.—to blind its possessor to his very real weakness.

Self-deceit, self-assertion, complicated ways of preserving our own ego-ideal or of avoiding responsibilities—these are all obstacles to the full development of human personality. They are obstacles, too, to a man's fuller growth in grace for they close his soul to divine invitations to greater self-forgetfulness. Their ultimate source is original sin;

hence their ultimate author is the evil genius who still finds them ideal material to use in obstructing the workings of God's grace. From them we can be fully freed only by the Spirit of Truth who will lead us, along the way of faith, humility and obedience, to self-forgetful surrender to the love of God.

NOTES

[1] I Pet. 5:8; Eph. 6:12.

[2] D. Barsotti, *Vie Mystique et Mystère Liturgique*, c. XI.

[3] L. Lochet, S.J., *Vie Spirituelle*, 100 (1959), 477.

[4] Philippe de la Trinité, O.C.D., "Le Démon dans l'oeuvre de saint Jean de la Croix," *Satan, Etudes Carmélitaines* (Paris: Desclée de Brouwer, 1948).

[5] *Spiritual Conferences* (London: Burns & Oates, 1858), c. III: "Self-deceit."

[6] A. Schneiders, *Personal Adjustment and Mental Health*, p. 317.

[7] Cf. art. "Démon" in *Dictionnaire de Spiritualité*.

[8] H. Musurillo: "Symbolism and Kerygmatic Theology," *Thought*, 36 (1961), 67.

[9] A. Snoeck S.J., "La Pastorale du Scruple," *N.R.T.*, 79 (1957), 371–387; 478–493.

[10] Biot and Galimard, *Medical Guide to Vocations*, pp. 57–58.

[11] Dr. Charles Nodet.

[12] Snoeck, *art. cit.*

Chapter 15

THE CHRISTIAN PERSONALITY

———

Grace perfects the human person. The Christian personality is the *emergent totality* resulting from God's action through His grace on the human soul and our human cooperation. Hence it can be regarded from two points of view. It is viewed most truly if it is seen as the life of Christ coming to fuller measure in each of His members, as our being drawn more deeply into the mystery of Christ. But perhaps it is understood more clearly by our human minds if we approach it from the more tangible side of the human personality being formed and fashioned under the action of God. This will be our point of view in this chapter, while the other view will be studied in the next chapter.

Generally, the starting point of a "spiritual life," as it is studied in spiritual theology, is taken as "the moment one first conceives a sincere desire of advancing in the spiritual life." Consonant with what we have already written, we would express this as an experience of the living reality of faith, believing in God's love, and being drawn to Christ. From this starting point, with its desire of personal dedication to Christ, all true spirituality springs. And since the personal relationship with God in Christ is the definitive shaping force in the formation of a Christian spirituality, there can be no truly Christian personality without a man's consciously deciding to make that personal relationship the ruling force of his life.

1. Stages in the Growth of the Christian Personality

The customary divisions of the spiritual life (purgative way, illuminative way, unitive way; or beginners, advanced, perfect) are well known and have been well treated by many authors. We shall not, then, make any attempt to repeat or summarize what these authors have written. Rather, we shall trace the growth of the Christian personality from a slightly different aspect that would seem to be quite practical and helpful for one's own life and for the work of spiritual direction. We have in mind the majority of Christians called to the active life.

(a) THE FORMATIVE STAGE

Those who respond to the call of Christ to greater personal intimacy must be formed to fuller Christian living. The term *purgative way* is not altogether satisfactory as a classification of this initial stage. It fits perfectly those who, from a life of worldliness, were converted to the spiritual life. These were the ones for whom the phrase was first coined. It indicates that, during the initial period of the spiritual life, the "converted" person must consciously concentrate on "purgation," getting rid of his old ways, vices, tendencies to selfishness. It does not, of course, suppose that self-denial is limited to the first stage, but rather that this is the conscious preoccupation of the beginner. This does not apply to all classes of beginners. The living experience of a call to closer friendship with God and the desire to respond come to people in various ways.

Thus beginners can be a very mixed lot: (i) Those who are converted from a life of worldliness. (ii) Those who, as adults, are converted to the faith from other sects, in which they have lived lives of real natural or Christian goodness, according to their lights. These then, by their unselfishness, have built a sound natural foundation on which the supernatural can fit easily. (iii) Those who, educated in a good Catholic family, have always lived for Christ. The re-affirmation of their personal choice for Christ, as they leave their childhood behind, hardly seems any new step to them. (iv) Those who, after a rather selfish, or to some extent self-centered childhood, go through their adolescent crisis and, choosing to give their lives to Christ more fully, are conscious of a radical change in the direction of their lives. (v) Those adult Catholics to whom the desire comes to "do more for Christ," after a life that has been indifferent rather than worldly; the indifference is generally the lack of any enlightened knowledge about spiritual matters.

All of these are beginners. All have need of knowledge, of instruction, and of guidance. All will have need of dying to self to live for Christ, but not all will need to make this their chief conscious preoccupation. Such a need will be in proportion to the natural tendency to self-seeking that exists in each individual, which must be judged in each case. Each will have to learn self-knowledge, especially his own "dominant tendency" or particular form of pride,[1] in which he is naturally inclined to seek self. For all, this initial experience is a surrender to God. For those who enter a seminary or religious life, this surrender is lived out in the acceptance of whatever their superiors or the rules demand of them. This is why so much importance is placed on such an acceptance, for it is the external element which seems a normal necessity that the self-renunciation in a gift of self to God should be a lived reality. For others, it consists in the acceptance of spiritual direction as the will of God, which they are prepared to follow utterly. It should not be overlooked that, in the generous renunciation which a convert to the Catholic Church makes and the complete acceptance of all the demands of the Church, there is often a deeper and more radical death to self, a surer beginning of a fervent spiritual life than in many "vocations" within the Church. It is often because their surrender is not sufficiently deep that beginners in religious life or seminaries have a long period of internal struggle.

The first thing to ensure is that this surrender to God is sufficiently deep, that the self-renunciation is sufficiently radical. This is the reason behind the various trials and proofs (some of doubtful wisdom) to which beginners have been put through the centuries. Once the effective sincerity of a desire for complete gift of self to God, with its necessary self-renunciation, has been established, the beginner will be set on his search for closer personal intimacy with Christ, by prayer, instruction, reading etc.

This search will not really be sincere without a determined effort to get rid of the obstacles to that intimacy, notably, sin and the inclination to sin. In this regard, all the traditional teaching holds good. It would, however, seem particularly useful for our times to regard this initial period as one in which much thought is given, by directors and directed, to aiming at spiritual maturity. This, for practical purposes, will mean that all sound teaching about psychological maturity can be profitably utilized.

The spiritual life is first of all the reception of God's grace and our co-operation with that grace. The Spirit breathes where He will, and psychologists can set no limits to His action. But spirituality does not consist in sitting down and waiting for His grace to move us, nor merely in praying and waiting. Positively, grace perfects the human personality; negatively, it rectifies defects of personality which are obstacles to the workings of grace. The Spirit will not breathe in directions at variance with the full human perfection of man. All this we have seen earlier. The spiritual life and Christian asceticism do not aim at humanism, but rather at the divinization of man.[2] Setting out to perfect our personalities would be anything but striving for Christian perfection. But setting out to live for Christ, to live our personal relationship with God, demands, if there is any truth in it, that we live unselfishly, with our lives centered on Him and not on ourselves. Hence it demands that we take thought of all the ways in which we really do seek self, or exalt ourselves, or center our thoughts and activity around ourselves. For these are effects of original sin and obstacles to grace.

Therefore, this initial period of formation toward spiritual maturity will be one in which, in each individual case, we see what are the elements of immaturity, in which we work toward the positive development of the human person, toward maturity: responsibility, emotional control, facing reality, etc. Negatively, there must be an effort against irresponsibility, flight from reality, etc. With older "beginners" who have already achieved a certain maturity, there may be remaining elements of "infantilism." There will, generally, be more of self in their seeking God than they realize. Accustomed to run their own affairs, they will often bring to the spiritual life the conviction of their own sufficiency and the assumption of their own complete ability to live a life for God along the way they plan.

For all, a humble self-knowledge must be acquired during this formative stage. Without it, one never really passes beyond the stage of the beginners.

(b) TRANSITION STAGE

If one is to keep to three stages in the development of the Christian personality, the second would be that of spiritual maturity, which we shall shortly consider. From the formative period to the stage of spiritual maturity, there is a time of transition with its peculiar problems. Some never succeed in resolving these problems; as a result they never proceed to the fullness of spiritual maturity. This transition period, with all its inherent conflicts, psychological and spiritual, has had its classic treatment in St. John of the Cross, with his writing on the "night of the senses." Much of this we have already seen. Rather than repeat, we refer back to it.[3] It is during this period that a person has particular need of enlightened guidance and support.

The religious passes through it, to some extent, on leaving the novitiate or training period, especially if he is then engaged in the active apostolate. The young priest goes through something of it in the early part of his ministry. All pass through part of it as their prayer undergoes the necessary development from its early, more superficial character to deeper, more dedicated devotion.

Their period of formation was one in which they received detailed direction as to what to do; definite spiritual practices were prescribed with set times to carry them out. They learned the principles of the spiritual life but often identified the principles with the only practice of them they knew. They built up their own idealized vision of the future—and of themselves; for, in the relatively sheltered circumstances of their formative days, they took for inner strength what was only external absence of difficulty. In the transition period, they have to make their own decisions, their own applications of principles to practice, to make use of things they had renounced; they have to forgo some of the spiritual practices in which they felt so secure, to work in conditions in which recollection of mind, which seemed so easy, now seems an impossibility. Many of the principles of the spiritual life which they were taught they cannot now apply; they will often tend to think that they do not apply at all. They will see others interpret them differently, and they will often not know whether these others are not living up to essential principles (whence the universality of rash judgment at this stage), or whether the principles are not as essential as they were led to believe.

All these conflicts they must learn to resolve. They must learn to accept reality, to accept limitations and frustrations without giving way to discouragement, to distinguish between principle and practice, and to take up their responsibilities by accepting their individual liberty and striving to fulfill their own personal call in fidelity to their own personal grace. When they have done this, to some extent, they may be regarded as at the stage of spiritual maturity.

(c) THE STAGE OF SPIRITUAL MATURITY

Within this class, one should distinguish between the earlier and the later stage. The earlier period is one in which people have really surmounted successfully the crisis of transition, but still have much to learn in the school of experience. There will still be certain imprudences, quick reactions, temporary rebellions and frustration, and deep emotional reaction to success and failure. There will be some self-seeking; there will be a lack of complete unification of the various constituent elements of their lives; certain natural attachments will remain or revive. There will be a certain lack of patience with the shortcomings of others and some lack of regard for the personal dignity of every human soul.

At a later, more advanced stage of spiritual maturity there will be, together with steady onward striving, deep devotion and personal dedication, a steadier generosity, a greater calmness, patience, tolerance, and regard for others. There will also be a further elimination from their lives of all that is useless and not directed toward union with Christ and work for Christ. For those who over the years have steadily grown in faith, hope, and charity lived in a devoted dedication to God and His will, the step into the third stage, which we call the *active unitive way*, will be almost imperceptibly taken. For the less generous, it will be a more difficult step to take. Some will never summon the generosity required to make it.

(d) UNCLASSIFIED

This brings us to a category of persons who do not fit into the framework of "Progress in the Spiritual Life" or "Growth of the Christian Personality." They have ceased to progress, ceased to develop. They are variously designated as: retarded souls, the mediocre, the lukewarm, the merely pious. Their number is said to be many.[4] They lack a serious and efficacious desire for progress and a truly interior life. They have never effectively resolved all the conflicts of the transition stage from the period of formation of beginners; or having passed through it successfully, they have grown weary and disillusioned along the way. Their merit may be great, and their devotion to duty quite satisfactory; but the spark has gone from their lives, the dynamism from their faith and hope, and the fervor from their charity. Or, at least, although their piety may be fervent, it lacks the breadth and depth, the vision and understanding that mark the man who has grown to his full stature in Christ.

Some have never succeeded in surmounting fully the

crisis that should have been the door to fuller maturity. When they are faced, at that stage, with the call to fuller liberty, to leave behind the more dependent days of formation, some fail to adjust themselves to reality, recoil from the risk involved, and try to live all their lives as they did in the period of formation. They never succeed in adapting themselves to a wider world and remain always "merely pious," *simpliste*, and small. Others, paralleling the ordinary adolescent crisis, reject almost all of the old; thus they show that they did not profit by it but work out their spiritual way according to their own lights. Unfortunately, these lights are too often natural and mixed with much self-seeking, which they usually succeed in "rationalizing."

Still others, after passing the crisis, fall back into older ways of self-seeking and lack of generosity. Their predominant tendency reasserts itself in some other sphere. This can be either because their original self-renunciation did not go deep enough, or because they never succeeded in coping with disillusionment and difficulties. Again, rationalization fortifies them in their situation. Some are too easily discouraged and lose heart—"perfection is not for them." In one form or another all fail to mature fully.

(e) THE ADULT CRISIS

Given all the factors which can be obstacles to a man's growth in perfection, it would seem to be a rare thing that a man continues an unbroken, steady, forward movement after he has entered the way of spiritual maturity. Much more frequently, at a later stage of maturity, many people can settle into a phase that contains some characteristics of the state of spiritual stagnation which we have just indicated. The frequency of such a happening would be less if more thought and spiritual writing took account of what has been found of the psychology of the adult. Those who give themselves to a deeper spiritual life are, during the period of their training, put on guard against inclinations to sin, against all the immature ways of seeking self. They master their emotions, channel their forces, and with the strength they have acquired under God's grace, set out to work for Him. They must always be vigilant, they know, but the vigilance is usually directed against old enemies, and their care is lest they fall back into the weakness from which they have been delivered.

They can think that, freed from the dangers of youth and immaturity, they are now secure; and they can, imperceptibly, fall into the "terrible self-sufficiency of the adult," with little regard for other persons, with little sympathy or care to understand them. In this way, a man can enclose himself in the self-centered world of middle age. The adult, especially a man, tends naturally to egoism: "Conscious of his professional importance . . . jealous of his majority . . . proud of making his own decisions . . . finding it repugnant to ask for advice. . . ." The adult can be even more certain than a youth that he knows all the answers, and that he is always right; thus he can be more determined to have his own way.

If he settles down in this "terrible self-sufficiency," or even if it affects him only slightly, this is something from which he must be delivered if he is to advance to the fullness of faith and hope and complete surrender to God. No natural sense of self-sufficiency can stand with complete openness to the action of grace. The "I live, now no longer I," must be thorough and total, if Christ is to live in us according to our capacity.

Examples of this self-sufficiency are known to us all. Good test questions are: How many of us are ready to learn from our inferiors, from those younger and less experienced than we are? How many of us are convinced that we have nothing to learn from them, and that they must learn from us? How many of us are always right, unwilling to admit that someone else may have better ideas? How many of us condemn out of hand whatever other people do, or think, or are interested in if these things are not according to our own judgment or inclinations?

To take the first question: How many superiors resent suggestions by subjects; how many priests refuse to learn anything from the laity, etc.? "Who does he think he is? He's only a youngster, a layman. . . ." And yet, there are few, if any of us, who can not learn from others, even those inferior to us in experience, age, or status. There is a good example of this self-sufficient rejection of true knowledge in the Gospel story of the man born blind (John 9:30–34). When he was cured, after much questioning by the Pharisees, he said: "Here is a man who comes you can not tell whence, and he has opened my eyes. And yet we know for certain that God does not answer the prayers of sinners; it is only when a man is devout and does his will, that his prayers are answered. That a man should open the eyes of one born blind is unheard of since the world began. No, if this man did not come from God, he would have no powers at all." He was right, of course; perfectly right. But they answered: "What, are we to have lessons from thee, all steeped in sin from thy birth?" Who was he to try to teach them? So it has always been, for this is not Pharisaism, but human nature in its self-sufficiency.

There is need of further purification—passive purification—to be delivered from "pride, personal judgment, and self-will."[5] This self-sufficiency of the adult is the psychological reason for the necessity of the second passive purification: that of the spirit. It would seem obvious that, parallel to the night of the senses, the need for any intense purification is less in proportion as the mature Christian has been generous and devoted in living fully the virtues of humility, faith, and hope; and that knowledge of the ways of the spiritual life will lessen any anguish and worry at this period, which otherwise can be a period of real crisis. He comes to a profound conviction of his own insufficiency, feels a great solitude, and feels often that his whole life has been useless. Given way to, these feelings can bring on true nervous depression. It is well enough known that some priests and religious suffer a breakdown at this stage. But, with the help of God's grace, the adult should pass through this trial (whether it be intense, or spread out over the years, and not perceived as anything special) to a humbler and purer faith, hope, and charity.

(f) THE ACTIVE UNITIVE WAY

Although this terminology may not be common, the reality it denotes is quite certain and could well receive more stress—to the encouragement and consolation of the great army of devoted apostles of whom the Church is justly proud. It indicates that higher ways of the spiritual life, the deeper degrees of intimacy with Christ, are not denied to those whom Christ has called to spend their lives and their energy in active work for the spread of His Kingdom. St. Alphonsus distinguishes between "active union" of the will of man with the will of God in the active life, and the "passive union" of the mystical states. "That the soul should attain to perfection, passive union is not necessary; it is enough for it to arrive at an active union. Active union is perfect conformity with the will of God, wherein certainly consists the whole perfection of divine love."[6]

St. Teresa of Avila also wrote something very similar: "True union can quite well be achieved, with the favor of Our Lord, if we endeavor to attain to it by not following our own will but submitting it to whatever is the will of God . . . when you have obtained this favor from the Lord, you need not strive to that other delectable union which has been described, for the most valuable thing about it is that it proceeds from this union which I am now describing. . . . The Lord can enrich souls in many ways and bring them to these Mansions by many other paths than the short-cut which has been described [the way of infused contemplation]."[7] Of this passage Dom Cuthbert Butler says: "The French Carmelites in their translation rightly interpret it as meaning that St. Teresa recognizes two ways of arriving at union, a mystic way and a non-mystic way."[8]

This is also very much in accord with the Church's "present norms of holiness" which we have studied in a previous chapter.[9] There we saw that sanctity, even in heroic degree, is described as "simple conformity to the divine Will expressed in an exact and constant fulfillment of the duties of one's state."

St. John of the Cross writes that the transforming union "consists in having the soul, as regards the will, so much transformed into the divine Will that there is no longer anything in it contrary to the will of God, but that in all and for all, what moves it is only the will of God."[10]

As spiritual authors stress, there can be no perfect sanctity without habitual docility to the inspirations of the Holy Spirit, i.e., without the gifts of the Holy Spirit operating more fully in our lives. These inspirations are not necessarily perceived as such.[11] Generally they will not be distinguished from the continued readiness to devote oneself to God's will and His glory. This readiness to give our lives to God in personal dedication was His gift in the first place—God's grace. New grace, drawing us to deeper personal intimacy with Christ, to continued faithful dedication to His will, will not appear as separate movements in a life constantly lived for God. As for the Gifts of the Holy Spirit, whose operation increases as charity grows— as we have seen—in practice their increased influence means that we live more consciously the personal love of charity, with which is found always that "instinctive" knowing of the demands of a personal love. Furthermore, as we have said before, it seems un-Christian, illogical, and un-Thomistic to assert that the operation of the Gifts of the Holy Spirit, in the degree necessary for full Christian perfection, can be found only in the exercise of infused contemplation. As Gabriel of Mary Magdalene says, no one can carry out perfectly the duties of his state (the conditions of which often make infused contemplation a practical impossibility) without being habitually moved by the Holy Spirit.[12] He simply states the fact, not deeming it necessary to give a theological explanation. One aspect of such an explanation is that of the ordination of the Gifts to action. Another point is that "The Holy Spirit personifies the will of God. Vivified in the Spirit, means being vivified in the will of God."[13] The Holy Spirit is the will of God personified. He who, out of personal dedication to God, lives in alertness to the manifestations of the divine will, faithful to embrace it and carry it out, is following the guidance of the Holy Spirit.

It goes without saying that, at this stage, the virtues are practiced in an eminent degree: "great spirit of faith, perfect humility, almost unalterable patience."[14]

There can be no sanctity without a life of prayer. Prayer, in the active unitive way, will be perseverance in the prayer described in Chapters 12 and 13. "It is certain that habitual union of mind and heart with God is necessary for sanctity. This union may be effected by thinking lovingly of God and divine things even when engaged in

other affairs; or by a supernatural spirit and a deep penetration into the truths of faith, or by some other means
(or by the continued living of one's personal dedication
to God, being more and more completely possessed by it).
It is also certain that the spiritual life becomes, as a consequence, more simple, more unified, more profound."[15]

2. The Emergent Totality

Personality is defined as: "The organized emergent totality of a human organism's individual characteristics, dispositions, values, and attitudes that regulate his adjustments to
self and environment." The Christian personality, then,
will be one who, taking his values and attitudes from
Christ, has under God's grace regulated his adjustments to
self and environment accordingly. Decisive among the interpersonal relationships, whose unselfish living brings him
to his human perfection, will be his personal relationship
with God, in whose love he has learned to believe, whose
demands he has accepted totally. Other human persons he
regards as persons with their individual dignity and destiny
as children of God.

Having made this personal relationship with God the
guiding force in his life, he has co-operated with God's
grace to establish emotional control, subjecting his human
affectivity to the rule of the Spirit, that his soul might be
ruled by God. That is to say, he has achieved unselfishness—living for God and for others as persons related to
God.

He has accepted reality: the reality of God in His transcendence, in His condescending and uplifting love; the
reality of self in all its finite limitation and weakness; the
reality of the imperfection of all created things. He has
accepted all these things with the joyful optimism of one

who believes in God's love for the world, but with the sane realism of one who knows the reality of sin and its effects. In other words, he has come to live the virtues of hope and humility in their true peace-giving combination.

He has thus been able to accept his responsibilities before God: those of his own personal destiny as an individual and as a member of the human race and the world, to whose fate he cannot be indifferent but for whose welfare he must work under God in whatever way is possible to him, knowing that, while he may not be able to achieve great things, he must yet achieve what he can.

He has succeeded in unifying his life, in blending into harmony all the various principles and truths of Christian living. He will not have establishd any false distinction between the natural and the supernatural, regarding as given to God only what is "spiritual." He will have learned that, while he must be "detached" from all things created, he can gratefully accept the natural human pleasures which God wills him to have. He will be the most "human" and understanding of men, sharing in the breadth and tolerance of divine wisdom. His will be the "hospitable mind," which is the mark of humility and charity, seeing the value in other ideas and other ways, condemning what is wrong but not what is "different."

He will, finally, in God and under God, have achieved the fulfillment of his basic psychological needs:

(a) The need of loving and being loved: first, in the love of God in which he has learned to believe; secondly, in created loves under God.

(b) His need of security is filled basically by his living hope and trust in the infinite loving power of God, and by his faith in divine Providence.

(c) His need for recognition, the need to be regarded as someone of some importance, the need to have one's efforts appreciated, is also fundamentally fulfilled in God—in the God who has said: "I know of thy doings. . . . I know how little thy strength is, and yet thou hast been true to my message, and hast not denied my name" (Apoc. 3:8). Yet this involves no spurning of human recognition, but gratitude for it, as a gift of God.

(d) His need for creative expression is satisfied in his work for God, and for the world under God—or for the contemplative—in the knowledge that whatever he does out of love for God will draw down God's blessing on the world.

(e) The need for new experience, as well as its natural fulfillment, also finds material for satisfaction in the further penetration into the mystery of God's love, the mystery of Christ, and their manifestation in the world and in his own soul.

(f) The need for a reasonable independence, and the need of self-esteem come, to some extent, with normal growth to maturity; and to a large extent are transcended in complete surrender to God, and in the acceptance of being what He makes us, in the humility which finds its joy in accepting our nothingness, that the power and love of Christ might dwell in us. Together with this, there is the dynamism of hope, which urges us to effort in the spiritual life, and in working for the Kingdom of Christ.

3. The Christian Personality and the Modern Crisis

There is always a modern crisis, at least for us who have left behind the days of our youth. We live in a changing world. Formed in the past, we live in the present, and the longer we live, the slower we are to change—from the merely natural point of view. There will always be something of the clash of the older and newer generations.

Youth wants to change all things; age wants to continue the "good old ways." The mature personality is adaptable, able to judge what is good in the new, ready to see what changes in method of work, etc., are demanded by new conditions. The Christian personality clings to eternal truths and unchanging principles of moral and spiritual life. But the Christian knows that the eternal can become incarnate in any period of history, that the Church's mission is to live in, adapt herself to, and transform the world of her time. He can bring a mature judgment to bear on adaptation. His is not the unreasoned: "It has always been done this way"—which, of course, to the young, seems the best reason for doing it differently now. In a Church in which tradition has always been seen as an essential, in which Modernism was a heresy to be condemned, there will always be, in some quarters, an unenlightened clinging to the old, because there is comfort in the old and it requires effort and enlightenment to change. Much has been said and written in recent years of adaptation of religious orders, particularly of nuns, to the needs and conditions of modern times. But let us not think that it is only or chiefly nuns who needed to adapt themselves to modern times and methods. "As a priest, I can affirm that the average nun is more ready and better disposed to adapt her apostolate to the needs of the modern world than the average parish priest."[16]

The opposite error—that of too eagerly embracing all that is modern, just because it is new—is also obviously something to be avoided. The mature Christian personality does not give way to uneasiness before new needs and new ways; nor does he reject old ways out of hand. Conscious of the unchanging value of his faith and the principles of Christian living, he is alert to the need to live and work in a changing world, able to adapt himself and to bring the eternal strength and youth of the divine into his life at all times.

4. Formation of the Christian Personality: Spiritual Direction

"Spiritual direction is necessary if one is to advance in perfection." This is a principle that is repeated in many books and to many audiences, as if it held good for all people at all stages of their spiritual life to more or less the same extent. The result of such insistence—without any explanation—is a certain amount of uneasiness of conscience of many directed, and a certain amount of useless formalism by some directors. Why is spiritual direction necessary? What is it supposed to give? How does its exercise differ according to the different stages of personal development of the subject?

Some hear it repeated that spiritual direction is a real necessity for spiritual progress, yet receive very little direction or seem to get very little out of what direction they do receive. Hence they feel that they are not receiving one of the necessary contributions to their spiritual life. Yet, in reality, they are probably getting all they need. The necessity of spiritual direction differs according to personalities, circumstances, and stages of the spiritual life.

For beginners in the spiritual life, spiritual direction is an obvious necessity. "It seems to have been, and to be, the general conviction among teachers of true wisdom that to attain perfection man has to find a teacher or a leader who controls the steps of the beginner, warns him of the mistakes he makes, and points out to him the pitfalls besetting the way to progress. Progress is not possible without self-knowledge; but to attain this the advice of a master and a special technique seem to be indispensable. The idea of a spiritual director is not a peculiarity of Catholicism . . . Chinese, Mohammedan, or Indian wisdom recommends that a man desirous of progress ought to choose a 'director.' "[17] The aim of direction for the beginner will be:

(a) To excite in him or purify a true supernatural desire for perfection.

(b) To teach him to know God and the ways of God, theological truths, the means to acquire perfection, virtues to be practiced, principles of spirituality, etc.

(c) To train him in the application of these principles to particular cases and circumstances.

(d) To teach him and guide him in the practice of prayer.

(e) To teach him to know himself: character, temperament, talents, defects.

(f) To help in particular difficulties; to help in the choice of vocation; to enlighten and encourage in times of trial.

(g) To help judge of "lights and inspirations"; to help form the judgment of the beginner to make his own enlightened decisions in all matters which he is likely to meet.

Direction is, to a large extent, the education of a person to spiritual maturity, i.e., toward a reasonable independence and an ability to face up to and solve most problems in the spiritual life. The need for instruction, the need for self-knowledge do not remain in later stages. Often it will only be a matter of recalling old truths afresh.

During the first transition stage, from that of beginners to that of the spiritually mature, direction, particularly in the way of assurance and encouragement, will be needed. This obviously has special application with regard to prayer. Then, after the crisis has been passed, there will often be the need to talk over the application of principles to individual cases which are different from what one has previously encountered. After that their need is mainly one of friendly criticism. Furthermore, much of what is supplied by the spiritual director in the early stages is given to religious through their rule, spiritual exercises, conferences, retreats, and spiritual reading.

"Later, its necessity is felt less, except at difficult periods when some changes take place, or again when an important decision must be made."[18] The aim of spiritual direction is to help a human person surrender himself completely to the love of God, i.e., to free himself from all self-seeking, self-deceit, and self-will so that he be led by the Spirit of God. A director must lead his *dirigé* to independence of him. When the subject who is directed is able to meet with God and respond to His demands in humility and spiritual maturity, the director's role is finished. Where can he "direct" him further? His office will now, if anything, be that of friend and counsellor. If the *dirigé* is always dependent on his director, the director has not fulfilled his role of educator to spiritual maturity.

However, there is another important aspect of Christian spiritual direction that is something more than the education and guidance which even natural reason dictates. This aspect is put forward by Leo XIII in *Testem benevolentiae*. It features largely in the teaching of the early Fathers of the desert and is intimately connected with the nature of faith. Faith is the complete surrender of man to God: surrender of mind and heart to supreme truth and love. Man has his own ideas of what is entailed in surrender to God. But God's ways are not our ways, and what man works out as a "reasonable" surrender is often no surrender at all, for it is surrender on our own terms. The Jews had faith of a sort, yet they refused to believe in Christ and to accept God in human nature; they refused to submit to what was seemingly less than what they thought God should be. The Jew "goes away giving himself an answer, closing himself up in his own logic, in his own view of the world and history; he reassures himself, forges a good conscience for himself. . . . He has restricted his messianism to his own measure; he has made it too human. . . ."[19] Faith, in the Gospels, is acceptance of Christ as the Revealer-Savior. Some, who thought they submitted to God, refused to submit to Christ. They could not renounce themselves, for they would not renounce their own judgment and their own ideas of the way in which they would submit to God. Hence they did not really submit at all.

This same rejection of God is manifest in every heresy which has, while claiming to submit to God, refused to see the action of God and the will of God mediated through a human Church. This is what Journet calls the "Law of the Incarnation": God coming to man and giving His gifts to man through created instruments of authority in the Church, of sacraments as continuations of the law of the Incarnation begun in Christ.[20] We do not have to explain God's dealings with men; they have their reason in the infinite wisdom from which they flow. But it would seem that, for fallen man subject to pride and the self-exalting effects of original sin, it is impossible to renounce self effectively, really submitting to God, without doing so through the humiliating self-abasement of surrender through a created intermediary. If man would go to God "in his own personal dignity," he goes in independence, and with much self-assertion in his "self-renunciation," which is evidently an inherently contradictory attitude.

The convert to the faith surrenders to God—but does so through the created intermediary of the Church and her authorities. The convert to greater self-surrender, in the way of greater spiritual perfection, can make such an effective self-renunciation only through submission to others. Pope Leo XIII wrote: "The general law of Providence has laid down that men be generally saved by other men, and that, in the same way, those whom it calls to a higher degree of sanctity will be led to it by other men." The masters of the spiritual life have always seen a refusal to seek direction as a lack of complete surrender to God, a clinging to self-will, and the vestiges of pride.

In the early Church men went out into the desert to live more spiritual lives in the practice of virginity, poverty, and prayer. They performed practices of penance and austerity. But it soon became evident that in these practices there could be, and often was, much self-seeking; much of their rivalry was far from being holy. Although they had left all things behind, they had not left themselves. Hence they saw that to renounce self, they should submit to some "director" whom, because of his learning and holiness, they could regard as indicating God's will to them. Spiritual direction, in its first beginnings, had much of the nature of the vow of obedience. As a matter of fact, it was because these men saw that obedience to a human director was the most effective way of giving oneself completely to God that the vow of obedience was later approved by the Church. Leo XIII sets spiritual direction within the general framework of the sanctifying mission of the Church: It is exercised as part of a mission which one receives in the Church to lead men to God.

Now from this aspect, the necessity of submission to a director also varies with the stages of the spiritual life. In the beginning it is absolutely essential. The one who wills to give himself completely to God must renounce himself completely. This he does not do if he retains his own ideas of how he is going to serve God, if he surrenders on his own terms and in his own way. It must be an utterly complete "Lord what will you have me do," a complete preparedness to do whatever God indicates through the director.

But, similar to the surrender of faith, this surrender of the second conversion, with its death to self, turns out to be surrender to life and liberty—the liberty of the children of God, and not subjection to man. The director must never forget that it is not to him that the human person has submitted, but through him to God, and that his role is to lead this person forth to fullness of life in Christ.

If this surrender has been complete, then, at the transition stage when the person is being set on his own feet to lead his life in spiritual maturity before God, he will, for a while, feel that he should be receiving more guidance and more support. He will feel that he may no longer be living his complete surrender, but seeking himself. (If he does not feel this, but joyfully embraces his independence, it is a sign that his renunciation of self-will was not complete.) The director's task is then to help the other grow to maturity and independence.

During the following stages, a mark of genuine self-renunciation in gift to God will be a readiness to receive direction and advice. By a strange irony, once a man has left the stage of beginners, the one who is always ready for direction does not need it; and the one who does need it is the one who feels that he needs none and really is not ready to accept it. If he has fallen into the "terrible self-sufficiency of the adult," he may seem to seek counsel, when all he really wants is confirmation of what he wants to do in his own self-will and self-sufficiency. If he is to be delivered from what is really a state of stagnation as regards genuine spiritual progress, he must, by some means or other, seek direction to which he is prepared to submit utterly.

5. The Supernatural and the Christian Personality

"One of the worst and most common of the ills of modern Christianity is to stick a label of "the supernatural"—which is only in ideas, sentiments, arbitrary will, and attitudes—on to the 'natural' which is not qualified to take it. . . ."[21] One of the most aggravating things in our life in the Church is to see an appeal to "the supernatural spirit" used as an excuse for not using common sense. Subjects who are overburdened with an unreasonable amount of work are told to have a spirit of faith and trust in God. Human persons, with many of their human needs unhealthily frustrated, are expected to live a fully "supernatural" life. Subjects naturally unfitted for religious life are admitted, with the pious rationalization that "we must set no limits to the power of grace." In so-called spiritual formation or direction, "natural attachments" are ruthlessly cut in order to destroy selfishness.

These things may not be universal, but in one form or another they are more widespread than they ought to be. Their root cause is what has been mentioned before—the cleavage between our ideas of "natural" and "supernatural." Their remedy is a full realization of the "personal nature" of the supernatural with all its consequences. The spiritual life is not "the continual exercise of a will which, in the strength of an heroic hope, surmounts the repugnances of nature. . . . The religious ideal, on the contrary, is to reduce interior conflicts, in order to fight the battles of God with a more integrated and radiant soul."[22]

To this end, we can never forget that the spiritual life cannot flourish where man's basic psychological needs are not fulfilled. We have seen that, as a man grows in grace, he finds that his basic needs are fulfilled more and more completely by his love and life for God. This means that, if he renounces, or is deprived of, their fulfillment on the natural or merely human level, he can, in the strength of his living for God, accept the loss of the less in the possession of the greater. But this does not mean that his life will be richer—naturally and supernaturally—if he has no human friendships, no sense of achievement, no happiness in the knowledge that he is esteemed and regarded by others. The more he grows in love of God, the more will he see these things as God's gift to him, for which he can be only grateful and never proud. Further, those whose task it is— as directors or superiors—will do their task well in proportion as they take careful account of the personal needs of their subjects: recognition, esteem, fulfillment of their talents in a work they can do well, lawful personal preferences, new experience, etc. While the perfect may be able to find the fulfillment of their basic needs only in God, those who are not perfect are not yet able to do so, and normally speaking, even the perfect are not expected to.

One last remark on fraternal charity, which, as we have said, means regard for others as persons. Personal charity, which can help others along their way to God, will also know how to take into account the personal needs of others and to help others with signs of esteem, recognition, etc. These can be a most valuable help to other men to rise to a greater appreciation of their own worth and meaning in the eyes of God.

NOTES

[1] See Ch. 4.

[2] F. X. Durrwell, *Dans le Christ Rédempteur* (Le Puy: Xavier Mappus, 1960), p. 198.

[3] Ch. 10.

[4] J. de Guibert, *The Theology of the Spiritual Life*, p. 341.

[5] R. Garrigou-Lagrange, *The Three Ages of the Spiritual Life*, II, p. 359.

[6] Instruction on the "Direction of Interior Souls," Appendix to *Homo Apostolicus*, translation given by Dom C. Butler, *Western Mysticism*, p. xli.

[7] *Interior Castle*, Fifth Mansion, ch. 3. Allison Peers translation.

[8] *Op. cit.*, p. xliii.

[9] Ch. 8.

[10] *Ascent of Mount Carmel*, I, 11, n. 2.

[11] De Guibert, *op. cit.*, nn. 129–130.

[12] *Conflict and Light*, pp. 164–165.

[13] F. X. Durrwell, *Dans le Christ Rédempteur*, p. 194.

[14] Garrigou-Lagrange, *op. cit*, I, p. 245.

[15] De Guibert, *op. cit.*, p. 258.

[16] G. Huyghe, *Equilibre et Adaptation* (Paris: Ed du Cerf, 1960), p. 39.

[17] R. Allers, *Difficulties in Life* (Cork: Mercier Press, 1947), p. 38.

[18] Garrigou-Lagrange, *op. cit.*, I, 258; See also G. Kelly, S.J., *Guidance for Religious* (Westminster, Md.: Newman, 1957).

[19] Decourtray, "La Conception johannique de la foi," *N.R.T.*, 81 (1959) 563.

[20] *L'Eglise du Verbe Incarné*, Vol. II, 80.

[21] J. Regamey, O.P., "L'Aspect définitif de l'engagement religieuse, sa signification théologique," in *Supplément de la Vie Spirituelle*, n. 56 (1961), 19.

[22] *Ibid.*

Chapter 16

CHRISTIAN SPIRITUALITY

---

1. Many Ways Are One

There are many ways to God, just as there are many mansions in our Father's house. But there is one house, one God and Father of all, one Lord and one faith; the many ways to God are all different manifestations of the life of Christ in each of us. We must admit the diversity and be glad of it, for this helps us avoid the error of seeking a unity in elements which need not be the same in all expressions of Christian spirituality. The unity and diversity are perhaps best seen by considering briefly the theology of the "Schools of Spirituality" on at least one central point. First of all, it is evident that no true Christian spirituality can exclude or neglect any of the fundamental principles and essential means of sanctification. In these, all spirituality is one. But the many elements can be combined with stress and accent on different aspects of the whole, and the total synthesis colored by special points of view and practice.

This is the point on which I would put much stress:

The history of spirituality shows that in no case is this synthesis the fruit of a cold elaboration made by a theorist seated at his desk. There is, at the root of all spirituality, a factor of personal experience, for which there can be no substitute. This personal experience, summed up in a central intuition, has a double effect: it gives to each of the traditional elements (which substantially are invariable) a new color or nuance. . . . Further, and by way of consequence, each of the traditional elements takes on a new relative value . . . (i.e., as colored by the central intuition and related to it). . . . This (personal experience) explains the vital character of the unity of a spirituality.[1]

Now this is true of schools of spirituality because it is true of all spirituality. The spiritual life begins in the vital experience of a personal meeting with Christ. From that meeting flows forth a real spiritual life, embracing all the essentials of Christian spirituality, but in a way which varies according to circumstances, state in life, personal gifts, and the guidance of the Holy Spirit. This, as we saw, must be kept in mind when comparing the contemplative life and the active. They are one—not in the resulting accent and color with which the essential principles of life are viewed and lived, but in the basic vital experience of a personal encounter with God, which then expresses itself through the living of the same essentials, but in quite different fashion.

2. The Way of Many: Thoughts on a Spirituality of the Laity

A clear grasp of what we have just said has enabled spiritual writers to formulate clear principles of a spirituality for men of action. They have seen that there is no vigorous nor completely true spirituality of the apostle if one tries to make it a watered-down version of monastic or contemplative life. They have seen that it was a mistake, in treating of the Christian life outside monasteries, to regard "the only really sanctifying part of it . . . as . . . those elements borrowed from the monastic rule." Hence, it has rightly been insisted that the spirituality of the diocesan priest does not consist in being as much like a monk as his duties permit. Apostolic spirituality has found its true vigor by not trying to be an imitation of the contemplative life.

Today, efforts are being made to formulate clear principles of a spirituality of the laity.[2] Some of the writing on this subject has been excellent, although a completely unified and practical "spirituality of the laity" in its definitive form has yet to be written. However, in some quarters there seems to be, in this matter, the same illogicality which attempted to make apostles into strict contemplatives—to the extent that the obstacles of their apostolic work permitted. While many of the "apostles"—priests or religious who care for souls—have rightly resisted the attempts to impose on them a spirituality that does not fit their conditions of life and vocation, many of them, in turn, have, in effect, tried to impose an attenuated form of their own "spirituality" on the laity. This is to repeat an error which is precisely the one from which they themselves have been delivered.

Let us examine this contention a little more fully. The spirituality of the priest is built up around his personal vocation, his Mass, prayer, and God-given apostolate. So is that of the active religious. Now, if a lay person asks many of these how they should go about living a more spiritual life in the world, what answer will he receive? Often enough, he will be exhorted to go to daily Mass, or at least to Mass during the week sometimes, to join one or other of the branches of Catholic Action in which he can carry out the apostolate, to live the liturgy and the apostolate—and that is all. If that is all, it is to make the spirituality of the laity an attenuated form of priestly or religious spirituality, and not a proper "life style" in its own right.

Up to a recent date there were two clear kindred problems of spiritual theology: a spirituality of the apostolate, and a spirituality of the laity. The one has been basically rethought; so must be the other. As the one came to life and strength and liberty by going back to its basic personal experience and vocation, making that inform the whole, so will the other be vital and practical only if it does the same. Both have the same starting point; both must integrate the essentials of Christian spirituality, but both are distinct and special life styles; the one is no more the model of the other than contemplative monastic spirituality is.

The source of any layman's spiritual life is the universal source of God's grace and the personal experience of a personal encounter in faith. Taking this as our starting point, we should be able to construct a spirituality of the laity from the same essential materials we have seen in previous chapters, since they are common elements of all spirituality. The synthesis must take into account the practical conditions of the life of the laity; it must show, parallel to the spirituality of the apostle, how the layman can sanctify himself in his life and work, and not in spite of those things.

(a) A LIVING FAITH

Belief in the love of God, belief in the Providence of God, giver of all gifts, material and spiritual; belief in a personal God who guides and rules the world, who loves all men and wills to lead them to eternal salvation—these basic truths must take hold of a man's mind and heart before there is any question of a real spiritual life. Then there must be a deep conviction of God's love for him personally, of his individual dignity and worth in the eyes of God, and of his personal destiny to a life of personal friendship with God.

(b) HUMILITY AND GRATITUDE

These also are basic attitudes of soul. They are intimately united in life, and one cannot exist without the other. Both require a deep conviction of the value of God's gifts, an appreciation of their worth and of our own undeservingness.

(c) PERSONAL ENCOUNTER AND PERSONAL DEDICATION

It is unfortunate that, in spite of the insistence that *vocation* must be understood in a wider sense than that of a call to religious life or priesthood, many young people on the threshold of adulthood ask themselves whether they have a vocation or not. Asking themselves such a question, the majority conclude that they are not called to dedicate their lives to Christ. The answer is false because the question is wrongly asked. The only real question is: In what way am I, a Christian, called to dedicate my life to Christ? As long as many of the laity see their lives as "not being called, not having a vocation," they will not live the Christian life very deeply. Each must know that he is called to personal intimacy with God, that his is a role that no one else can fill—on the level of personal life for God. Each has a special part to play in God's general plan for the salvation of men, and the spread of the Kingdom of Christ, and God's will for the world. One must, however, accept this fact of one's individual worth and destiny with humility and gratitude. The opposite attitude has been encountered, not infrequently, in certain sections of Catholic Action (at least in its beginnings), when some were inclined to "thank God that they were not like the rest of men," that *they* were really doing something for God. Such an attitude is, of course, destructive of true spirituality which begins and grows in humble gratitude for the privilege God has bestowed on us by lavishing His love upon us, and calling us to take part in His work for the world. Here there is no place for pride, but only for a delicate and generous solicitude that we do not fail in our response that it is our honored and grateful duty to give.

(d) NATURAL AND SUPERNATURAL

In order to have the sense of personal dedication to God in the work and life of the layman, it is essential for him to see the "personal" character of the life of grace and to avoid the too-common division between the "spiritual life" of prayer, etc., and "other things," which take up most of a man's time. He must see his activity, work, and leisure as entering into the plan of God's will for the world, and thus entering into his personal life for God.

(e) APOSTOLATE

(1) *Personal Witness*

The general doctrine of the principles and practice have been seen above.

There are three chief fields of application: (i) within the family; (ii) in one's work or profession; (iii) among one's acquaintances.

The first two will be considered in detail later; the third has been sufficiently covered—or rather, a more detailed coverage is easily enough made and is beyond the range of this "outline."

(2) *Official Consecration*

"Be mindful of your dignity." At baptism, Christians are consecrated children of God and members of His household. By the sacrament of confirmation "the Holy Spirit is given to them to strengthen them, as He was given to the apostles on the day of Pentecost, that they might boldly profess the name of Christ."[3] Officially consecrated as witnesses and apostles, they receive, through the strengthening grace of the Spirit of God, continued helps all their lives to live up to their high calling. Every layman should live in the consciousness of his mission.

(3) *Active Endeavor*

Witness to Christ by what he is, he must also be witness to Christ and apostle in his active endeavor:

(i) FOR THE SPREAD OF THE KINGDOM: by this I mean the layman's part in working in the Church for the Church; for his local parish Church, for the Church universal in her whole life and missionary enterprise. This includes his material contributions, his part in such lay-activities as are open to him, his prayer for the spread of the faith.

(ii) FOR THE REIGN OF CHRIST AGAINST THE EFFECTS OF SIN: This is an apostolic work he carries on in the world and in society. It includes all his efforts—in his profession, organizations, politics, in public affairs or private—against error and ignorance, prejudice, injustice, poverty, misery, and oppression. All these are obstacles to the reign of Christ, and every effort against them is an effort to "restore all things in Christ." It is an effort that Christ expects from His lay apostles; it is part of the mission He has entrusted to them. A good Catholic cannot but *be* a devoted citizen. He sees his efforts in a higher plan of reference, for he knows that anything that helps a human person to reach the fullness of personal life helps him to be a fitter subject for the grace of God.

(iii) SOCIAL DIMENSION OF CHARITY: In reality, the exercise of charity in what is sometimes called its "social dimension" coincides with what we have just summarily indicated. In the conditions of the modern world, although there will always be scope for individual acts of alms-giving and charity, the most effective way to combat pauperism and misery and want will be through collaboration with others through institutions and social means. The Christian will see this work as part of his charity, "loving his neighbor" out of love for God.

The greatest work of charity is to help men to the love of God, to receive divine life and salvation from Him. We have already pointed out that this work is falsely conceived if it is thought of as no more than teaching "religious" truths or "spiritual realities." It is the whole human person who practices virtue, who lives a religious life. He will not normally do that in conditions that are unfavorable to the practice of religion. When housing is poor, when employment is irregular and poorly paid, when men and women suffer great anxiety about material security, etc., they find it more difficult to give the necessary time and thought to matters of religion.

The Christian layman, then, will see as the practice of Christian charity all that he does by way of personal activity, collaboration with others, in influencing public opinion to see that social conditions are such as to help men live according to their personal dignity, and thus help them to live according to their dignity as children of God.

(f) PERSONAL PRAYER

Prayer is more than an exercise—it is the atmosphere in which we live. A man cannot live his personal dedication to God through the various activities of his life unless he has made profoundly his own the attitudes listed in the first part of this section. To make and keep them a vital part of his whole living, he must return to them in thought and prayer; he must conserve and foster them by the practice of prayer. The vocation of every apostle begins with a vision of God and ends with a mission to men. The mission to men will be less divine if the vision of God grows dim. Prayer alone can keep it alight and alive. By *prayer* more is understood than the mere recitation of set formulas; it means, especially, the prayerful thinking over of the various truths of our life in Christ—as we see them in the Gospels and Epistles—some of which are set forth in this book.

What prayer is required of the layman? It is not easy to give a practical answer to this question. To suggest daily Mass is an impractical answer for many people in modern conditions—especially country people and mothers of families. However, Mass on a weekday would not seem to be asking much from many people. If a layman is sincere in his desire to live the spiritual life—which is first of all his rendering a personal tribute of worship to God—he should be able to do something over and above his Sunday Mass in the way of worship in the Church, as Mass on a weekday, benediction of the Blessed Sacrament, a visit to Our Lord in the Blessed Sacrament, etc. It goes without saying that Sunday Mass and weekly Communion will be central focal points of his spiritual life.

There is much to be said for the old Christian practice of morning and evening prayers, particularly if they are

[290]

impregnated with the spirit of personal devotion to God, and not just "practices" to be performed. Lochet has a fine passage on which the lay-person could well meditate and make part of his spiritual life:

The night has its development and its liturgy. It supposes an evening and a morning. The evening is this return (when obscurity dims the contours of the world that is passing, brings the worker home, and gathers the soul at its center where it finds God), this recollection, this meeting, this remission, this gift of self and one's work. The hour of Compline delicately marks for us its essential themes. This is the glance over the work of the day, the regrets, the pardon. The world of which we have taken charge today, we place tonight in the hands of God again. Here man sinks into this peaceful night, the image of death, this definitive and blessed meeting with the Saviour. Behold the child who falls asleep in the arms of the Father who holds up for him the whole universe . . . who has need of refreshing his strength to labor again tomorrow at the perfection of the world for the glory of the Father.

The morning is the time for prayer, but it is not the exclusive "time given to God," or "time of intimacy with God," for all time is to be such. It is the awakening of the soul to the spiritual life, the conscious resuming of its life in Christ and of its duties in the Church—faith waking and watching: the apostle who places himself in the Church at the disposal of God for the fulfilling of a mission. Morning prayer is the conscious resuming of intimacy with God; the total offering of our strength to receive from Him the grace which will sustain us and the mission which will direct us. Prayer, each day, is an "Ecce Venio."[4] With Him and in Him we enter anew into the world each day, there to accomplish the Will of the Father and to work for the spreading of the Kingdom.[5]

Practical circumstances, which vary so much in the life

of the laity, will have much bearing on deciding the practical question of what time should be given to prayer. Hence, it is impossible to formulate a general rule. But in the life of each one who tries to live a deeper spiritual life there must be some time habitually set aside, in which in prayerful silence he refreshes and deepens his personal intimacy with God.

(g) FAMILY SPIRITUALITY

The majority of the laity live in the married state. Since this is a state consecrated to God by the sacrament of matrimony, it will be in this state that they find the chief elements that constitute their living for God.

(i) THE SACRAMENT OF MATRIMONY: We have already explained something of the sacramental significance of marriage and of its aptitude to help husband and wife to live the personal reality of their union with God in grace and charity. This view, in faith, of the symbolism of marriage can do much to help them live a spiritual life. Hence the more this view is shared by both, the more can they help one another in the deeper life of the soul. This should be so in the normal nature of things. For what God has joined together is meant to be united in a shared vision of the greater values of life and love. If a wife tries to live a spiritual life "in spite of her husband," or vice versa, that may be an unfortunate necessity, but it is not what is meant to be.

(ii) APOSTOLATE IN THE FAMILY: If all Christian parents realized the importance of their vocation to educate their children to the fullness of Christian living, and if all carried it out with enlightened dedication, the world could well be a wonderfully different place. The most important work that parents can ever be asked to do is to work, under God, that the children that he gave them might live gladly and generously as children of God. They have no more sacred trust than this, none to which they should give more thought, and prayer, and study. Whatever they leave undone will take years of labor to remedy, if it can be remedied at all. How many priests and brothers and sisters spend years of labor in efforts that should not be necessary? How much of their time and effort is spent on work that would not be necessary if parents performed well their God-given duty? And all this is time and effort that is urgently needed in other directions too.

The work of the apostolate, as we have seen, must be regarded as the complete formation of a Christian personality—unselfish, generous, living his personal relationship with God as the greatest thing in his life. It is a long work and is early begun. "We have taught them their religion, and sent them to Catholic schools." Yes, but have you trained them to unselfishness; have you taught them to see religion as a privilege and not primarily a duty; have you let them see something of your own personal attachment to Christ? If you have not done these things, you have not "taught them their religion" at all!

Education of the Christian child prepares him to surmount the difficult years of adolescence, to make his adult "fundamental choice" for a personal God, to dedicate his whole life to Christ in the loyalty of a living faith. That he might do this, he must early come to know something of God's personal love for him; he must be formed to unselfishness, to a grateful appreciation of God's gifts, both natural and supernatural.

This formation of the child can only be done if he lives in a family atmosphere of personal faith and personal prayer, learning that true joy and content come through living his relations with God. A very important item of education, which Pope John has recently stressed, is that of sex education. If boys and girls come to the crisis of adolescence seeing human love in its right perspective, they grow into adulthood with an inner peace and an external poise that is normally denied to those who see sex as a mysterious, unexplained urge surrounded by taboos and a vague and sinister cloud of sinfulness.

It is an absorbing and rewarding task, this work of the apostolate, of forming the fullness of Christian personality in those persons whom parents, co-operating with the Creator, have brought into the world. It is also a responsible task: the chief work for God that Christian parents will be asked to do.

(iii) FAMILY WITNESS: In our days, much of the discontent and dissatisfaction that exists in certain families is the result of husbands, wives, and parents seeking pleasure rather than true contentment. That pleasure they often seek in amusements and other things *outside* the family circle. Hence children, especially when there are more than two, seem to be a burden and a hindrance to "having a good time and enjoying life." The truly Christian family, in the realization of the dignity of family life and the true happiness that comes from this realization, can and should be a living witness to the world of the worth of the faith and Christian values. Charity within the family circle and extended beyond will be, as Our Lord promised, a sign that men might know who are His disciples; a sign that will set others thinking, and so, with God's grace, set them on the way to Christ.

(h) LOVE AND SACRIFICE

As Congar points out,[6] until recently, husbands or wives were not canonized unless they had left their families. Examples of such saints are St. Jane Frances de Chantal and Nicolas von Flue. Behind this practice was some vestige of the idea that "lay life was a sort of degenerate monastic life which simply permitted the married state." For many a layman there still exists an unresolved difficulty with regard to his living a life of real sanctity. Most of the saints were priests or religious. Sanctity demands renunciation of created things for the love of God. Yet he has not renounced "creatures"; he enjoys the pleasures of family life. Must he then choose between living in his present state or a more perfect life which would demand its renunciation? Common sense gives the only practical answer, but it does not resolve his theoretical difficulty.

To solve that, we must recall and apply some principles already seen. First of all, renunciation of creatures is not a rejection of the things which God has made good. It is a measure to ensure one's internal rectitude in the use of all created things. The alcoholic gives up drink not because drink is bad in itself, but because he cannot make a right use of it. Others renounce drink because, even though they can make right use of it, their act of renunciation is one way in which they can express and make effective their gift of self to God and union with Christ for the redemption of the world. Priests and religious give up marriage because, under the attraction of grace, they are drawn toward a direct personal union with Christ.

But the married Christian finds, in and through the sacrament of marriage, through the personal, total, and definitive gift of himself to another person, the means whereby he may give himself totally to Christ. The fidelity of his married love is something he promises and lives as part of his fidelity in love to Christ, for he "marries in the Lord." Marriage is a sacrament: a sign of Christ's indefectible love for the Church. The married parties, in receiving the sacrament, pledge themselves to show forth, to one another and to the world, a fidelity in self-forgetful love which is an image of, and a sharing in, the unfailing love with which Christ cherishes His Church and all her members. This fidelity "until death do us part" is promised by each partner as something far more sacred than a human constancy which is confident that "our love is too great to fail." It is promised because, since marriage is a sacrament, each one who receives it solemnly and irrevocably pledges himself to signify to the other partner, by his own fidelity, the total and definitive gift of divine love given to men in Christ. In their mutual love, given and received, there is the double significance of Christ loving the Church and its members, and of the Church loved by Christ.

Whence, "the first responsibility of a married Christian is his home. It is first of all to his wife and children that he must express, by his affectionate devotedness, the love of Christ for them. It is first of all for them and with them that he must seek God in prayer and moral effort; before them and with them that he must be, his whole life long, a witness of the risen Christ. If he neglects these duties, he will express very imperfectly, by the incomplete gift of himself, the love of Christ for this household and for the Church. Inversely, the insufficiency of a moral and religious tone indicates, between Christian spouses, the imperfection of mutual self-giving and increases the risk of conjugal crises."[7]

This is the married Christian's way of living his personal love for Christ and his personal dedication to Christ. As we have seen, such love and dedication can be real and generous only if there is self-renunciation and self-sacrifice. But the self-sacrifice must be found where the love is found; it must be lived, not as a negative thing, but as a positive gift of self. Even on the natural plane, a successful, happy marriage demands continual and progressive self-sacrifice: "Love is a contrivance for inducing man to perform voluntarily what is most repugnant to him, to know self-sacrifice." It is in this continued self-dedication to other persons—wife or husband, and children—with its continued, ever-fuller self-renunciation, that, on the natural level, the married person reaches the fullness of human personality in self-transcendence.

Just as his natural human love is transformed and made sacred by the vision of faith which sees and lives it as a sharing in the love of Christ, lifting it to personal union with Christ, so will that same vision enable husband and wife and Christian parents to see self-renunciation and self-sacrifice as their chief way of bearing the cross of Christ, of losing their life of selfishness in a self-surrender which is made in and through their family life to God. There they will find the central section of their cross, just as they find there the core of their love lived for Christ. Their love, and their sacrifice too, are no longer merely natural, but consecrated by the sacrament that rules their whole life.

(i) WORK ACCORDING TO GOD'S WILL

It is admitted by some modern writers that "we do not yet have a theology of work."[8] Various points of doctrine are put forward to enable a man to integrate his life of work into his whole life for God. Some stress the fact that work is a sharing in God's creative activity: part of the work of restoring all things in Christ. For work, which is clearly seen as creative activity, this can be a helpful consideration, as also is the thought that sickness, hunger, and ignorance are part of the effects of sin, and that all work of healing, teaching, succoring the needy is a continuation of Christ's work of restoring all things. But some cannot easily fit their work into these categories—except in an abstract and theoretical way. If they can so see their work, it will obviously be a great help in living their personal dedication to God in their work.

Others stress the fact that work is a duty that perfects our human personality, or that God's will for man extends wider than things merely spiritual. According to our nature, we must work. Hence that we work in the world and for the good of the world, is also part of God's will, which is sanctifying in itself.[9]

There is a further consideration (more extrinsic to the work itself, but often efficacious in helping to integrate work into one's spiritual life) which is that, if a man does his work well and thoroughly, he is a more effective witness to the faith because of the respect that he wins. "Normally the witness which converts souls is prepared and rendered possible by the esteem which is won by professional competence."[10]

These are all good considerations, and one or another has helped many a layman to make his work an integral part of a life which is ruled by complete dedication to God. It is important for a really vigorous spiritual life that it be unified, and that one's work be seen and lived as integrated into one's personal life for God.

There may be another aspect which, for many years of their lives, will prove more helpful to many people, fitting as it does into the general unity of a spirituality lived in and for the family. If their love for Christ is lived out through the sacramental reality of conjugal and parental love, if their self-sacrifice to Christ is made through self-sacrifice for the persons who make up their family circle, will not their work be done for Christ if it be done for those persons with whom Christ has united them in a love which is a share in His own? All work is of value insofar as it is the expression of our personal dedication to Christ. For husband and wife, father and mother, the work that is done to sustain, cherish, and care for those others who are united to them in human yet spiritual love, is a work that is done for Christ. Just as their personal dedication does not stop at the created persons, but rises higher to a personal God, so is their personal dedication in work transformed by that same higher personal dedication. They work for God in working for those to whom Christ has linked them in a love that unites them with Him.

NOTES

[1] P. Lucien Marie de S. Joseph, "Ecole de Spiritualité," in *Dictionnaire de Spiritualité*, cc. 121–122.

[2] We have already quoted and referred to the works of Congar, Philips, and Leclercq.

[3] Council of Florence.

[4] Heb. 10:5, the words attributed to Christ: "See I am coming . . . to do Thy will, O, my God."

[5] L. Lochet, S.J., *Finding God in All Things.*

[6] *Op. cit.,* p. 389.

[7] J. de Baciocchi, S.M., "Structure Sacramentaire du mariage," *N.R.T.,* 74 (1952), 916 ff.

[8] *Theology Digest,* vol. IV, n. 1 (1956), 37.

[9] Thus Congar, *op. cit.* K. Truhlar, S.J., treats these points well in *Structura Theologica Vitae Spiritualis* (Rome: P.U.G., 1958).

[10] G. Huyghe, *Equilibre et Adaptation,* p. 72.

Chapter 17

IN CHRIST JESUS OUR LORD

---

1. Life in Christ

By way of a concluding summary, I wish to indicate more explicitly what has, I hope, been evident enough in the course of this work, namely, that these various "aspects of the spiritual life" are aspects of our life in Christ, or the life of Christ in us: the life of grace, sanctifying and actual. Under the influence of a personal attraction toward Christ, in whom God makes Himself known to man, we are drawn by God the Father into fellowship with His Son, sharing His life of personal intimacy with the Father and the Spirit of love. Led by the Holy Spirit and lifted by His transforming power, we accept Christ in a living faith as the Revealer-Redeemer and Lord of life. We give our life to Him in personal dedication; we ask Him to live in and through us, that this mind might be in us which was in Christ Jesus Our Lord, that His Spirit might lead us, enlighten and strengthen us to forsake all sin and selfishness that we might live for God in Christ. Our whole life is centered on the person of Christ: "Since I have known Christ, nothing seems beautiful enough for me to look upon it with desire,"[1] unless we see it transformed with the beauty that links us with the love of God.

Drawn to Christ, we are drawn into the twofold movement of His love: for the Father, that He might be loved and glorified; for men, that they might be the children of God. This love finds expression in the twofold movement of our prayer: worship of the divine majesty in union with Christ, "the perfect Adorer of the Father," and intercession for all men, united with Christ, who "lives on to make intercession on our behalf."

Attracted to Christ, we find that our life in Him is an ever-fuller entry into His redemptive mystery, into the death and Resurrection of Christ into which we were baptized. His death was His complete renunciation of all in His human nature that clung to its own existence: the complete surrender (of whatever "self" there could be in a sinless humanity) to the personal love of God. The Resurrection was the complete possession of the humanity by the Spirit, the personal love of God, transforming and uplifting His human nature, perfecting it in the glory of its complete surrender to the divine. The whole life of the Christian consists in living a surrender to divine love, as complete as possible: and this takes with it a self-renunciation, a death to "self" which must be ever more complete. It will reach its perfection only when, through the final surrender of death, we give ourselves entirely into the hands of God. Thus is our entire living a fuller entry into the redemptive mystery: death and resurrection, and death in view of the positive transformation of possession by the love of God. Our risen Lord and Savior, by the power and influence of His own Resurrection, draws us ever more deeply into His own mystery of life from death.

Sharing in His mystery, we share in His victory over

sin and Satan. His victory is the source of our confidence; for He, the Victor, continues the battle through us who are His members. Our faith gives us victory, the faith which is a convinced clinging to the strong and victorious protecting love of Christ. In a blessed hope, in confidence in Christ, we look forward to the final victory, in our own lives when the power of God will possess us, and in the world, when Christ's enemies will be subject to Him and Christ will be all in all.

In faith and love and confidence, we give ourselves to the cause of Christ, working for the glory of God and the salvation of men. Through our self-forgetful dedication to God, assuming our responsibilities in grateful and humble recognition of the dignity that God has given us by calling us into intimate association with His Son, we grow in Him to spiritual maturity. And so growing, we forget ourselves, only to discover that, in losing our lives, we have found Life more fully: "It is no longer *I* who live, but Christ who lives in me." The spiritual life thus develops from the stage of our living for Christ, through the stage of living in union with Christ, to the consciousness of Christ's living in and through us.

2. In the Body of Christ

Christ came into the world to gather into one those whom sin had dispersed and divided from one another. United with God, all those who were "in Christ" were to be united in the one Body of Christ which is the Church. Within the communion of the Church, the faithful live their union with Christ in charity, which is the bond of perfection, for fraternal charity is the sign and expression of their love for Christ. In the unity of faith, they find that their submission to God and total surrender to the divine truth and divine will is embodied in their acceptance of the teaching and ruling authority of the Church, which they see and accept as Christ continuing His royal power of ruling men's minds and wills. And if their faith is to be complete surrender to God, it must, for its truth, be complete renunciation of self-will and self-direction. This "death to self" is, as every man who has accepted it can attest, more deep searching when it is an acceptance of the divine, mediated through human representatives of God, with all their human limitations and weakness.

Through created channels of human ministers and material sacramental signs, the wonders of grace and life are given to men: life which flows from Christ the Head through the Body to each of its members.[2] Recipients of divine life, the members of the Body of Christ are not merely passive, but are drawn into the active worship of Christ their Head and High Priest, who continues the exercise of His priesthood in and through the Church. It is within the community of worship that each member of Christ renders praise and homage and thanksgiving to God.

Our active dedication to God is, again, not a matter of individual enterprise. It is Christ who, by the consecration and sharing in His priesthood which He gives us through the sacraments of baptism, confirmation and orders, entrusts to us a mission within the Church. The mission is to be exercised in submission to the Church, for only then is it a mission from Christ.

3. Union with Christ in the Eucharist

Pope Leo XIII in his encyclical letter, *Mirae caritatis*, referred to the Eucharist as the center, summary, and source of the whole Christian life. This it is from various points of view.

a. It is our *"Eucharist,"* and by its very name takes us into the biblical atmosphere of the eucharistic blessings, which are first of all a grateful recalling in wondering gratitude of all that God has done for man. It recalls God's marvellous works in which He has shown His grandeur, shown clearly that He is the one true God; in which He has shown His kindness in that He has wrought His wonderful works on behalf of man. The Christian Eucharist is a calling to mind of all God's gifts of creation, life, and eternal destiny, but above all, a calling to mind of what God has done for us in Christ: a remembering of Christ's death and Resurrection, whence comes our deliverance and our life. From this recall, we turn, naturally, to the expression of our praise of God, our gratitude, confidence and joy, and thence to prayer that His blessing will be upon us at all times.[3] This is an atmosphere that fosters a personal life for God.

b. *The Eucharistic Sacrifice.* Sacrifice of its very nature is the expression of man's deepest yearning for union with God: "that we might adhere to God in holy fellowship." Sacrifice is the offering of a gift; a gift can be expressive of many things. But when sinful man offers a gift to God, it always includes something of what is expressed by the disobedient but repentant child who makes a gift to his parents. His gift indicates love, sorrow, the promise of obedience—but above all, it expresses his yearning to be taken back into the personal family intimacy from which his fault has excluded him. His whole action is an effort to enter into the love which he has lost.

It is through Christ's sacrifice on Calvary that humanity regains God's friendship: in that sacrifice, through His self-renunciation in death, Christ gave Himself into the hands of God who accepted His sacrifice and took possession of His humanity in the glory of the Resurrection. The Mass is given to the Church that we might unite ourselves to the Sacrifice of Christ and have His offering as our own. From our personal point of view, each Mass at which we assist is our renewed will to enter more fully into the mystery of His death and Resurrection, to renounce ourselves in order that we might enter more intimately into the love of the Father. In each Mass we consecrate ourselves anew to His love, to the doing of His will, so that possessed by the power of His love, we might give glory to God.

c. *Communion*. In all the official documents of the Church there are no more beautiful passages than those which treat of the effects of Holy Communion. There is no act of devotion that means more to the Christian than this. That is as it should be, for here, in a mysterious intimacy, man is closely united to Christ, and for a brief period he lives what his whole life should be. The effects of this Blessed Sacrament, the fruit he should draw from it, the dispositions with which he should approach it, should be a constant subject for his thought, reading, and prayer. For Communion has, as its proper effect, a life of personal intimacy with Christ. Technically, this is expressed as "the fervor of charity," or "an increase of charity, habitual and actual." This means that the special effect of Communion is the conscious living of personal intimacy with Christ—in all its various aspects, some of which we have studied in previous chapters.

d. *Permanent Presence*. As Pope Pius XII recently reminded the world, we can draw great spiritual consolation and strength from the thought of Christ's continued presence in the sacrament of the Eucharist. "He is their counsellor, their consoler, their strength, their refuge, their hope, in life as in death."[4] Visits to the Blessed Sacrament will always be visits to a Person permanently present; present as "remembrance of His sacrifice and passion" since "it is by the sacrifice of the altar that Our Lord makes himself present in the Eucharist."⁵ Christ's eucharistic presence is thus a permanent reminder of the love that led Him to the cross and a permanent invitation to surrender ourselves more fully to the love of God. He who is present is the risen Christ, who in heaven "lives on to make intercession on our behalf." Christ is in continual prayer before the throne of God, and our adoration of the Eucharist is the expression of our will to associate ourselves with the eternal adoration and intercession of our High Priest in heaven.⁶

4. In the Heart of Christ

In his recent encyclical letter, *Haurietis aquas*, Pope Pius XII wrote that devotion to the Sacred Heart of Christ was a most excellent way of practicing the Christian religion. He repeated the words of Pope Pius XI: "This form of piety leads our minds more quickly than any other to an intimate knowledge of Christ the Lord and inclines our hearts more effectively to love Him with greater vehemence and to imitate Him more earnestly."

The teaching of the Popes does not need our proofs. But if proof were needed of the value of devotion to the Sacred Heart, it could be found in the effectiveness of this devotion in helping us to live the aspects of the spiritual life we have outlined. The value of devotion to the Heart of Christ is that it helps to make the practice of our religion a fully personal life. Devotion to the Sacred Heart

. . . teaches us the absolutely unique importance which our relations with Christ have in Christian spirituality. Founded on a common nature, they have the character of relations particularly intimate and spontaneous; and it is yet by the facility and simplicity of these relations that man enters into the very heart of God, for he does not unite himself to the person of a man, but to the Person of the Word. . . . God is no longer infinitely distant and inaccessible: He has become our friend, our companion. What is devotion to the Sacred Heart but the most perfect and fullest expression of "our" friendship, a mutual friendship between Him and us. Only devotion to the Sacred Heart shows us Christ as our brother who loves us and asks for our love. . . .

People speak often . . . of the sublimity of the Prologue of the Fourth Gospel; but . . . the end of the Gospel is at least as sublime as the Prologue: "Simon Peter, do you love me more than these others?"—the Word was made flesh to ask men for their love. That God should love us is a mystery, and that he should want our love is an even greater one. Both are taught as reality by devotion to the Heart of the Word Incarnate.[7]

Devotion to the Sacred Heart, with its stress upon the personal love of God, on the human and divine love of Christ has, through the centuries, kept this personal tone in Christian life, in spite of human tendencies toward overabstraction, exclusive stress on law and duty, and toward a separation of the "supernatural" from the humanly personal. The symbol of the living, human heart of the risen Christ, the heart pierced on the cross, has been a living summary of God's love for man and an invitation to return that love in living personal dedication. "The faithful . . . consecrate themselves with all they have, to their Creator and Redeemer, as regards both their intimate affections and external activities of their life . . . dedicate themselves more easily and promptly to the divine charity."[8]

Every devotion "creates a perspective," a viewpoint from which we see the whole of religion, and "traces directive lines," showing us what our practice of the spiritual life ought to be.[9] Devotion to the Sacred Heart gives us this perspective: the Incarnate Christ at the center of the twofold movement of God's dealings with men, and man's return to God. Christ is the supreme manifestation of the "love of God in our regard" in which we have learned to believe the divine creative and redemptive love. In the Heart of Christ is also the ascending love of a human nature, a filial love, for it is the love of the Son of God, a love which expresses itself in worship and adoration. It is the meeting place of the love of God and man.

This devotion also traces strong and directive lines for our life toward God: of prayer and loving worship toward the Father, of charity and zeal for those whom God loves with an everlasting love.

Pope Pius XII wrote that the Heart of Christ is a symbol of His threefold love: (a) divine; (b) human spiritual love, charity; (c) human emotional love. With regard to this last point, the Pope quoted some fine texts from the Fathers: "He wished by sharing our emotions to provide for them a healing remedy" (St. Justin); "All things therefore [of our nature] He assumed, that he might make all holy" (St. John Damascene). There was a wisdom in these words that had been too often forgotten. We have to sanctify our whole nature, not a disembodied "spiritual" part of it. Stripped of all sentiment, made unfeeling and insensitive, man may be a stoic; he will not be a saint. A man is sanctified, not by having affection cut out of his heart, but by having it centered on the beauty of God and all its human manifestations in the Person of Christ. In Him was the most sensitive human nature, the kindest and most understanding, "able to feel for us in our infirmities." All loves in the heart of Christ were sensitive and strong, unified in the Person who possessed them. God gave us human "hearts to know Him" in all their human need and sensitivity.

They will find strength and peace—and sanctity—through surrender to the Person who wills to possess them, divine love binding the heart of man to the heart of God in a fully personal spirituality.

NOTES

[1] Lacordaire.

[2] J. Gaillard, "Les Sacrements de la foi," *N.R.T.*, 59 (1959).

[3] J. Audet, "Esquisse historique du genre littéraire de la 'Bénédiction' juive et de l' 'Eucharistie' chrétienne," *Revue Biblique*, 67 (1958), 371–399.

[4] Allocation to the First International Congress on Pastoral Liturgy, Sept. 22, 1956 (A.A.S. 48 [1956]), pp. 711–725.

[5] *Ibid.*

[6] P. Michel-Jean, "Eucharistie et Prière incessante," *Maison-Dieu*, n. 64 (1960).

[7] D. Barsotti, *Vie Mystique et Mystère Liturgique.*

[8] *Haurietis aquas.*

[9] "Dévotion," *Dictionnaire de Spiritualité.*

Index

A

"Abandonment to Divine Providence," 104–105

Activity, spiritual, 114–117

Adam, role of, in cross, 131–132

Ad Conditorem (John XXIII), 102

Adler, Felix, on importance of security, 151

Adoption, divine, St. Thomas' concept of, 26–27

Adoration, prayer of, 202

Aggression, 252–254

Alexander, on psychoanalysis, 34

Alexander VI, 113

Anxiety, as keynote of purification, 160, 161

Apostolate, the, 162–166; as Christ's work, 116–117; devil as adversary in, 236–237; in family, 292–294

Armenian liturgy, on baptism, 82

Ascent of Mount Carmel, The (St. John of the Cross), 102–103

Asceticism, aims of, 141; adult, 147; characteristics of, 138; Christian, 135; personal, 140–150; transitional stages of, 143; of young, 147

Authority, Church, human element in, 113–114

Autonomy, development of, 36–40; personal, 36–37; social, 37; as step in development of liberty, 38–39

B

Benedict XV, on sanctity, 103

Benildus of Christian Schools, devotion of, to duty, 106–107

Bérulle, Cardinal, on virtue of religion, 112

Bouyer, L., S.J., on balance between positive and negative, 128

Butler, B., on second stage of prayer, 208

Butler, Dom Cuthbert, on St. Teresa's dual method of achieving union with God, 267

C

Carmelites, on prayer of simplicity, 203; terminology of, regarding contemplation, 217–218

Chapman, Dom, on second stage of prayer, 208

Charity, and double law of growth, 98–99; fraternal, 91–97, 280; social dimension of, 289; as source of apostolic activity, 230

Chesterton, G. K., on attitude, 134; on pride of timidity, 47; on self-control, 135

Children of the Father, 24–27

Claudel, Paul, on dynamism of St. Teresa, 171

Commitment, personal, 121–122

Communion, special effect of, 305

[311]

A NOTE ON THE TYPE

IN WHICH THIS BOOK IS SET

This book is set in Janson, a Linotype face, created from the early punches of Anton Janson, who settled in Leipzig around 1670. This type is not an historic revival, but rather a letter of fine ancestry, remodelled and brought up to date to satisfy present day taste. It carries a feeling of being quite compact and sturdy. It has good color and displays a pleasing proportion of ascenders and descenders as compared to the height of the lower case letters. The book was composed and printed by The York Composition Company, Inc., of York, Pa., and bound by Moore and Company of Baltimore. The typography and design are by Howard N. King.